GOOD FOOD: BETTER SEX

A Guide to Intimacy and Love Using
Traditional Chinese Medicine and Food

Written & Published by Joanne Faulkner
Shiatsu & Conscious Cooking

PUBLISHED BY JOANNE FAULKNER
www.joannefaulkner.ie

EDITED BY
Faith Amon
www.frecklefootcreative.com

BOOK DESIGN BY
Leila Aguilera
www.leilaaguilera.com

ILLUSTRATIONS, PHOTOGRAPHY AND ARTWORK BY
Joanne Faulkner

A catalogue record for this book is available
from the British Library.

joanne
FAULKNER
SHIATSU - CONSCIOUS COOKING

TABLE OF CONTENTS

INTRODUCTION

CHAPTER 1 YIN/YANG

CHAPTER 2 KIDNEY/BLADDER

CHAPTER 3 LIVER/GALLBLADDER

CHAPTER 4- HEART PROTECTOR/ TRIPLE HEATER

CHAPTER 5 - HEART/ SMALL INTESTINE

CHAPTER 6 SPLEEN/STOMACH

CHAPTER 7 – LUNG/LARGE INTESTINE

FULL CIRCLE

QUICK REFERENCE GUIDE
HOW DO YOU FEEL AND WHAT DO YOU NEED?

KEY

CV - Conception Vessel (Yin)
GV - Governing Vessel (Yang)
K - Kidney
BL - Bladder
LV - Liver
GB - Gallbladder
H - Heart
SM - Small Intestine
HP - Heart Protector
TH - Triple Heater
ST - Stomach
SP - Spleen
LU - Lung

Candida/Thrush/Vaginitis/Prostatitis

Points CV1&2/BL23&52/TH4/LV3/GB41/ST28/ST40/SP6/LU7&K6

Building sexual energy

Points CV6/GV4/K3/K1/BL23&BL52/TH4/ST36/SP1/SP6

Aphrodisiac

Points CV6/CV17/GV4/BL10/BL23/BL52/HP2/HP6/LU7

Dissolving Lumps, Bumps, Adhesions and Scars

Points GV24.5/HP3/TH4/LV3/LV5/GB41/ST18/ST40/SP6/LI4

Erectile Dysfunction

Points CV1&2/CV6/GV20/GV4/K1/K3/ BL23/ BL52/SP12&13/LI11/LU7

Fertility

Points CV4/CV6/GV4/K3/BL23/BL52/TH4/GB41/ SP1/SP6/LU7&K6

Heartbreak

Points CV6/CV17/GV20&GV24.5/HP2/HP6&K6/ GB9/H6/H7/LI4/LU1/LU7&K6

Libido

Points CV1&2/CV6/GV4/GV20/K3/BL23/BL52/ BL10/TH4&ST42/ST36/SP6

Sexual Control and Premature Ejaculation

Points CV1&2/K1/GV4/K1/K3/BL23/BL52/TH4/ GB13&CV4/ST36/SP12&13

Post Baby

Points CV6/CV17/GV20/GV4/K6/BL10/BL23&52/ TH4&ST42/H6/ST18/ST36/SP1/SP6/LU7&K6

Vaginal dryness

Points CV1&2/GV4/K6/K3/BL23&52/LV3/GB9/H6/SP6/SP12&13/LU7

- Love Lube 105
- Wheat and Gluten Free Drop Scones 315
- Herby Lime Noodles with Cashews 151
- Sea Buckthorn Fizz 282

Falling in Love/ Relationships /Pleasure

Points CV6/CV17/GV20&24.5/GV26/K1/HP2/HP6/LV3&LV5/GB13&CV13/H7/SM17/LI11/LI4/LU1/LU7

- Anchovy Pesto 156
- Black Olive and Lemon Courgetti 155
- Sacred Hot Chocolate 211
- Roasted Chickpeas 207
- No Shame Millet Muffins 290

Hormone and Nerve function

Points CV17/GV24.5/K7/K6/BL10/GB20/HT6/SM17

- Oatmilk Pancakes 097
- Chilli Relish 313
- Avocado, Barley and Arame Salad 088
- Red Rice and Minted Pea Salad 241
- Bone Broth 057

Sexual Addiction

Points CV1&2/CV6/CV17/GV26/K1/LV3/GB9/GB13&CV4/H7/SP6/LU7

- Liquorice Stick 293
- Sweet Potato Falafel 273
- Coconut Pancakes with Sweet Sauce 198

Increasing Circulation and flow

Points K3/BL23/BL52/HP3/TH4/LV3/GB41/SM17/ST28/SP6/SP12/SP13/LI11

- Green Beans, Black Ear Fungus and Sesame Salad 099
- Three Colour Noodles 153
- Black Wood Ear Noodle Soup 320
- Roasted Peaches with Dark Chocolate 363
- Insalata Caprese 246
- Special Umeboshi Sauce 129

Menopause / Andropause

Points CV4&6/CV17/GV20&24.5/GV26/GV4/K1&K6&K7&K3/BL23&52/BL10/HP6/TH9or10&ST36/LV3/GB20/H6&H7/ST36&CV6/SP6/LU7&K6

- Sexing the Cherry 230
- Chrysanthemum Tea 132
- Gomasio Green Beans 073
- Shaved Fennel Salad 141
- Beet Marmalade 139
- Poached Egg with Grilled Mackerel 133
- Sage Tea 181

Reducing Inflammation and Pain

Points CV1and2/CV6/BL10/HP3/TH9or10&ST36/LV3/LV5/GB9/GB21/ ST18/ST28/SP6/LI4

- Chilli con Barley 093
- Chilli Pesto 313
- Anti-Inflammatory Tea 309
- Chocolate Cherries 252
- Barley Water 085
- Ginger Compress 237

WHO AM I TO TELL YOU?

It was 1999 in the kitchen of Lois Dana Retreat Centre, during my Shiatsu training, I first tasted Miso and Kudzu soup. As one of my teachers, Josephine Lynch, explained the energetic properties of this salty paste in Chinese Medicine, I felt my kidneys relax. My spine soften and the muscles across my chest ease.
My whole nervous system was calmer than it had been for weeks. It was at that moment I understood that food was more than just fuel, it was medicine.

Using the Five Element System of Shiatsu and Traditional Chinese Medicine *(see graphic on page 12)* I began to deepen my knowledge of the energetics of food. My previous culinary experiences had been during travels in my early twenties, preparing breakfast, lunch and dinner for eight hundred people on an Israeli Kibbutz plus making egg and chips for British tourists at a beach bar in Greece. In these instances, food had been the function for the day ahead or to soothe the night before. However now I was having a relationship with food. I knew it's season, it's colour, it's flavour. I knew which body part, which emotion and sensory organ it affected. At this epiphanal moment, I experienced food in a whole new way. It made perfect sense to me that the liver would need sour food to cut through fatty sluggish congestion that slowed energy flow and metabolism. I found it obvious that the immune system, housed in the large intestine, would be improved with pungent food such as ginger and garlic. When I thought of the colour orange I could taste sweet on my tongue, my saliva increased and therefore I knew that the spleen was responsible for the regulation of blood sugars.

For me, the connections seem easy and with many hundreds of clients in my practice over the years, the solutions that the Five Element System offers works for them too. Memorably, I once had a client who wished to get pregnant. I diagnosed her as having suffered shock in her early childhood which resulted in her having become cold and stagnated in the lower abdomen and small intestine. She also suffered anxiousness, insomnia and cold feet. This all pointed to the heart and small intestine lacking in Chi to move and warm the body and blood. I prescribed warming and red foods such as tomato and coconut soup, roasted peppers with fresh coriander, calming chamomile, valerian plus a bedtime practice that included self shiatsu points and breathing practices; within two months she was pregnant.

My postgraduate studies in Chinese Medicine, Tantra and Taoism have deepened my experience, my courage, my understanding and my relationship with food. In 2013 I began teaching regular, drop in, Conscious Cooking Classes in Dublin City Centre. Over six years, a community developed and I taught a wide range of people, not trained in Chinese Medicine, to use the Five Element System for maintaining health, balance and wellness. In my books and blogs, I share recipes, insights, health practices and personal experiences that have helped transform pain and trauma for myself and my clients. Asking simple questions such as "How am I feeling?" and "What do I need?" are the first steps into connection with the power we all have to affect our well-being. Food and the Five Elements can guide us to answers. We are energy made manifest and as such we are constantly changing. To maintain balance and understand the body's ever-changing symptoms, cravings, feelings and emotions we can use the Five Element system and let food be our guide.

"The Five Elemental energies of Wood, Fire, Earth, Metal and Water encompass all the myriad phenomena of nature. It is a paradigm that applies equally to humans."

The Yellow Emperor's Classic
of Internal Medicine 2BC

I have used the Five Element System and all the tools within this book to heal my hot flushes, sexual dysfunction, heartbreak, panic attacks, ice cream addiction, low libido, terrible tinder dates, dizzy spells, urinary tract infections and more. My appetite for life is better than ever. Generating and circulating sexual energy with its passion and desire I believe, keeps me youthful, healthy, happy and in love.

joanne
FAULKNER

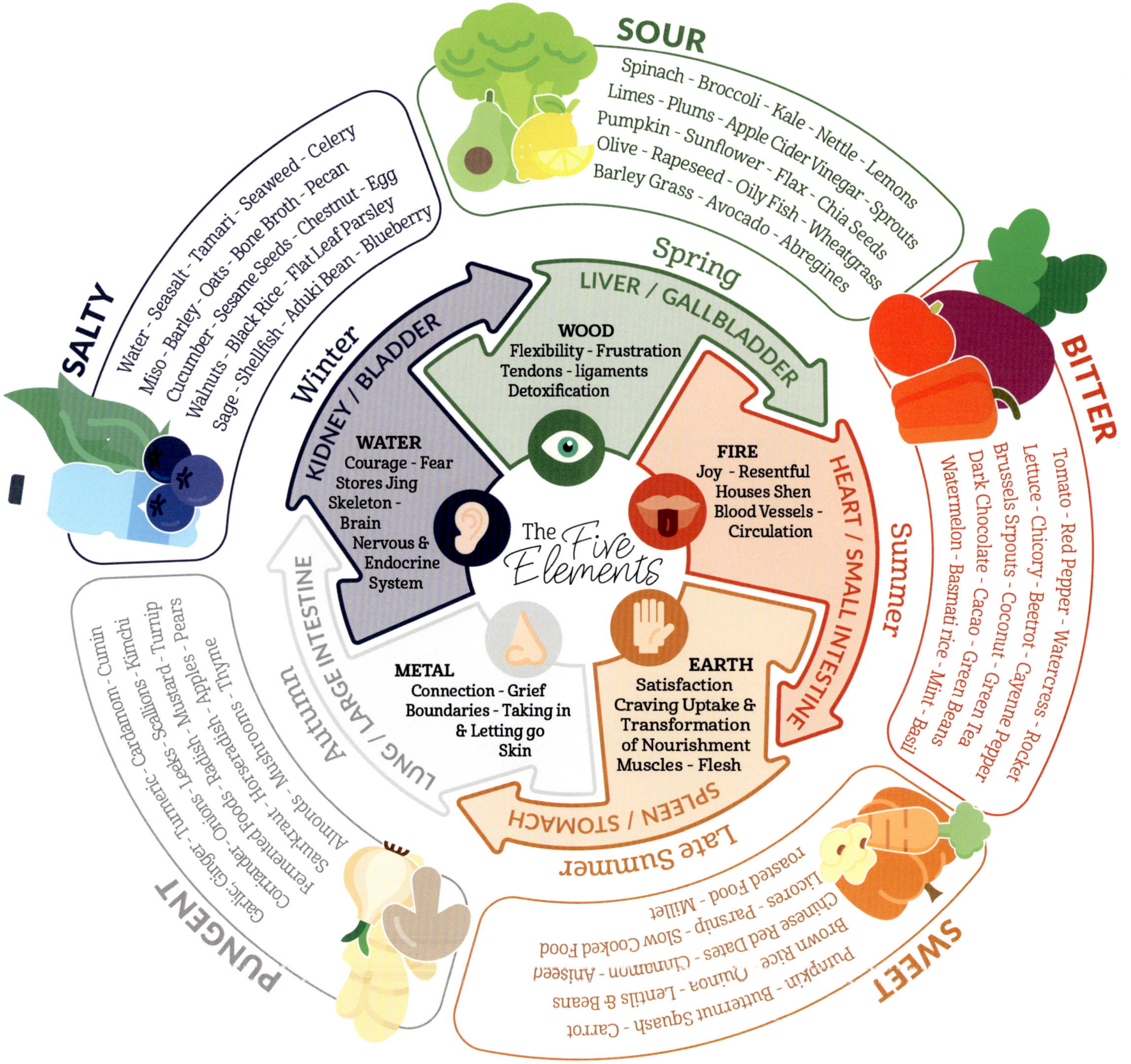

SOUR
Spinach - Broccoli - Kale - Nettle - Lemons
Limes - Plums - Apple Cider Vinegar - Sprouts
Pumpkin - Sunflower - Flax - Chia Seeds
Olive - Rapeseed - Oily Fish - Wheatgrass
Barley Grass - Avocado - Abregines
BITTER
Tomato - Red Pepper - Watercress - Rocket
Lettuce - Chicory - Beetrot - Cayenne Pepper
Brussels Srpouts - Coconut - Green Tea
Dark Chocolate - Cacao - Green Beans
Watermelon - Basmati rice - Mint - Basil
SWEET
Pumpkin - Butternut Squash - Carrot
Brown Rice - Quinoa - Lentils & Beans
Chinese Red Dates - Cinnamon - Aniseed
Licores - Parsnip - Slow Cooked Food
roasted Food - Millet
PUNGENT
Garlic; Ginger - Turmeric - Cardamom - Cumin
Corriander - Onions - Leeks - Scallions - Kimchi
Fermented Foods - Radish - Mustard - Turnip
Saukraut - Horseradish - Apples - Pears
Almonds - Mushrooms - Thyme
SALTY
Water - Seasalt - Tamari - Seaweed - Celery
Miso - Barley - Oats - Bone Broth - Pecan
Cucumber - Sesame Seeds - Chestnut - Egg
Walnuts - Black Rice - Flat Leaf Parsley
Sage - Shellfish - Aduki Bean - Blueberry
Spring
LIVER / GALLBLADDER
WOOD
Flexibility - Frustration
Tendons - ligaments
Detoxification
Summer
HEART / SMALL INTESTINE
FIRE
Joy - Resentful
Houses Shen
Blood Vessels -
Circulation
Late Summer
SPLEEN / STOMACH
EARTH
Satisfaction
Craving Uptake &
Transformation
of Nourishment
Muscles - Flesh
Autumn
LUNG / LARGE INTESTINE
METAL
Connection - Grief
Boundaries - Taking in
& Letting go
Skin
Winter
KIDNEY / BLADDER
WATER
Courage - Fear
Stores Jing
Skeleton -
Brain
Nervous &
Endocrine
System
The Five Elements

MISO AND KUDZU SOUP

150 ml water
1 spring onion
1-2 tsp. Miso Organic Paste
1 tsp. Kudzu
Sprinkle of wakame seaweed

In a small saucepan, bring the water to the boil, add the spring onions to let the flavour of the onions infuse for a minute or so. Meanwhile, dissolve 1 level teaspoon of kudzu powder in a glass containing 1 tablespoon of water. Add this paste to the water after it has reached boiling point and been turned down to a simmer. The kudzu will begin to thicken the water, remove from the heat, sprinkle with seaweed and stir in the miso paste. Overheating or cooking the miso will damage the living bacteria contained in the fermented miso paste so take care of this precious salty ingredient. The deep blue black of the seaweed further fortifies the kidneys ensuring a balanced, relaxed nervous system.

You can add to the dish with noodles, egg and/or simplify it by just pouring water from a recently boiled kettle over a tablespoon of miso and stir until dissolved.

GLOSSARY

Traditional Chinese Medicine – ancient system of well-being which uses diet, herbs, bodywork and exercise to maintain balance and prevent ill-health.

The Yellow Emperors Classic of Medicine (*Huángdì Nèijīng*) – original source document for Traditional Chinese Medicine which is over 2000 years old. Written as a dialogue between the Yellow Emperor and his ministers and physicians, explaining the how the laws of the natural world apply to the life of man and how diet, lifestyle, emotions, environment and natural aging can be used to stay healthy.

Holistic – views the physical, emotional, spiritual body as a whole inseparable system.

Yin/Yang – complementary natural forces whose balance is essential for health.

Five Elements – used to explain the relationship between the different energies found in nature and the body. Each element has its specific characteristics, such as organ, body part, sense, flavour, colours, time of year, etc.

Shiatsu – Japanese form of bodywork that combines acupressure plus massage to balance Chi, nourish Jing and Shen in the body.

Shiatsu & Conscious Cooking – Uses Shiatsu plus dietary advice from the Five Element system of diagnosis and treatment.

Chi (Qi, Ki) – Bodies vital energy that animates life and flows through the meridians.

Shen – Consciousness or spiritual connection, housed in the heart.

Jing – the energy with which a lifeform is given at conception housed in kidneys.

Acu point – a specific point, usually found on a meridian, where heat, pressure or needles are applied to effect change in the body/mind energy system.

When using the acupoints in the chapters following, be aware that the meridians are on both sides of the body so the points are mirrored on either sides. For example, you have two arms, so the same point is used on both arms. Only the extraordinary meridians of Conception Vessel and Governing Vessel which run the midline of the body use singular points.

Meridian – a channel for energy which is part of a network that connects the whole body as a living system.

Dan Tien – major energy centre in the body where the Chi pools as a "field of elixir" to be flowed around the body for nourishment and health. Traditionally there are three Dan Tien – Upper (between the eyebrows), Middle (heart level) and Lower (approx two fingers below belly button).

Burning Centres - three centres in the body – **Upper Burner** controls intake, **Middle Burner** controls transformation, **Lower Burner** controls elimination, all maintained by the triple heater.

Conception Vessel – one of the extraordinary meridians that begins inside the body at the lower dan tien and is numbered externally from the perineum up the front mid-line of the body to a point under the lower lip. It is Yin and nourishes blood and Jing.

Governing Vessel – one of the extraordinary meridians that begins between anus and the coccyx, runs up the mid-line of the spine, over the skull, forehead, nose and finishes on the mid-line above the top of the upper lip. It is Yang and moves the body to action.

Ming Men – Gate of Vitality acupoint on the Governing Vessel that distributes kidney Yang.

Autonomic Nervous System – regulates key involuntary functions of the body, including the activity of the heart, the lungs, the glands and the digestive tract.

Sympathetic Nervous System - accelerates the heart rate, constricts blood vessels and raises blood pressure in preparation for intense physical activity in response to impending danger and stressful situations. Functions not necessary to immediate survival, such as digestion and procreation, shut down.

Parasympathetic Nervous System – conserves energy slowing the heart rate, relaxing muscles, increasing intestinal and gland activity (excluding sweat glands) including the ability to become aroused and maintain an erection.

INTERNAL CONDITIONS OF:

Dampness – collection of moisture causing heavy and foggy energy - generating sticky secretions and protracted, dense pain especially in the middle and lower burner.

Dryness – linked to dehydration and scant body fluids especially in the mucous membranes of the body including lungs, nasal cavities, digestive tract, skin, hair and nails.

Heat – causes erratic movement of Chi and often associated with inflammation, redness of skin, irritability and inability for the Shen to settle.

Cold – creates contraction, obstructions and slow movement of Chi causing cramps and sharp pain.

Wind – often works with the other internal climates to invade the body, moving energy, pathogens and symptoms erratically causing tremors, spasms and twitching.

All eggs are Free Range Organic and Stock unless otherwise stated is a Vegetable Bouillon free from MSG and colouring.

INTRODUCTION

HOW TO USE THIS BOOK

Good sex is about more than physical penetration. It's about intimacy, openness, truth, connection, timing, playfulness, vulnerability, giving and receiving. It's about being in a body that functions well and that you love. This book is full of food, poetry, paintings and acupressure points. It is full of the juiciness of life. Its purpose is for you to engage with your body in a deeply connected way that is full of love. ***It is not essential to have a partner to use this book and strengthen the experience of love in your life because after all, how much love is in your life is really up to you. It's never about the other person.*** Can you see the beauty in life, new-born babies, flowers, trees, food and the sky? How much joy, happiness and pleasure you experience depends on you. Like a muscle, we have to practice generating and receiving love so it is plentiful. It doesn't diminish by giving it away rather it grows, spreading like light from one candle lit to another.

I have spent long periods of my life without having sex with another person but I always considered my life to be deeply sensual and sexual because I am willing to experience all that life flows my way. Just like every human being, life has been full of pleasure and pain; both emotions helped me understand who I am and what I need. ***People join us on the journey for many reasons. Some bring heartache and some ecstasy but our emotional response is ultimately our responsibility.***

It is possible to create conditions in which love flourishes. For example, where you live, the partner you choose, the food you eat, the colours of your walls or how much time you spend in nature. For me, Chinese Medicine has given me a tool to show my body and mind that I love it. I ask how it's feeling and see what it needs. Sometimes I need to watch Judge Judy, sometimes I need a cup of tea, a massage, time in bed by myself, an orgasm, barley water or a chat with my mum. I am my ultimate, beautiful, fantastic lover and so I treat myself as such, with love, affection and attention. I am tender with the little girl inside who is nervous and confused. I am cautious with the rebellious teenager that loves to be out of control and I am generous to the woman that has borne heartbreak yet still stands tall and has the courage to love.

The most important aspect of love is not in giving or the receiving: it's in the being. When I need love from others, or need to give love to others, I'm caught in an unstable situation. Being in love, rather than giving or taking love, is the only thing that provides stability. Being in love means seeing the Beloved all around me. When we see the Beloved in each person, it's like walking through a garden, watching flowers bloom all around us.

Ram Dass

HOW COULD YOU LOVE YOURSELF MORE?

Would you spend time in nature, make a beautiful meal, read poetry, watch the clouds, watch a box set, have an early night with a good book, go dancing, buy yourself flowers or lie down next to your child and listen to them sleep? If you were to take yourself on a date, what would you do? *When you are able to love yourself and do loving things for yourself then you can spread the love to family members, intimate partners, lifelong friends, and even strangers.* Ultimately, this unconditional love can be spread to everyone we meet – loving others as we love ourselves. The place to start is with ourselves, which can be the most difficult place. *It is far easier to love the small baby, the handsome hero, or the helpless princess and lay blame for lack of love with an abusive, forgetful, distant husband, a frigid, nagging, unavailable wife, or the selfish, smelly teenager but ultimately it's our choice how we love.* Things may happen to us but our reaction, our thoughts, our feelings and how we live life is up to us. Use this book with recipes and sensual practices as a way to love yourself more everyday. Start by asking: How am I feeling and what do I need? What do I want to eat? Use the Quick Reference Guide, Five Elements Chart or the interactive website[1] to find the food and the flavour that's good for your body today.

---

1 www.Shiatsu-ConsciousCooking.com/app

A WORD OF ADVICE

This book is about staying well and healthy – about maintaining balance and wellness. Certain foods are recommended for certain conditions and organs but if you have a serious condition please consult a qualified health practitioner. No two cases of the same condition are alike therefore the same solution for every body does not apply. We require different doses, different combinations of medicines and different time scales for convalescence. This book aims to give you power and connection with your own lovely body. We are all unique with our own decisions, attitude, consequences and life journey. Use the information here to stay well and healthy, in connection with your body, feeling what it needs and making the best decisions to nurture and love yourself more.

"Love is not relational, it's who you are"

Krishna Das, Kirtan, Dublin 2019

We can let the
circumstances of our lives
harden us
so that we become
increasingly resentful
and afraid,
or we can let them soften us
and make us kinder.
You always have
the choice.

- Dalai Lama

THE TAOIST/TANTRA BIT

I find the word Taoism and Tantra mean different things to different people so I thought it best to be clear at the beginning of what they mean to me in the context of this book.

We are all familiar with energy, we bask in the radiant energy of the sun, we feel the power of the wind and watch the surge of the rolling sea. The Tao in Chinese Medicine is the understanding of that energy, not as a concept but as a natural order of life unfolding. Following the Tao means understanding this energy and how it manifests in our everyday life with flow and ease. To live within the Tao means to be present, flowing this natural energy for tip-top mental, spiritual, emotional, and physical health, rather than fighting with it, forcing life be the way we want it.

As humans, we transform energy constantly from the food we eat and the air we breathe. We also generate energy deep within our bodies. It feels joyous, excitable and expansive. It is the sexual energy of creation that brings new life into being. If allowed to flow, it begins new projects, it inspires everyday choices and it guides life. It's not just about having sex and making babies. ***Sexual energy can be used internally to heal our bodies and even bring relief to the mind. It is precious energy not to be squandered looking for external attention or easy satisfaction***. If our sexual energy flows freely all around our body, without tension or blockages, this can be our original blissful state of being, which is flexible, exuberant and delighted to be alive.

"He who denies sex is a filthy person who smears in the lowest way his own parents who have begotten him"

Egon Schiele

In India, thousands of years ago, they realized that by becoming aware of this sexual energy, by harnessing and directing it through mental and physical training, they could attain heightened states of consciousness. Thus, Tantra was born. This book doesn't contain sexual acrobatics or directions on how to sustain lovemaking. There are plenty of good books out there that do, I have listed some of my favourites at the "Recommended Reading List" at the back of the book. This book begins with the bodily senses and how they respond to food. Focusing in on the senses brings us into the body right here, right now in this present moment. ***When you are fully present with your food you smell it, you see it, you hear how it is in the mouth, you feel it with your tongue and you taste it.*** However, if you eat your dinner watching the TV you might not even realize you have eaten it before its all gone.

Tantra makes the practice of engaging with the sensual body a sacred experience. If I consciously eat a raw chocolate ball, I taste it right then and there, I smell it, I hold it, I feel it only at that moment. If I share the food with another, we taste it together, we experience it together, deepening and strengthening our connection with each other. Often to do this effectively means eating slowly, mindfully, really engaging with the senses, taking time to connect.

THE BASICS - TO EAT OR NOT TO EAT

Shiatsu originated in Japan but it has its roots in Traditional Chinese Medicine. In the 6th Century, a Buddhist monk introduced the ancient system of massage, acupuncture, and herbalism to Japan but it was adapted to suit the culture. In particular, the Japanese developed the manual healing and diagnostic art of using the abdomen (*Hara*) and the back in the treatment. Shiatsu is sometimes described as acupuncture without needles, which to an extent is true. Shiatsu practitioners use the same meridian pairs, same points, and the same structure found in acupuncture and Traditional Chinese Medicine. The core belief is the same, that everything is energy, therefore nothing ends, it simply changes form. ***This changing energy, called the Tao, makes up absolutely everything in the universe and is explained and understood through Yin/Yang and the Five Elements (see diagrams on page 12, 26 and 38).***

In Shiatsu and Traditional Chinese Medicine, the body is classified into Yin/Yang organ pairs and meridian pathways which correspond to emotions, flavours, seasons and colours. There are no good or bad foods – simply foods which do and do not suit us at this time. It's all about connecting with the body, seeing what it wants and loving ourselves more. My mission is to explain the connection between physical symptoms, emotional conditions and the food we eat However, you must take the information and make it your own. Don't blindly follow mine or anyone else's ideas, instructions or dogma. To do that is to do a disservice to your own divine knowledge and intelligence. Search out your own way that brings you a healthy happy life. Question things and remain curious, this is the flow of the Tao.

"How shall a man judge what to do in such times?
'As he ever has judged,' said Aragorn. 'Good and I'll have not changed since yesteryear...It is a man's part to discern them, as much in the Golden Wood as in his own house."

J.R.R. Tolkien

Facts and figures surround us in this technological age, our own discernment is essential so that information becomes wisdom. There are many therapies, many therapists. Find a path that speaks to you, that you understand, that you can integrate and make your own. For example, the world is full of languages. Simply because I don't understand Arabic doesn't make Arabic poetry any less beautiful. Rumi, the famous Sufi poet, wrote in Persian, Turkish, Arabic and Greek. His words, which have been translated for me to understand, unlock something in me and I find peace in the moment of reading. The way he puts words and syllables together creates harmony and colour that resonates with my heart and my smile. Hopefully, my interpretation of Traditional Chinese Medicine speaks to you and you find some enlightening moments, where you can see food for the healing powers it has and that you understand the symptoms your body gives you as directional messages towards joyous, balanced health.

The Five Element System

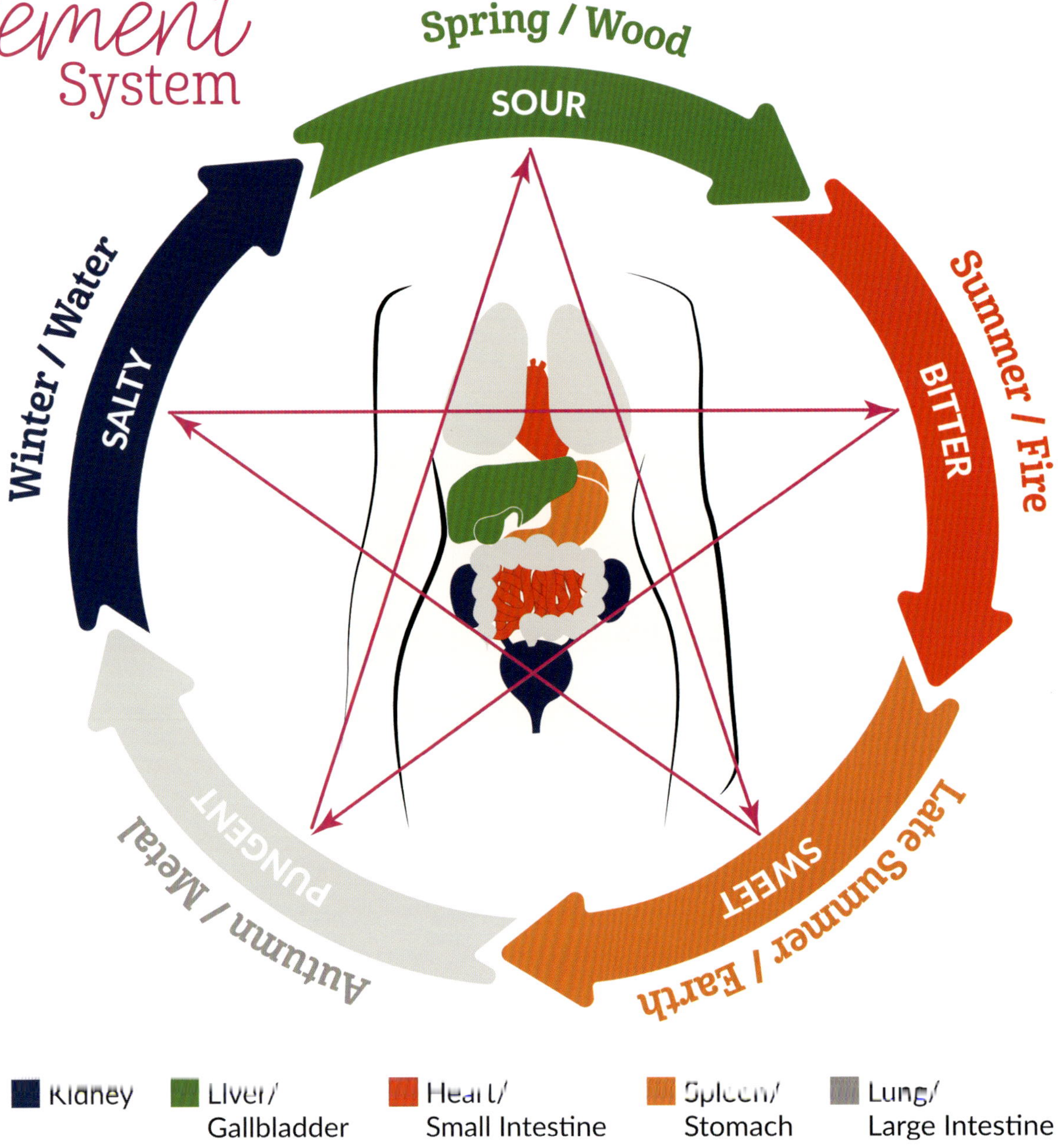

THE FIVE ELEMENTS

Traditional medicine differs from modern western medicine in that it doesn't view disease as stemming from germs or bacteria. It doesn't rely solely on strong medicines or surgery to stop the invasion or growth rather it looks to balance the whole system as a method of prevention. Bacteria, germs and cancers require a very specific set of conditions such as temperature, moisture and PH balance to survive and thrive within the human system. It is our responsibility that we listen to our body to keep it in balance so that pathogens cannot lodge and grow in our system. Sometimes there is a tendency to wait until a condition becomes chronic before we make changes to diet or lifestyle. Only when a symptom becomes intolerable do we make a change because we have no choice. Even then I have seen people carry on living the same lifestyle expecting the medicine to make the change, rather than accepting that a problem has occurred due to a lifestyle imbalance. The symptom may be treated with medicine but unless the lifestyle cause is addressed there will be no real healing. I invite you to make conscious choices regarding food. Make balanced decisions otherwise the luxury of choice may not always be yours to take.

The System of the 5 Elements guides you to make informed choices that relate to your unique body and emotional soul.

"Yin and Yang and the Five Elemental Energies form the main roots in the Taoist tree of health. The Five Elemental Energies... Illuminate the internal functional relationships between the body's various vital organs and explain how external elements such as foods and medicinal herbs influence the organs and their functions."

The Complete Book of Chinese Health & Healing - Daniel Reid

The Five Element graphic shows how all Five Elements interact. The outer circle is supportive. For example, wood/liver and gallbladder supports fire/ heart and small intestine. In our body, this means blood, detoxified by the liver, is easier for the heart to circulate. Whereas the internal arrows demonstrate the destructive cycle, for example, Earth/spleen and stomach weaken water/kidney and bladder. This means too much sweet sugar creates an acid environment which weakens bones and puts pressure on the nervous system.

Meridians & Organs	Liver/ Gallbladder	Heart/ Small Intestine	Spleen/ Stomach	Lung / Large Intestine	Kidney/ Bladder
Element	Wood	Fire	Earth	Metal	Water
Season	Spring	Summer	Late Summer	Autumn	Winter
Flavour	Sour	Bitter	Sweet	Pungent	Salty
Property	Dynamic, flexible and effective	Expansion	Centring and supporting	Protection & Boundaries	Core foundation of calm & being
Energy Quality	Generative	Expansive	Stabilizing	Contracting	Conserving
Emotion	Creativity/ Anger	Joy/ Bitterness	Satisfaction / Craving	Grief / Letting Go	Fear / Calm Flow
Attribute	Planning	Intelligence	Memory	Evaluation / Judgement	Will Power
Colour	Yellow/Green	Red	Orange / Brown	White	Blue / Black
Sensory Organ	Eye	Tongue	Lips	Nose	Ear
Sense	Sight	Speech	Taste	Smell	Hearing
Sound	Shouting	Laughing	Singing	Crying	Groaning
Body Part	Tendons & Ligaments	Blood Vessels	Flesh, Fat Muscle Tone	Skin, Body Hair	Bones, Teeth, Bone Marrow, Hormones
Bodily fluid	Tears	Sweat	Saliva	Mucous	Urine
Adversely affected by					
	Wind	Heat	Damp	Dry	Cold

Please Note: heart protector/triple heater are under the domain of the heart.

Some examples using the chart:
If you have floaters in the eyes or the eyes are **becoming yellowish or green**, begin by asking questions about the liver. If your tears are blocked, look at perhaps are your **emotions flowing**. Are you feeling **frustrated**, do you wake **tense and stiff**? Treat

the liver with plenty of fat clearing sour foods such as lemon, rhubarb and plums and green foods which stimulate the gallbladder.

If someone was **red** all over the face that would signify the blood was not being dispersed throughout the body properly and perhaps there was too much **heat accumulating**. This assessment points to the heart. The same too if there was not enough **circulation** and **the extremities became cold** causing Reynards or chilblains. To make sure the blood is healthy and strong eat plenty of antioxidant red food such as beetroot, peppers and tomatoes.

If someone constantly **craved** things, especially sweet things this would point to a spleen imbalance. The same if they had an **overproduction of saliva** or fat deposited around the body. With all these symptoms I usually find clients complain of **poor memory or brain fog**. So don't reach for the chocolate bar – rather have naturally sweet **orange** foods such as carrots, sweet potato and butternut squash.

Skin conditions such as eczema or psoriasis would begin in the large intestine. Often when people experience the **death** of a loved one or any deep loss it can affect the lungs and manifest in **chest infections and mucus build up**. Emotionally, People can become isolated in their **grief** and their boundaries too protected from anyone offering support. Support your body at this time by eating pungent foods such as ginger and garlic to clear sticky mucus from the lung and large intestine.

Blue /black circles around the eyes are a sign that **adrenals** are overworked and the body hasn't rested enough. Exhaustion sets in and only **will power keeps us going**. Sometimes we might get a sore throat or a urinary infection. These symptoms clearly say kidney and bladder energy is being depleted. Make sure you are getting enough rest, enough **minerals**, salt and water. Interpretation is personal, ask yourself, how much is enough?

Often symptoms may not be clear cut. You may have menopausal symptoms of weight gain and hot flashes. This combines three sections: kidney - correlates with hormonal change; spleen - with weight gain and heart/triple heater - with the temperature change of a hot flash. Take care of these three organs with seaweed, to supplement the kidneys; sweet vegetables and whole grains for the spleen; and plenty of detoxifying foods such as tomatoes and lettuce to calm the heart.

This system can take years to master but there's always time to learn and now is a good time to start. I find the five Element System gives me a language in which I can speak to the body, hear and interpret its symptoms. To listen and be heard is essential in any great relationship, that's how you feel loved. So begin with yourself... How do you feel right now and what do you need?

Rule No. 1 in eating for health -
If it does not ripen and rot, it is not food - don't eat it.

So called foods, made with preservatives such as BHA (Butylated Hydroxyanisole) and BHT (Butylated Hydroxytoluene), Propyl Gallate, Sodium Nitrate and Sodium Nitrite are not foods. Also, ingredients such as artificial sweeteners, high fructose corn syrup, and Monosodium Glutamate (MSG - often labelled

as yeast extract) are added to food to stop it going rancid before it gets to the table. All these ingredients can cause serious problems for the nervous, detoxification and digestion systems. It is best to avoid food that has been pre-packaged and ready made as these meals have to wait a long time from manufacture to table, to your body. For this reason they contain chemicals to make them taste better and last longer. For optimum health, choose fresh ingredients and cook from scratch.

Some preservatives have been used for thousands of years such as salt and vinegar. Where appropriate it can be fantastic to eat these in small amounts as the concentrated energy found in umeboshi plum (see liver chapter) or the bacteria that is found in fermented foods such as kimchi, miso or sauerkraut (see lung chapter) can maintain balance and vitality in the body. Again it is important to follow your connection to your own body's symptoms. Too much Umeboshi plum can drain the body of energy and too much Kimchi can disrupt the large intestine. How much is too much is up to you and your body. If you are not sure, start with what you think is a small amount and work up from there. If you are attempting to remedy a condition, work together with a health practitioner who has experience and can assist you in finding your path.

FIVE ELEMENTS OF TOUCH

As previously discussed, there are five basic meridian pairs and these equate to flavours, colours, seasons and emotions. We use these indicators to help us diagnose the cause of the symptoms. In this way, Chinese Medicine uses a very distinct system to help diagnose a problem, treat the symptom and address the cause. The practice uses a holistic system of diet, massage, acupressure and lifestyle practices such as meditation and Chi gong. This repertoire of tools at your fingertips is essential to satiate an ever-changing physical and emotional body.

In the same way that we need a variety of foods, we need various forms of touch. Each meridian pair responds differently to tactile interaction. It could be that you start with stomach/spleen and move through all the elements finishing with liver/gallbladder or perhaps you want the feeling of flowing water of the kidney meridian through your hands and fingers. Talk with your partner to see how they feel and what they need. You don't have to have a partner for this, try these forms of touch on your own body.

Stomach / Spleen
Element Earth – Use pressure of the palms to push into the hollows of the body. (Backs of the knees, crook of the elbow, under the collarbone, small of the back, waist, ankles, arch of the foot). Hold these spaces like you are filling them up with substance.

Kidney / Bladder
Element Water – Use your hands, arms, elbows to flow over the body with a medium touch and pressure. As if your limbs were water flowing over your or your lover's body, cover them from head to toe.

Heart / Small Intestine
Element Fire – Wake the entire body up with light pummeling, flicking, slaps and using nails to enliven the skin.

Lung / Large Intestine
Element Air – Use the lightest of touch, your hair, a feather, the tips of your fingers even your breath to brush over the skin of the body.

Liver / Gallbladder
Ether – massage the space above the body, comb the air, making circles and swooshing over the arms and chest down toward the pelvis and legs. Use your imagination and create patterns and circles, see if you can feel areas of ether that feel heavier or solid and others that feel light and spacious.

Ask yourself what you need and find the element to match this. Use the free quiz at *Shiatsu-ConsciousCooking.com/app* to practice connecting how you feel with the correct meridians, organs and flavours.

Professional therapies span a myriad of ways to talk to and nourish the body physically. **Sports massage** can be deep, physical and fiery. **Shiatsu and Ayurvedic** massage can tend to the need for nurturing and holding. **Bioenergy** work often uses the etheric field to change the physical and emotional state of the receiver. **Lomi-Lomi** uses long strokes and the whole body to relax the nervous system. Remember there is always self practice, using your own hands to respond to your own levels of touch. Your body will really thank you for it. You will feel relaxed, alive, nourished and loved.

FOOD IS NOT JUST FUNCTIONAL

Food, for many, has become pleasure laden. We eat fast and die young. Using food as a reward or to soothe and comfort. Sometimes eating is just a habit. However, we can build a better relationship with food. Much of the world is struggling to deal with the health effects of overeating while millions are malnourished or starving to death. This Yin Yang balance needs to change and consciousness of imbalance is a beginning. In the extreme, not eating or overeating because you hate your body is a way to become sick. Extremes weaken the body sometimes to the point of death. Balance your intake of food with other earthly pleasures. Eating less and receiving energy and pleasure from other areas of life is entirely possible.

In this book the emotional component of why we choose to eat and drink the food we do is clarified. Take a look at how you define yourself with your diet. Do you use food to stay social and in connection with others? Do you eat food for comfort or out of habit? When was the last time you allowed yourself to feel hungry? Do you let uncomfortable feelings or memories arise before you suppress them with food or drink? Being conscious of our eating patterns is a place to start. My friend and mentor, Erik Forsmark used to say "You have to dig where you stand" or put another way, if you want things to change you have to recognize, accept and take responsibility for where you are right now.

I live in a city, it is busy and fast-paced. Physical space is a valuable commodity, mental space can be scarce with so many people and so much noise. It's hard to find gaps to unpack your mind, understand your feelings and give space for emotions. They pop up at inconvenient times only to be squashed back with food, drink, drugs or other distractions like TV or social media. If you don't allow the metaphorical golden fields of space in your life, suppressed emotions can break you and can make you sick. ***Food is a mirror for your relationship with life. Allow space, allow your body to live. Fill your life with other things not just fodder at designated feeding times.*** Fill it with all the things you love — sex, dancing, sitting in nature, massage, making love, stroking your children's hair, walking on the beach, swimming in the sea, watching films, teaching, listening, laughing until you cry or walking in a forest on a rainy day. You will feel the benefit of eating less. The hunger will subside because you are filled with life. It's not about control it is about flow. Allow the energy of the world to fill you up. There's energy all around you. Sit quietly and allow yourself to be loved, touched and stroked by it. Lie on the ground and feel it entering your meridians. Breath it in then feel yourself connected as your energy flows back to the earth. This is your lover, feel the heartbeat and magnificence, it will fill you up.

Love is the key. Loving yourself, and loving the food you choose is essential. If you don't like brown rice or green smoothies then don't eat them. Fill your life with the love of food. There will be consequences if you eat 3 pizzas and drink 10 pints of beer every day but if you are truly in love with your life you will make conscious choices that reflect your relationship with life. Food and drink won't be used to escape or mask pain or other uncomfortable feelings. But be easy on yourself. Use the 5 elements but don't be a slave to them. Enjoy your journey and the communion between how you feel and what you eat. Feel good and eat well.

In these pages I share many personal experiences and methods that have improved and healed my relationships, love, pleasure and sexual experiences. There have been times in my life where I have had a love affair with food. Mabrouk in Sardinia with Paula where we ate dish after sumptuous dish, with no menu and no idea what was coming next. My birthday in Galicia with Simon where we ate a platter of seafood with hammers, tweezers and other operational tools, washed down with saucers of cloudy local white wine. Afterwards we cycled down a dark unlit hill, full of hairpin bends, with only our dynamo bike lights to guide us. If we wanted to see where we were going we had to cycle faster and faster. So we flew down the hill, high on crab, wine and the wind in our hair.

Use flavours, food and the Five Elements as a tool for communication with your physical and emotional body. There's no getting it wrong and there's no correct diet.

Everyday is different so drop the anxiety about being perfect and follow your joy, follow your bliss, follow your ecstasy. I feel that joy as I run around the park in the rain, as I walk on the beach at new years, as I kiss my kids goodnight and as I watch the trees behind my house. There is joy to be experienced everywhere.

Don't fill your life with food so you feel nothing else. Choose food consciously.

For some, a go-to craving is chocolate, crisps, cheese or chips. For me, I love alcohol. Gin, wine and a good Guinness being my preferences. But I have to take care how and when I partake. From an early age, binge drinking was part of my culture. I used stolen alcohol from my parents drink cabinet to find courage to be me on a Friday night. It was my crutch. I have drunk out of boredom and sometimes to excess when I wanted to release a pressure valve of responsibility. Drinking in this way does not serve me. I end up putting on weight, getting cystitis and feeling frustrated. I am quick to anger, low in energy, creativity, motivation and suffer bouts of insomnia. Alcohol isn't the problem but rather my use of it. It isn't the best friend that backs me up and brings me bravery. I have to be my own best friend. As I get older and approach menopause, alcohol plays havoc with my hormones and my libido so I am very careful with gin and tonic intake. I still really enjoy the experience of drinking but I'm conscious of it's consequences. The following dish is more a sharing than a recipe. It was one of my most memorable, fun-filled sexual food experiences. I was bursting with the joy of the adventure, the decadence and sheer pleasure of the food. Sometimes filling ourselves with the love of food is just as important as the nutritional content.

12 OYSTERS AND 2 GLASSES OF DRY WHITE WINE

Oysters in Chinese Medicine are a valued superfood that feed the Jing of the body. They increase longevity, nourish blood, improve libido, fertility and reduce premature ejaculation. This corresponds with western nutritional medicine as they contain more Zinc than many other food sources, fantastic for boosting immunity and providing antioxidants to repair the body and reduce inflammation.[2] Oysters are rich in omega 3 fatty acids improving heart health and blood circulation[3] plus Zinc deficiency in men can lead to low testosterone and impotence.[4] In women, Zinc boosts progesterone which helps with fertility, menopause and irregular menstruation.[5]
The high levels of minerals such as calcium, magnesium, iron, and selenium and slightly salty flavour support the kidneys in Chinese Medicine which stores the jing, strengthens bones and manages sexual desire.

Ireland is an amazing place for fresh oysters. It has an unspoilt and diverse coastline perfect for cultivating bright, fresh oysters. Always make sure your oysters come from a trusted source. Eat them regularly but as with everything else, in moderation or else you may become a Casanova who reputedly ate dozens to fortify himself before a tryst.

12 Oysters
A squeeze of lemon juice
2 drops of Tabasco sauce
2 Glasses of ice cold Verdicchio

It was a grey wintry Wednesday afternoon. My children were sitting at the kitchen table receiving their maths grinds and would be for the next couple of hours. So my partner and I took the opportunity to head off for a sneaky snack in Howth, a little fishing village, ten minutes from my house. There were only a couple of people in the little restaurant overlooking the harbour but we wouldn't have noticed anyone as we loosened the oysters from their shells, drizzled them with lemon, a few drops of Tabasco and fed them to each other. All the while laughing and giggling like teenagers. We were there together, oblivious to others, supporting each other in our erotic, courageous food play. The oysters were cool and slippery, the wine was sharp and crisp. It was escape, it was decadence and it was heart bursting, fingertip licking tingling, joy. We looked at each other with the knowledge of the pleasure that was to be enjoyed later, when we were alone. The excitement heightened with every salty, spicy, juicy oyster we fed each other.

With giddy animation we talked of how oysters fed sexual drive, how they raised the libido and how they would fit into this book yet to be born.

2 www.sciencedaily.com/releases/2013/02/130207131344.htm
3 www.ncbi.nlm.nih.gov/pmc/articles/PMC5067287/
4 www.ncbi.nlm.nih.gov/pubmed/8875519
5 www.letsgetchecked.com/articles/naturally-increase-low-progesterone-levels/

I no longer yearn to be seen
That little girl who wants
to be heard
Who screams and whines
for attention
is appeased
I am woman, all grown up
Strutting it and sexual
Without the need
to be noticed
desired or admired
-
I will add to the world but not
to take glory
Or to earn love
Nor attract moths
As I shine in love to add light
to the world
I say to myself
You are enough
You are it all
My faith is in you

Chapter 1
YIN/YANG

The Five Element System

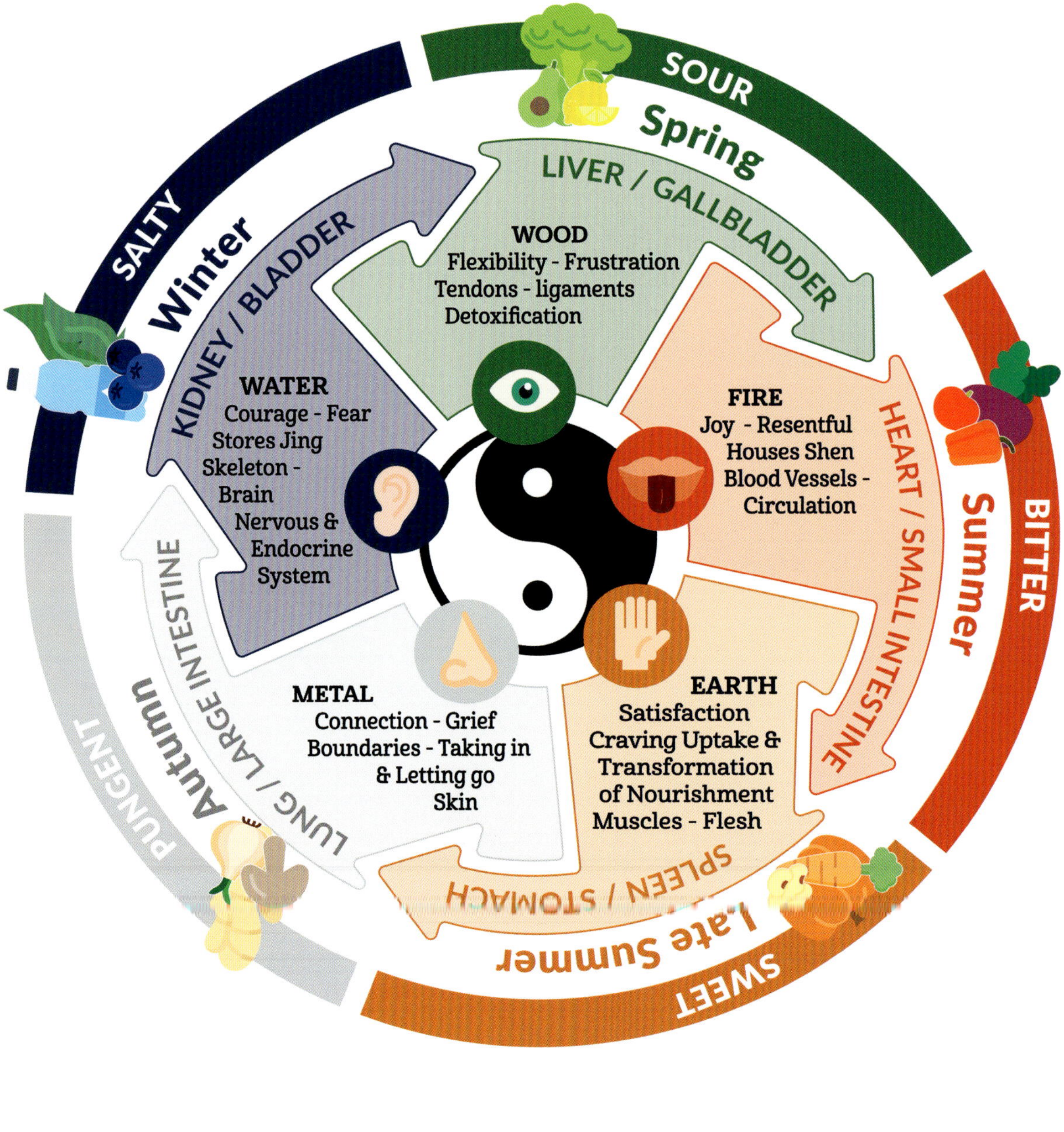

OVERVIEW: FUNDAMENTALS OF ENERGY

The underlying foundation for Chinese Medicine is that everything changes. Why does everything change? Because everything is energy. Nothing can be created nor destroyed, it is merely transferred from one state to another. The coffee I drank two minutes ago is becoming my energy and the fingers I'm typing with will one day cease to exist and become fertilizer for the earth. Everything is changing from one state to another. Energy never disappears it merely transforms its material state. In Chinese Medicine, this energy is depicted as a circle in which everything is held, from the wind, the seas, the amoeba, the giraffe, the planet, to the cosmos and the universe. In that circle is the infinity of energy, always changing, always transforming. At an atomic level it's all the same, all atoms used like bricks to build different structures, but still with protons and electrons swirling around a nucleus. Even before the introduction of modern science Chinese Medicine understood this truth, that energy is infinite, always changing, always transforming.

The giant circle of infinite, flowing, universal energy is always looking for balance. Whether at a cosmic, earthly or human level, it creates reactions and feedback loops to bring systems to homeostasis and wellness. This is represented in Chinese Medicine with the Yin and Yang, the black and white in which nothing is separate, but understood in relation to its energetic counterpart. When our body is hot it sweats to cool down, when our stomachs are empty they crave to be full, we feel happy because we have experienced sadness. Every atom is in relation to another, constantly seeking equilibrium to balance Yin and Yang.

The key to mastering health is to regulate the Yin and the Yang of the body. If the Yin and Yang balance is disrupted, it is like going through a year with spring but no winter, or winter but no summer.

- Yellow Emperors Handbook

In Chinese Medicine energy flows in the body through channels known as meridians. These meridians are grouped in Yin Yang pairs and relate to organs within the body. The system can get complex and intricate but at its core it returns to Yin and Yang balance.

Yin	Yang
Body	Mind
Sensual	Spiritual
Instinct	Insight
Flesh	Spirit
Blood	Energy
Destiny / Fate	Thought / Consciousness
In breath	Out Breath
Earth	Cosmos
Nature	Weather
Calm / Restorative	Active / Creative
Cool / Cold	Warm / Hot

From Yin's stability, its inward direction, it's quiet, dark and cool to Yang's ability to act, to be light and warm, to move up and out. For a healthy, happy, sexy body we walk a line balancing the two opposite energies.

A healthy long life, well lived, seeks to balance and allow the forces to dance rather than see them as opposing sides without hope of reconciliation. We can't eradicate sadness so that we are always happy. There will be times when we are sick and times when we are well, times when we are angry and times when we feel peace. We cannot eradicate the negative so that only the positive exists.

A definition of harmony can be the combination of simultaneously sounded musical notes to produce a pleasing effect. Life is never one thing or the other - it tends to ebb and flow of all sorts of everything. Searching for happiness means we have to seek equanimity in all things. As everything is constantly changing this means we are always up and down on the Yin Yang see-saw with endless opportunity for balance. Understanding that these laws of the universe apply to the microcosm of our body and mind can guide our choices and help us relax into the ebb and flow of love and life. Nothing is ever perfect, nothing is ever finished and you never get to the end of your to-do list. Balance your passionate desire for pleasure with surrender and receptivity from everything in life that wants to love you.

Quick Yin food

If you want to open, nourish, hydrate and lubricate the body for calm, smooth, silky softness eat more:

Parsley	Miso
Cucumber/Celery	Bone-broth
Apple/Pear/ Pomegranate	Seaweeds and algae
Lemon/Lime	Sesame Seed
Watermelon	Almond
Sea Salt	Spinach/Kale/Dark Leafy Greens
Kidney Bean/Adzuki Bean	Grapes
Honey	Tofu/Tempeh
Egg	Sprouted seeds and beans
Oyster	Peas

Quick Yang food

If you feel you need to stimulate warm moving energy, promote ardour and passion eat more:

Chickpea	Sage/Rosemary
Ginger	Turmeric/Chilli/Ginseng
Garlic/Onion/Chive	Millet/Quinoa/Brown Rice
Coconut	Shiitake Mushrooms
Squash Family	Radish/Turnip/
Chestnut	Black & Green Tea
Cinnamon/Clove/	Cardamom/Star
Anise/Fennel/	Coriander/Cumin

YIN YANG SEXUAL ENERGY

It is important to remember that all Yang comes from Yin – all action must come from stillness. Time and again there is a "to-do" list and only at the end can we rest. This quickly depletes the body, emotionally and physically. So a word of caution, rather than taking the Yang food to raise energy, ensure you rest and have enough energy in the tank before enacting any action. Far too often we assess our worthiness by what we create, what we have amassed and how much we get done. This is Yang, doing, giving energy. To balance this we need to be still, to listen and to receive from the world. This is the way to remain joyful, vibrant and sexually alive for longer.

Enjoy the stillness of winter Yin, know that in this season everything is in quiet preparation for sexual spring where every animal feels the rise in temperature and acts on the Yang upsurge in sexual energy.

"The source and preservation of the Yin form the five flavours of food in the diet ...... therefore, one should be mindful of what one consumes to ensure proper growth, reproduction and development of bones, tendons, ligaments, channels and collaterals. This will help generate the smooth flow of qi and blood, enabling one to live to a ripe age."

The Yellow Emperor's Classic of Medicine
(Neijing Suwen)

SEXUAL PRACTICE FOR YIN YANG

CIRCULATION OF SEXUAL ENERGY THROUGH THE GOVERNING AND CONCEPTION VESSEL

Energy in the body can seem like an abstract concept. There are machines to measure blood pressure, liver function and heart rate but nothing that can measure energy. When I write of sexual energy, it's not tangible, it can't be calculated, but most people will know how it feels. The area of the pelvis and genitals begins to pulsate, tingle and fill with bubbling, dynamic drive. Where energy and attention goes, then blood flows, both male and female sexual organs become aroused, enlarged and filled with energy and blood. From a Chinese Medicine perspective, it's important to be in touch with this energy using it daily to keep the body relaxed and flowing. You can use this technique whilst self-pleasuring or with a partner. To reach climax with this exercise is not the goal, its purpose is to spread this energy throughout the body. This doesn't decrease pleasure rather, it increases the sensations to be felt throughout the body and in this way it can heighten the orgasmic experience. Sexual energy is deliciously vital for the body. It isn't healthy to deny it or reject it. However, it is essential to understand and have control over it.

Within Traditional Chinese Medicine, the body has two main rivers of energy, the Yin Conception Vessel and the Yang Governing Vessel. These perfectly balance and regulate all remaining 12 classical meridians and all basic life functions. The Governing Vessel runs from the point between the anus and the coccyx right up the mid-line of the spine, over the skull, forehead, nose and finishes on the mid-line above the top lip. Using the tongue to press the roof of the mouth behind your teeth, just like an on-off switch, helps the energy pass from the Governing Vessel to the Conception Vessel and form a Small Heavenly Circle or Microcosmic Orbit.[6] The Yin Conception Vessel then runs from under the bottom lip over the soft mid-line on the front of the body, over the genitals until you arrive at the start of the external Conception vessel, located between the anus and the scrotum in men, anus and lower labia in women.

"It is our imagination that is responsible for love, not the other person"

Marcel Proust

The following practice, which flows the energy in a circuit around the body, can be done at the bus stop, at the supermarket, in the shower self-pleasuring or whilst in the act of making love. It all starts by generating sexual energy and that begins in the mind. Use your imagination to picture flights of fantasy. Or if you don't want to use an internal movie reel, imagine a ball of pulsating warm red light all around your genitals, it's soft, warm and intimate, bringing gentle relaxation and increased arousal. Once you feel energy circulating around your sexual organs, use your breath to pull up the muscles around the vagina, testes, perineum, and anus. Do this using

6 To learn more about the Microcosmic Orbit I would recommend books by Mantak Chia, especially Healing Light of the Tao

short clenching movements sending the energy from the perineum up the spine. Exhale and relax. Repeat the process until you feel the energy rising. Don't get too caught up in the muscle clenching and breath combination the important thing is to feel the build-up of energy. Once you have developed a connection to the sensation, use the muscle to pulse like a pump to help to move the energy up the spine. This doesn't have to be quick, you can take your time enjoying the feeling of softness and control this brings up your body and the release you feel as you relax and the energy falls. Breathe in and send the energy from the genitals up the spine to the top of the head and as you breathe out, allow it to fall like water over the front mid-line of the body.

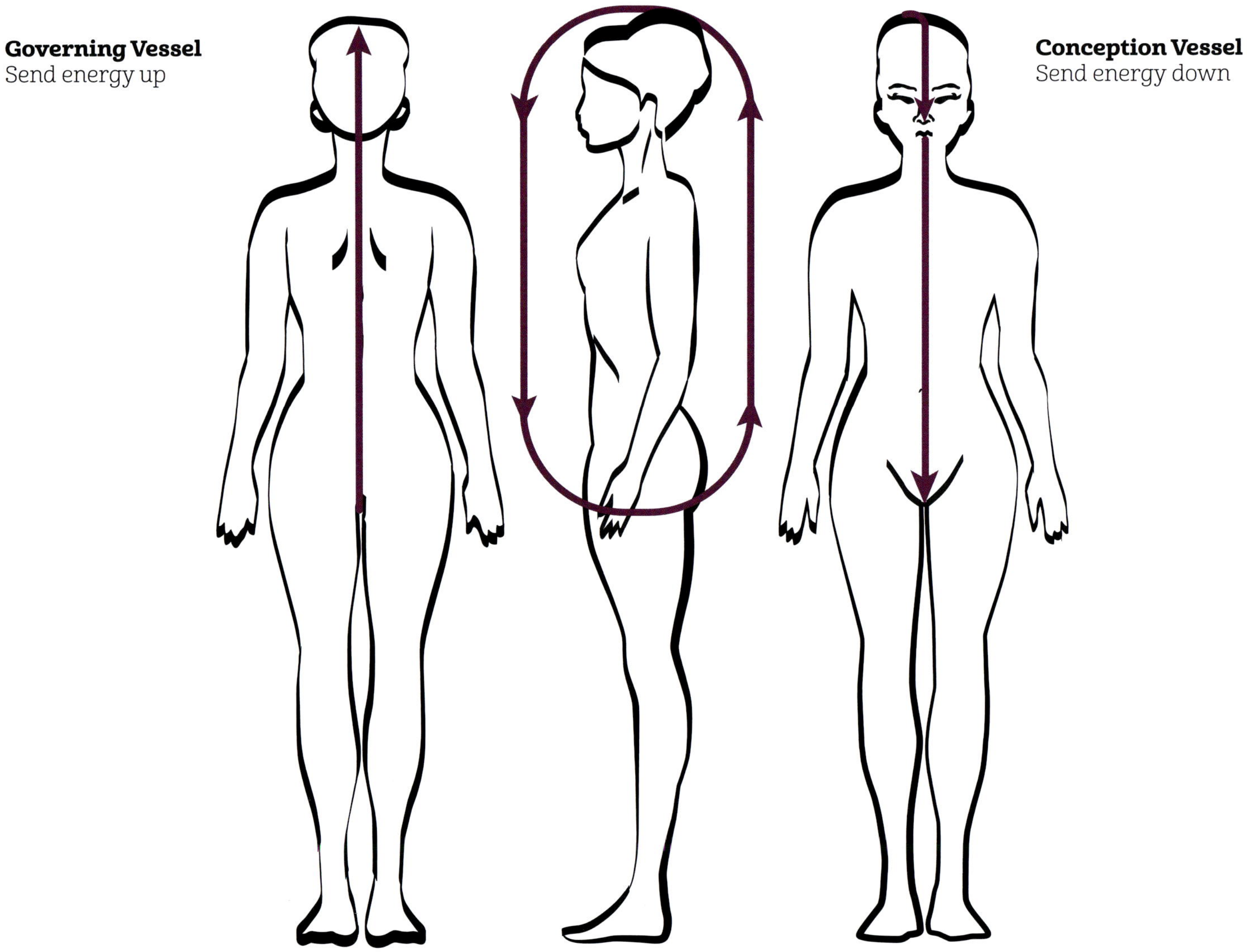

To see the beginning and end points of the circuit, find CV1 and GV1 at the end of the chapter.

If you wish you can pool the energy just below the belly button at CV6, before bringing your attention back to the genitals and the perineum to start the circulation of energy once more.

CV6 POINT

The point, two fingers below the belly button is the Dan Tien Point, sometimes referred to as the Sea of Chi or the Pool of Elixir. This is a fantastic spot to bring all your attention to. Rest your energy at this point to help regulate and build all sexual energy and regeneration in the body. It helps fertility in all parts of the body including smooth menstruation and the production of semen. This is where all movement should arise from and why it is referred to as "the root of the tree of life" [7] in many Tai Chi and Chi Gong forms of movement. Chop your vegetables from this spot, dance from this spot, talk from this spot and your energy can be controlled and enhanced.

At first, you may be able to feel this movement of energy stronger in certain areas of your body than others. The important thing is to relax. Rock your pelvis back and forth or make circular movements, whatever relieves stress and builds sexual energy. If you become tense around your neck drop the chin to forward to the chest allowing it to bob up and down. Use your hands stroking the front mid-line to reinforcing the image of energy moving downwards or hold them at the navel so you can feel the energy and heat pooling there.

If you do nothing else, no other sexual practice, no other massage, eat no seaweed, drink no green tea, but just focus on this point, allow your breath to rise up your spine, flow down your front and rest there, this daily practice would be enough to increase health, vitality and happiness.

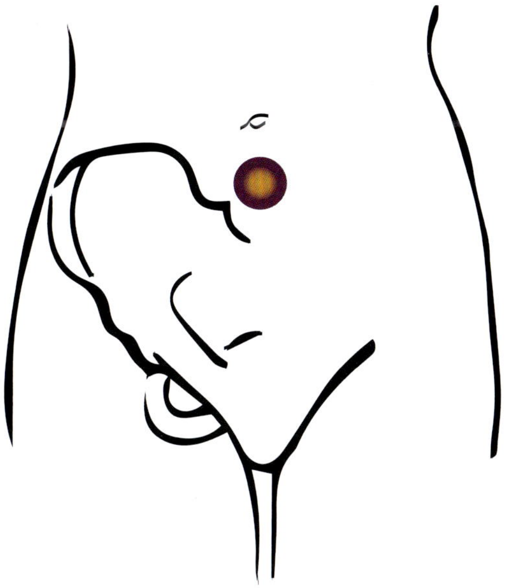

CV6 - LOWER SEA OF CHI

Rejuvenates the energy of the body, relieving weakness and fatigue. Increases fertility. Focus on this point and store energy here to increase libido. Very powerful post-partum recovery point. Relieves abdominal tension increasing sexual intimacy and pleasure.

Find CV6 on the midline of the body, 2 fingers below the belly button.

---

7 Cohen, K. S. (1999). The Way of Qigong: The Art and Science of Chinese Energy Healing. Random House of Canada. ISBN 0-345-42109-4

BALANCE AND THREE TREASURES

Put simply, Heaven creates the mind; Earth creates the body. These two Yin Yang powers flow and create our unique human life force. All three of these energies are precious and are labelled as the three treasures - Shen, Chi and Jing.

We are born with the Chi of Earth. It is represented as Yin, the solid, nourishing, cooling fuel for the body and is referred to as your essence or Jing. It is the inherited, pre-natal energy we are born with; genetic information passed on from generation to generation and stored in our DNA. Jing governs our biological instincts to eat, drink and have sex. The drive to maintain life and the on-going survival of our species is a primal and a deep-rooted energy.

The Chi of Heaven is Yang, it is the energy we gain following our birth. It is derived from the food, drink and air we breathe. Intangible, warming, transforming, and moving, this energy is said to be stored in the ethereal place which is our consciousness, spirit or Shen.

Chi of Heaven and Chi of Earth constantly move and mix to create our unique life force Chi.

The tension of two energetic opposites of Heaven and Earth create a dance between our consciousness and our basic natural instincts. Neither can exist without the other. It is possible to be celibate, consciously recycling and using sexual energy to replenish the whole body. It's also possible to be a spiritual being, taking pleasure in sexual experiences and encounters.

A healthy life must acknowledge both the spiritual and physical. This play of movement between heaven and earth in our physical bodies creates our unique human energy and way of being in the world.

Spirit without a body is a ghost;
Body without a spirit is a corpse

-Proverb

The following is a recipe that feeds, nourishes and balances all three aspects. Eating the marrow from the bones of an animal will feed the Jing of our body as it is the transformation of essence from the animal to be our own. In Chinese Medicine there are certain energetic properties that meat offers but if we have a balanced diet it is not an essential ingredient for good health. There are purposely not many meat recipes in this book because I think to maintain Yin Yang balance in the body and on the planet people need to consume less meat. If you want to include meat in your diet, make sure you give thanks and appreciate the animal that gave it's life to feed yours.[8]

The recipe should be cooked for at least an hour so the minerals can be drawn out from the bones and into the rice. The brown rice nourishes stomach and spleen in the body. It balances energy rising to transform the food into absorbable energy with descending energy of the food. The seaweed will nourish the kidney and bladder with its wide range of bioavailable protein and minerals. Slow cooked onions and plenty of garlic will open the lung and large intestine meridians, rosemary will open the heart whilst the final splash of green raw herbs added at the end will aid liver/ gallbladder's movement. This gives a complete meal in one easy to cook pot. Give thanks to the chicken and your hand that makes the dish. Feel it nourishing your bodily Jing whilst opening and calming the Shen mind, leaving you with deep peace to be and express the Chi of who you are completely. A total Yin Yang mix for your beautiful, sensual body and your generous, conscious mind. Treat yourself well, love both the light and the shadow.

ONE POT CHICKEN AND BROWN RICE

Serves 2

2 onions
100ml sunflower or rapeseed oil
2 sticks celery
6-8 cloves garlic
2 medium carrots
4 pieces of skinless chicken on the bone (preferably thigh)
200g brown rice
1 tbsp. chopped rosemary
1 tsp. wakame seaweed
2 tsp. sea salt
½ tsp. black pepper
¼ lemon
500 ml stock or bone broth
100g chopped Cashew nuts
125g chopped flat leaf parsley

Roughly chop the onions and fry on a medium heat. When they become translucent and soft add the celery and carrots, frying for another five minutes adding the roughly chopped garlic and chicken. Stir all together including the uncooked rice, rosemary, seaweed, salt, pepper and lemon, making sure it is thoroughly mixed and each piece of rice is coated with the juice of the onions and vegetables. Pour in the bone broth, don't stir anymore let it all sit. Bring to a boil with the lid on. As soon as it boils turn heat down to a very low simmer and leave for at least 45 minutes to an hour until all the stock is absorbed and the rice is chewy but not hard. Depending on your lid and stove top controls you may need to add more stock to make sure the rice is completely cooked. After the hour add the roughly chopped cashews and flat leaf parsley. You can stir them through or sprinkle as a heavy garnish. You may want to squeeze more lemon juice over the top if you feel the dish is too heavy and further stimulate the liver's powerful digestive enzymes.

8 If you want to find out more about the environmental impact on meat and the planet see here: https://www.theguardian.com/environment/2018/may/31/avoiding-meat-and-dairy-is-single-biggest-way-to-reduce-your-impact-on-earth

JING

Within the body, Jing energy, stored in the kidneys, governs fertility, hormone production, the structure of our bones and the hydration of the body. Your parents Jing created the vitality of the ovum and semen, which was then passed on to you. Western medicine describes this as our DNA, wrapped up in cells, bones and tissues, genetically carried from one generation to another.

The basic instinct to thrive, survive and procreate, is stored as Jing energy within the kidneys. This is the Chi of Earth. As discussed in the 3 treasures, this Chi of Earth must blend with the Chi of Heaven to create our own subtle way of being in the world. Despite our inherited genetic coding, we are not replicas of our parents and our grandparents. We do not mirror our siblings; even identical twins individually have unique ways of being in the world. We have an energetic quality, a Chi, that is uniquely our own. A blend of what we are born with and the choices we make.

No matter what we eat and drink, no matter how often we exercise or lifestyle choices we make, we cannot create or add to Jing. We can choose to squander and deplete Jing or we can protect and conserve it. It is a miracle with all the possibilities of sperms and ovum's that your unique Jing came into the world at all. Treat this Jing energy like a gift to be treasured and valued.

HORMONES AND JING

According to the ancient Nei Jing text in Chinese Medicine, every seven years strong hormonal changes take place in the body of a woman. For men, the cycles are every eight years, at which similar powerful hormonal changes occur. -

FEMALE JING CYCLES OF SEVEN	MALE JING CYCLES OF EIGHT
Her kidney energy becomes prosperous at seven years of age (1x7).	A man's kidney energy is prosperous, his hair develops and his teeth emerge at the age of eight (1x8).
Her menstruation appears as the ren (sea of Yin) channel flows and the chong (sea of blood) channel becomes prosperous at the age of 14 (2x7).	His kidney energy grows and is filled with vital energy, and he is able to let his sperm out at the age of 16 (2x8).
Her kidney qi reaches a balanced state, and her teeth are completely developed at the age of 21 (3x7).	His kidney energy is developed, his extremities are strong, and all of his teeth are developed by the age of 24 (3x8).
Her vital energy and blood are substantial, her four limbs are strong and the body is at optimal condition at the age of 28 (4x7).	His body has developed to its best condition, and his extremities and muscles are very strong at the age of 32 (4x8).
Her peak condition declines gradually. The Yang ming channel is depleted, her face withers and her hair begins to fall out at the age of 35 (5x7).	His kidney energy begins to decline, his hair falls out and his teeth begin to whither at the age of 40 (5x8).
Her three Yang channels, tai Yang, Yang ming and shao Yang, begin to decline. Her face complexion wanes and her hair turn white at the age of 42 (6x7).	His kidney energy declines more, the Yang energy of the entire body declines, his complexion becomes withered and his hair turns white at the age of 48 (6x8).
The ren and chong channels are both declining, her menstruation ends, her physique turns old and feeble, and she can no longer conceive at the age of 49 (7x7).	His liver energy declines as a result of kidney deficiency; the tendons become rigid and fail to be nimble at the age of 56 (7x8).
	His essence and vital energy is weak, as are his bones and tendons. His teeth fall out and his body becomes decrepit at the age of 64 (8x8).

Obviously these are broad brush strokes outlining the hormonal changes the body goes through. We have all heard of cases of women becoming pregnant after the age of 49, of boys becoming fathers at 14 and of men with all their own teeth at the age of 80. I am 50, my hair is not white and I still have a monthly bleed. However I use the generalizations to illustrate the changes in our hormonal body. It is the Jing that powers these transitions at whatever age they happen. If we treasure Jing, the transitions are smoother and we have the power to keep reproducing. Physically we may not be able to make babies but at a cellular level, our body constantly needs to reproduce We create new plasma cells daily; colon cells refresh after four days; we make a whole new skin every 2-3 weeks; white blood cells take more than a year to regenerate, and it takes an average of 10 years for a body to cumulatively regenerate bone cells to form an entirely new skeleton. The energy that makes reproduction happen is Jing. It's the energy that we are born with and we deplete it through overwork, pushing ourselves past our physical limits, emotional situations especially fear or anger. Overstimulating foods such as caffeine, sugar, and drugs (prescription or recreational) all drain Jing. Environmental pollution and ingested toxins also have to be processed and excreted by the body which consumes our energy. How we have treated our physical and emotional body will show up every 7/8 years at the times of hormonal change. Good amounts of Jing will bring energy to ensure a smooth transition of the seven year cycles. Often, long-term constitutional illnesses such as eczema, hayfever and arthritis clear up or appear at these pivotal points on our timeline. I personally "grew out" of acute hayfever at 35 which had begun at 7. I used my understanding of Chinese Medicine to make changes in diet and lifestyle coming up to this transitional time. As I type this I am 50 years old and am very aware of the need to support my Jing so that transition into menopause requires no medication or sweat-filled, insomniac nights. I don't want to become "feeble" or "decrepit". Whilst I don't want more children, I intend to value and nurture my Jing, to preserve my youthful ability to regenerate and reproduce at a cellular level. I wish to stay vibrant and juicy with desire for sexual pleasure, love and life.

The following diagram is a common analogy to describe Jing throughout life.

Source: Nei Jing reference: Yellow Emperor's Canon of Internal Medicine, China Science & Technology Press. - Interpretation BY DAVID TWICKEN, DOM, LAC

"The flame that burns twice as bright burns half as long."
Lao Tzu - Tao Te Ching

The light of the candle is your Shen (spirit), illuminating the darkness, given life from Jing and Chi.

The flame of the candle is your Chi, your vitality and energy, which should burn evenly. In health, this is replenished through food, breath and rest so that the wax doesn't melt and your Jing lasts longer.

The wax and wick of the candle is your Jing, the energy you were born with. If the light is too bright the candle will burn too quickly and the Jing be depleted signifying the end of life.

Jing determines the management, storage, and usage of all our Chi/energy. We cannot add to it but we can support it with good foods such as:

* Eggs, oysters
* Royal jelly, Bee Pollen
* Seaweeds and blue green algae such as Spirulina and Chlorella
* Almonds, sesame seeds
* Adzuki Beans
* Bone broth
* Goji Berries

This Jing also provides the spark between our two kidneys that ignites our fire for life. The point between the kidneys is referred to as the Mingmen, a Yang fire that comes from two Yin water organs of the kidneys. This spark enables Jing to pass to every organ of the body and as we move through life we use this energy naturally. Unfortunately, it's not possible to build on or add to this Jing energy but it is possible to squander the treasure by struggling on when we are exhausted, enduring draining situations or by using will power, drugs, or caffeine to succeed in completing projects. Sexual activity can also deplete this essence if, for a man, he ejaculates too frequently and for a woman if she bears too many children or struggles to regulate menstruation. For more information, acupressure points and an exercise to conserve Jing see "More on Mingmen" later in this chapter.

MINGMEN: GATE OF LIFE

The Jing is reserved in the two Yin kidneys and distributed by the kidney Yang Mingmen. Maintaining healthy kidney energy is about being in the flow. Water is the element that governs kidney and bladder energy. It is essential we drink plenty and use good quality sea salt to remain hydrated. The flow of water suggests surrender and acceptance rather than exerting effort to change what is. It isn't the same as being passive and just letting life happen to us. It is learning to walk the fine line between doing and being, Yin and Yang; finding the balance between acceptance and empowerment.

"Under heaven, nothing is more soft and yielding than water. Yet for attacking the solid and strong, nothing is better; it has no equal"

Tao Te Ching (verse 78)

Storing and conserving Jing is essential. But it is also important to understand what depletes this energy. In my experience, the following 3 factors are the main Jing depletors, which prevent the body from reproducing healthy cells and healing itself.

THE 3 STRESSORS

Physical Stress. When the body experiences physical injury such as broken bones, operations, trauma such as car accidents or abusive relationships, the sympathetic nervous system is on high alert. It is sensitive to impending dangers and sharply aware of real or perceived threats, ready to fight or flight at any moment. When in this state, digestion, assimilation, excretion and sexual functions are turned off. It is only when the body is relaxed and at ease in the parasympathetic nervous system that the body can rest, restore, regenerate and reproduce.

Environmental Stress. The introduction of pathogens, viruses and poisons into the body means the body is in constant fight mode to process and eradicate them. Hormones fed to animals make their way into our food chain. Additives and preservatives in food, pill-popping paracetamol, birth control, antihistamines and other over the counter medications as well as prescribed antibiotics, and inhalers all have to be processed by the liver and eliminated from the body. Chemicals in cleaning products, air fresheners, shampoo, makeup and moisturisers, fluoride, chlorine and heavy metals found in the water supply all mean the body is under stress as it tries to eliminate them. The air we breath often contains contaminants such as carbon monoxide, lead, hydrocarbons. These all require energy for the body to dispose of and remain in balanced homeostasis. Leaving the Jing weakened, compromised in it's ability to regenerate healthy cells

Emotional Stress. The expectations we have of ourselves and allow others to put upon us can drain physical energy and emotional joy from our lives. It is exhausting for Jing and destructive for hormonal and sexual health to live up to society's, families and our own idea of correctness and perfection.

There is no exact formula but I have seen that when all three of the stressors combine, and causes are not addressed, the body will create extreme, often debilitating, symptoms such as autoimmune and inflammatory illnesses such as fibromyalgia, arthritis, asthma, psoriasis, M.E., M.S., Lupus, Lymes Disease.

Nurturing Jing and being in the parasympathetic nervous system is core to self-regeneration. To ensure activation of the parasympathetic, treatments can include counselling, exercise, rest, meditation, mindfulness, dance, journalling, diet, breathwork, yoga, qigong and more. Over and above any therapy, we must take time to rest and heal. When exhausted, the body uses excessive amounts of Jing to reproduce and rebuild cells, which means premature aging and even death. Jing is essential energy, which must flow for life, be soft on yourself, don't push too hard, treasure you and your Jing.

**"The hard and stiff are death's companions.
The soft and weak are life's companions"**
[Tao Te Ching chapter 76]

I have treated a client who suffered sexual abuse and further abused their own body with narcotics and poor diet. They found it difficult to relax and allow touch. Their body was swollen and painful but through a slow process of trust, conscious breathwork and shiatsu, they have been able to receive, repair and reduce their pain.

I had a stressful birth experience, was given too much medication and then found managing twins and my own business very stressful. It severely depleted my jing and desire for sexual intimacy. As I entered perimenopause I suffered anxiety, dizziness and insomnia. To address this I changed my diet, my job, entered therapy and received shiatsu. It took time but as I enter menopause I have no debilitating symptoms.

I've worked with a client who lost loved ones and put themselves under enormous pressure to maintain a household, often using sugar or alcohol as a way to relax, which meant they developed stiff and swollen joints, diagnosed as arthritis. With changes to their diet and ways of thinking they were able to manage the grief process and approach life with flexibility and a reduction in pain.

I've had a client who suffered traumatic head injuries, worked themselves till exhaustion, ate on the go, suffered skin ulcerations and was unable to have any sexual function. Unfortunately they were looking for a magic cure. They made no changes to their diet or lifestyle and their condition didn't improve.

Finally a client who suffered a motorbike accident and underwent a painful divorce at the same time developed Parkinson's. Whilst the condition has not reversed itself yet with changes in diet, Shiatsu and establishment of a Chi gong practice, there is an increase in peace to the body and an intermittent reduction of pain and stiffness throughout.

BONE BROTH

The best recipe for restoring Jing is bone broth. As well as nurturing Jing it repairs and strengthens your large intestine which prevents the re-absorption of toxins back into the bloodstream reducing inflammation in arteries, joints, tissues, all over the body. The result being more flexibility and softness less hard and stiff, further from premature aging and death. From a western medicine point of view the body declines in its production of collagen at approximately 40 years old. Collagen is essential for connective tissues, bones teeth, tendons, ligaments, cartilage, hair, nails, skin and it supports all the hollow organs of your digestive system, from your esophagus, stomach, through to the small and large intestine. Collagen is often found in cosmetics to improve the elasticity and regeneration of the skin. The collagen from bone broth is bio-available to your body and easily absorbed. In fact, bone broth contains a wide range of easily digestible minerals. The slow cook time means they are easy for your body to assimilate. Bone broth is also high in Amino Acids such as glucosamine, hyaluronic acid, leucine and glutamine which build up connective tissue, to cushion and lubricate skin, joints and eyes. Amino acids help to repair and regenerate every tissue and organ in the body. They also help balance hormones and mood swings. Adding seaweed further increases the absorbable protein and Amino Acids. As I discussed previously to balance Yin and Yang, my recipes, on the whole, don't include the use of flesh. But for basic regeneration of the body and cherishing Jing, bone broth has it all. The Jing is said to be stored in the kidneys of all living creatures and the marrow of the bones. So give thanks to the animal that gives its essence that it may feed yours.

BONE BROTH

Serves 6

4 or 5 marrow-bones[9]
2 onions
3 or 4 carrots
3 or 4 sticks of celery
1 fennel bulb (optional)
1 small lemon
Medium piece of kombu or pinch of wakame or dillisk
Salt and Pepper to taste
1 tbsp. Cider vinegar or lemon juice

Pop all the bones in a large pot with a good fitting lid. Cover with water, the more the better. Add onions carrots and celery to add flavour. I like to add a fennel bulb as it aids digestion and helps to assimilate the nutrients into your body. Adding an astringent such as a couple of tablespoons of cider vinegar or lemon juice as this will help draw out the nutrients from the bones. Add a strip of Kombu or a pinch of Wakame or Dillisk, sprinkle in your salt and pepper. Bring it to the boil and then simmer for at least 10-12 hours. Strain away the bones and let the broth cool before placing in a container and storing it. As the broth cools it may develop a fat cap. This is useful as it will stop air getting to the broth and make it last longer. Bone broth can be stored in the refrigerator for up to 5 days. It also freezes well. Use the broth to make soups/stews/risotto/back to health soup it could even be added to juices if you like the flavour.

Additional options:
Roasting the bones before boiling can help with the flavour and colour but it's not essential.

For a perfect quick hot drink full of probiotics, add a teaspoon of miso paste to the bone broth, which has been preheated. Again sprinkle in seaweed and add a hard-boiled egg cut in half to further support Jing.

9 It is best to use bones from an organic free-range animal. You are extracting the very marrow of the animal so you don't want an animal that has been fed antibiotics, led a caged life or experienced a stress-full death. Seeking out a Kosher, Halal or any good butcher where you know the animals have been kept and killed humanely.

MINGMEN, GATE OF LIFE

As previously discussed, Jing is at our very core. In Chinese Medicine, it is the energy formed first within the foetus from which all other organs are formed. From between the two cool, Yin kidneys, the kidney Yang is formed and it is this warming energy that feeds all the other organs. Its name is Ming-men. For me this conjures up the Flash Gordon baddie, "Ming the Merciless", complete with tin foil boots, swishing cape, bald badness and sinister goatee. Of course, this is not how it is but it's sometimes helpful to see this energy as a powerful megalomaniac. It is the spark and warmth of kidney Yang, which has to penetrate and feed all the other organs so that they can function completely. In Traditional Chinese Medicine organs have more than just a physical function, they influence the way we think, feel and operate in the world.

- When the heart is nourished, consciousness is strong and it can make open hearted connections.
- When the small intestine is nourished it can disseminate both nutrients and information.
- When the liver is nourished it can plan.
- When the gallbladder is nourished it can make decisions.
- When the spleen is nourished it can transport.
- When the stomach is nourished it can transform.
- When the lung is nourished it can protect and regulate.
- When the large intestine is nourished it can eliminate.
- When the heart protector is nourished it can discern.
- When the triple heater is nourished it can keep clear the body's neurological and water pathways.
- When the bladder is nourished it can hold and store.
- When the kidneys themselves are nourished by Mingmen our body is full of vigour and va va voom.

'When the master is dim, the twelve officials are all in a state of crisis.'

Neijing statement

One of the foods that feed kidney Yang, so that Mingmen is strong and warm, are chestnuts. In Spain, I ate these a lot during the winter. On most corners in the city centre of Madrid, there were braziers with chestnuts roasting as an ideal snack on cold, crisp winters day. You can buy them pre-packed or roast them yourself by cutting a slit in the casing of the chestnut, so they have room to expand as they roast. Sprinkle them with water and place on a tray in a moderate oven for about 25-30 minutes. They work well chopped and tossed through rice or in a salad.

APPLE AND CHESTNUT SALAD WITH YOGURT AND SEAWEED DRESSING

Serves 4

4 medium carrots
2 celery stalks
2 apples
100g cooked and peeled chestnuts
1 tbsp. fresh chives, chopped

Dressing

150 ml cup plain yogurt
2 tbsps. olive oil
2 tsps. Dijon mustard
1 garlic clove, minced
Marinated (lemon juice and white wine vinegar) Dillisk or Sea Spaghetti
½ tsp. salt

Grate the carrots, thinly slice the celery and apples then add the roughly chopped chestnuts. Sprinkle in the chives and mix. For the dressing, marinate the Dillisk or Sea Spaghetti in the juice of half a lemon and a tablespoon of white wine vinegar until soft. Times will vary depending on the type of seaweed. When combined, pour over the vegetables, toss and serve.

Some other kidney Yang foods are:

Walnuts, Pistachio
Garlic, Ginger
Cinnamon, Cardamom, Cumin, Coriander, Clove
Lamb, Duck
Sage

Generally avoiding cold food and ice in drinks supports the body and especially kidney Yang.

SO WHERE IS MINGMEN

The Ming-men point is located on the governing vessel, which is a channel that runs midway between the coccyx and the anus up the mid-line of the back, over the skull and finishes on the top of the upper lip. You can then pick up the end of the conception vessel on the mid-line of the body under the lower lip and follow it down the front of the body until the perineum, midway between the anus, the vulva and the scrotum.

These energetic mid-line meridians are activated during the Sexual practice for Yin/Yang (see page 44). Keeping them alive and flowing supports the even distribution of Jing and the generation of healthy sexual energy.

GOVERNING VESSEL 4 – MINGMEN / GATE OF LIFE

Transports kidney Yang, warmth and energy to all organs in the body. Strengthens Jing and kidneys preventing infertility, erectile disfunction, premature ejaculation, incontinence, nocturnal emissions and enhances energy for libido

Find directly opposite the belly button on the spine. Midline of the back, below the spinous process of the vertebra L2. An easy way to find it would be to place your hands on your waist, turn them around so that the thumbs are on the front of the body and the fingers curl to the spine. Where the middle finger lands is approximately GV4 and your Mingmen point.

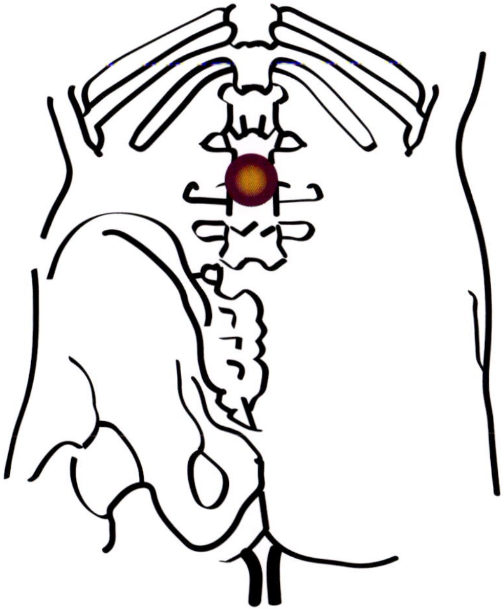

For more exercises to control jing preservation and develop Sexual Health I recommend Multi Orgasmic Man and Multi Orgasmic Woman by Mantak Chia.

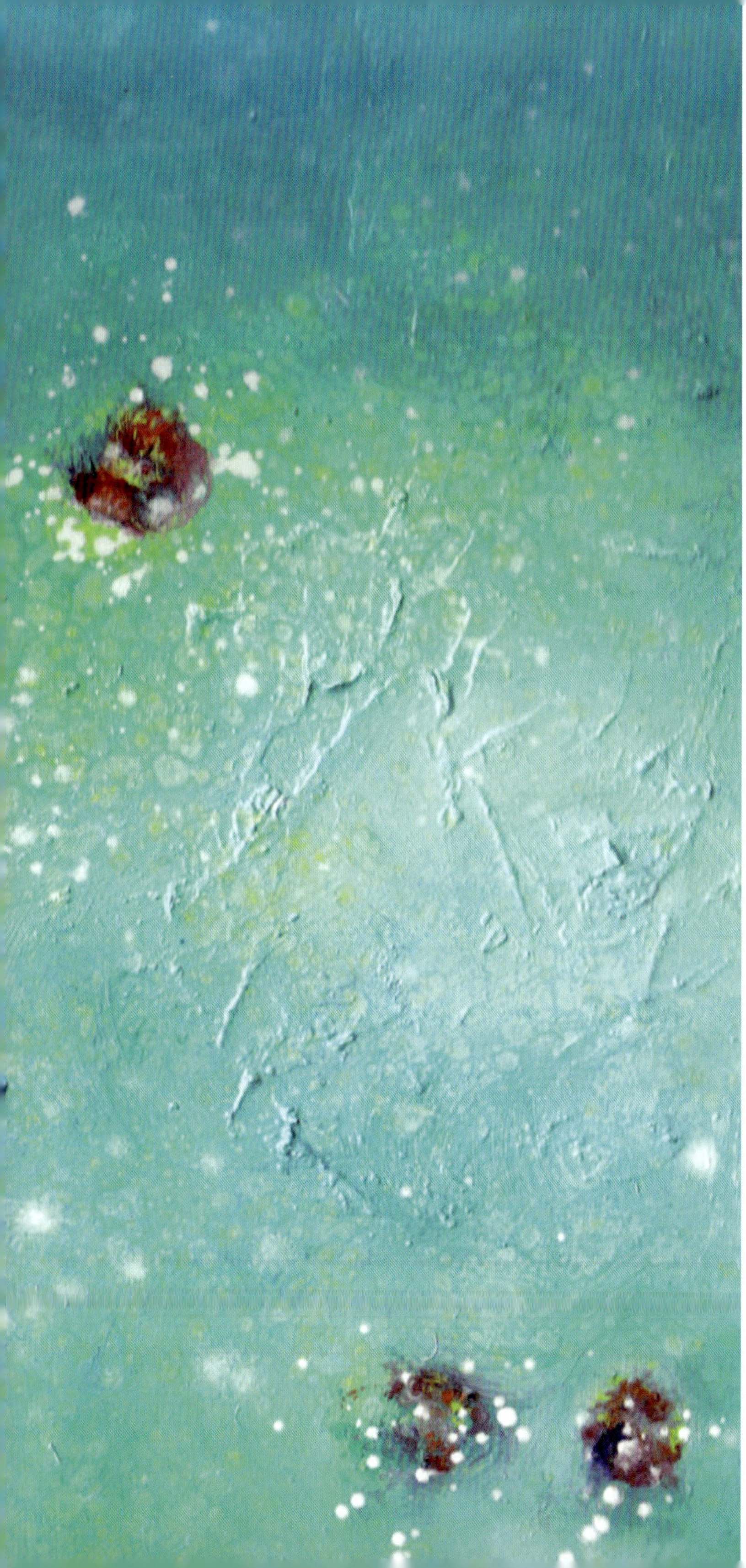

MORE ON MINGMEN

This is one of the gates of life located all around the governing and conception vessels. Mantak Chia, a Taoist Master talks about there being male Yin gates at the tip of the penis, the prostate gland and the anus. For women, it's the entrance to the vagina, the cervix and the anus. All of these gates of life must stay strong to prevent Jing leakage, premature aging and debilitating illness.

A simple exercise to nourish Jing and support its transportation around the body is to make the hands into gentle fists and massage either side of the spine at GV4 for approximately 30 seconds until you feel the area become warm. This will activate bladder 23 and bladder 52 on page 113, to either side of governing vessel 4. Then place your palms over the warm space and glide them around the waist until they meet just below the belly button. Hold them there and feel the warm girdle that you have made from the back of the body on the Ming-men point around to the front of the body at the lower CV6 on page 45 where your Jing is stored. This is a fundamental exercise that feeds our Jing.

ACUPRESSURE POINTS

CONCEPTION VESSEL 1 – MEETING OF YIN

Benefits Yin which builds and regulates fluids in the body. Benefits incontinence, impotence and seminal emission. Reduces genital dryness, itching, tension and pain.

A completion point forthe Circulation of Sexual Energy practice at the beginning of this chapter.

Find at the point of the perineum which is midway between the anus and scrotum in men and the anus and lower labia in women.

CONCEPTION VESSEL 2 – CURVED BONE
CONCEPTION VESSEL 3 – MIDDLE POLE

Warms the kidneys and regulates the lower burner. Helps with urination, eases pain in menstruations and assists in invigorating libido.

Find CV2 on the midline of the lower abdomen on the top of the pubic bone, one hand width below the belly button. CV3 is one thumb width above CV2.

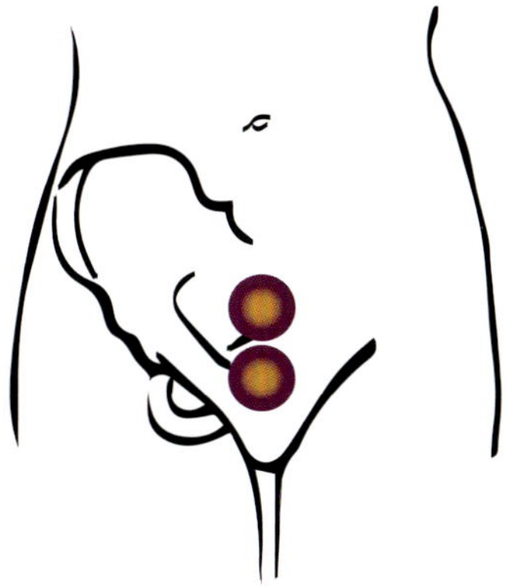

CONCEPTION VESSEL 4 – GATE ORIGIN/ORIGINAL CHI

Enhances/Tonifies kidney and Prenatal Chi. Strengthens blood helping reduce painful, cramping, scanty periods. Increases fertility.

Find by measuring 4 fingers below the belly button or one thumb width above CV3.

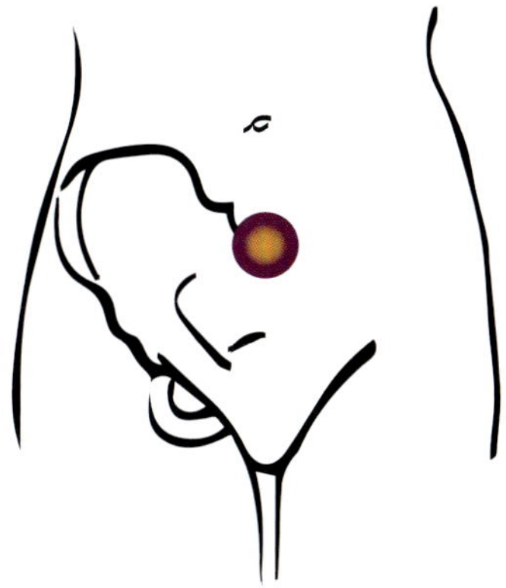

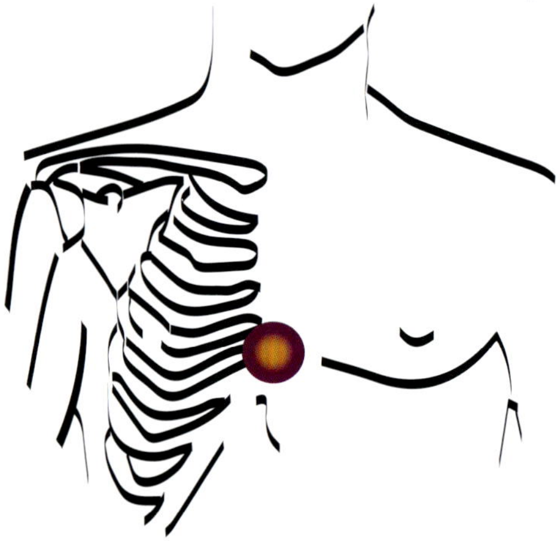

CONCEPTION VESSEL 17 – UPPER SEA OF CHI

Calming the Chi, relieving anxiety and panic for hormonal changes after childbirth and menopause.

Find on the midline of the sternum in the depression where a horizontal line is drawn midbreast/nipple to midbreast/nipple.

GOVERNING VESSEL 1 –LONG STRONG

This point activates the channel which runs up the midline of the back, up the spine over the top of the head to finish at the mid point under the nose and above the lip. Also treats haemorrhoids, enters the brain, calms spirit, relieves sacral pain and stiffness of the spine.

Find on the midline, mid way between the anus and the coccyx.

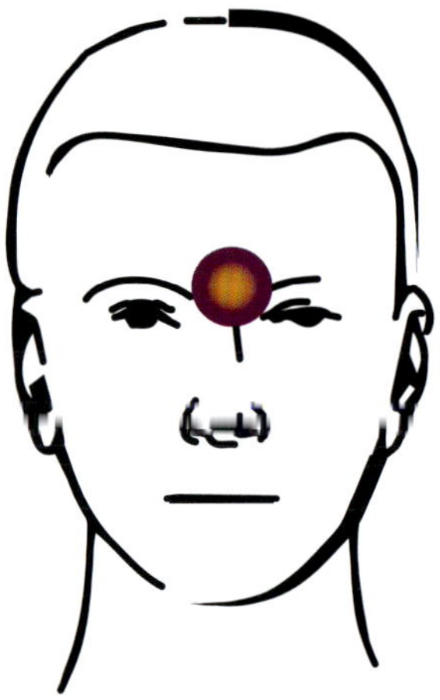

GOVERNING VESSEL 24.5 – THIRD EYE POINT

Regulates endocrine system and aids glandular imbalances. Used with GV 20 can help release emotional trauma.

Find in the midline of the body between the eyebrows.

GOVERNING VESSEL 20 – HUNDRED MEETINGS

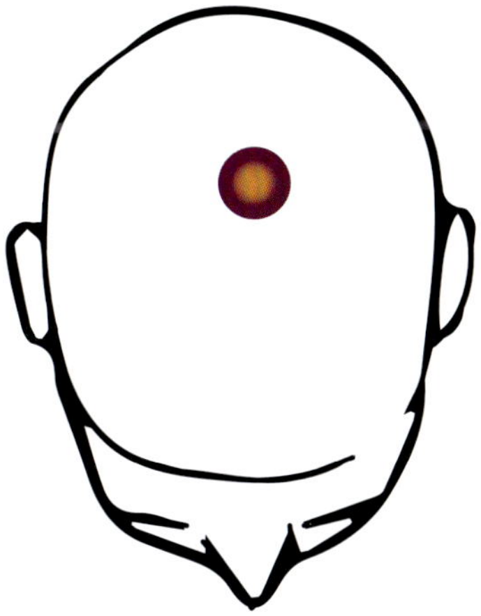

Crossing of 6 Yang meridians clearing the spirit balancing Yin/Yang.

Clears the mind, helps release excessive mental activity and increases the rise in physical energy. Strengthens the body against prolapse of internal organs such as stomach, uterus, bladder, anus or vagina.

Find by placing your thumbs on the apex of the ears and draw a line to the midline of the scull. Alternatively, imagine a golden string pulling up the internal midline of the body from the perineum and exiting the top of the body at GV 20.

GOVERNING VESSEL 26 – MIDDLE OF A PERSON

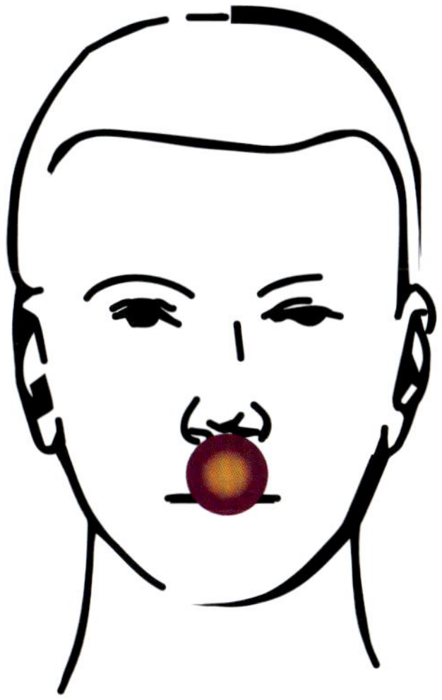

Brings the body back to itself, good to calm an insatiable desire

Find on the midline of the body, half way between the underside of the nose and the upper lip.

I want to know all of you
The curves of your back
The freckles on your skin
Your toes and how they flex
Your ears with the delicate
carteladge covered by thin
skin
How do they respond when
I whisper in your ear
I am here and I love you

Chapter 2

KIDNEY / BLADDER

My waking thoughts are
of you
Imagining the extra
presence in the bed
the extra weight
Solid
As you draw me in across
the white sheets
Over from the chasm
of sleep
to hold me in your arms

OVERVIEW
SURVIVE, THRIVE AND PROCREATE

Physically the bladder meridian runs like a train track, from the inside corner of both our eyes, over the top of our head, down the length of our spine and the backs of our legs, through our ankles to the outside tip of our little toe. The physical kidneys and the adrenal glands are also located in the middle of our back on either side of our spine. This bladder/kidney energy moves us forwards. It can be described as our determination, our will to survive, our will to succeed, our will to procreate and leave our mark on the world.

Fight or flight, thrive and survive; These are basic instincts and they are all governed by the energy of the lowest organs in the body, the bladder and kidney.

When we are in flow all is well, we are active yet calm, we accomplish a lot without stress and drama. However, when we use our will power to push past the limits of our body's energy the kidneys weaken and our Jing is depleted. We use stimulants such as drugs, nicotine or caffeine to boost our energy. Under stressful situations, our body, triggered by the kidneys, produces its own highly effective, addictive hormonal drug, adrenaline. It's a powerful chemical helping us to get things done. It gives us a surge of energy which is very useful if you need to escape a dangerous tiger or protect your children from invading Vikings but it doesn't serve us when preparing for Christmas or finishing a work project. It might get the job done but we pay a price in the long term with our kidney Jing. When it is depleted it causes hormone imbalance, adrenal fatigue, infertility, premature greying, lower back pain, loss of libido, premature ejaculation, tinnitus, weak bones, tooth decay and night sweats.

Too often, because of our wish to control situations and outcomes, we develop stressful reactions to situations. It's important to remember stress does not happen to us it's our reaction to situations that creates stress. When we become stressed adrenaline and cortisol enter the bloodstream from the kidneys and adrenals. Both these hormones are dangerous to our body, they increase blood pressure and blood sugar. Digestion and immune systems are compromised; access to the pre-frontal cortex of the brain is limited, preventing perspective, rational thinking and the ability to see alternative possibilities. Some studies show[10] that on-going stress shrinks the executive function areas of our brains and stimulates the habit-forming parts that keep us repeating negative patterns. However, it is important to remember, we have a choice. We can change how we operate in the world at any time.

Often I see clients who live very busy lives, juggling families, demanding jobs, they have high expectations of themselves and they simply burn out. Their kidney Jing is so depleted that their body and their hormones, don't function properly.

10 https://news.berkeley.edu/2014/02/11/chronic-stress-predisposes-brain-to-mental-illness/

There is a saying in Japan – "There's no use forging weapons when war has begun" meaning don't wait to take action. Don't wait until you have no choice. Your body's symptoms are telling you something. If you pop a pill without changing your lifestyle, the cause will remain so other symptoms may occur until you make the change. Don't wait until your body is shouting at you to listen.

If you are constantly using the strength of will to overpower the limits of your body, look at why you are doing it. Fear is the emotion of the kidney so be aware of what is driving your actions, is it the fear of failure, the fear of getting it wrong, the fear of being judged or is it the fear of change? Sometimes letting go of behaviours we know are not serving us creates fear.

Fear and stress can deplete our sexual energy. Intimacy is usually last on the to-do list because it takes time and focus. When all our attention has been directed elsewhere it's not surprising that there's nothing left for sexual stimulation, arousal and pleasure. The good news is that we can change the structure of our brains and our behaviour at any age just by intentionally focusing our attention. Fall into the energy of the spine and relax your thoughts to the back of the skull. Feel your brain relax and your need to get things done decrease. In Chinese Medicine taking your attention to the back of your skull enables all your ancestors who went before you to assist you. Relax in the knowledge you are supported.

Accept different things, different people and different outcomes. Tolerance for your own humanity and limitations is very important. Trying new ways of being can be a daunting prospect, the fear of which, can further tighten and chill the kidney/bladder.

Use the physical points, the food and the Tao/tantric techniques to focus attention internally to a deep fearless place. Deep within the marrow of our bones, this stability is always unshakably present. It is the marrow in bone-broth that feeds the Jing and kidneys. Go deep within and trust, be flexible and let go. Become fluid like water so that you never lose your centre. Life then, with its unexpected possibilities, will excite you rather than exhaust you.

On average the human body is made up of 60% water. The brain and heart are composed of 73% water, and the lungs are about 83% water. The skin contains 64% water, muscles and kidneys are 79%, even the bones are watery at 31%.[11] Water is a fluid essential for the function of every cell in the body. It regulates body temperature by sweating and through breathing. The body needs water to manufacture hormones and transport energy in the bloodstream. It also flushes out the body's waste including excess hormones.

Stress is a very Yang activity, it creates action and heat, to balance this, the body uses water and the body's Yin salt minerals to remain hydrated.

The following recipe contains good salts for hydration. Here I use it to support fertility and especially post-menopause. Minerals such as calcium, magnesium, zinc, and manganese help prevent osteoporosis and diminishing bone density, a common symptom of early aging and post-menopause. Zinc is especially good for increasing follicle-stimulating hormones, which decline with overuse of Jing.

---

11 https://www.usgs.gov/special-topic/water-science-school/science/water-you-water-and-human-body

We mustn't leak salts and minerals by overworked kidneys, weak bladder and stress.

"Flowing water never stagnates, active hinges never rust"

- Tao master Sun Simiao

Keep the body smooth soft and flowing with salty mineral rich Yin foods such as: seaweeds, chlorella, spirulina, cucumber, barley, millet, gomasio, feta cheese, miso soup, walnuts, broccoli, green leafy vegetables, brown rice, nuts, seeds and green beans.

GOMASIO GREEN BEANS

Serves 2

250g green beans
2 tblsp. Black and white sesame seeds
2 tsp. Sea salt
Sesame oil

Top the stalks off and steam the green beans for 5 minutes. Dry fry the sesame seeds for a couple of minutes, tossing them constantly to ensure they don't burn. When they look shiny and smell delicious pour them into a pestle and mortar together with the salt and grind. The high levels of vitamin E will be absorbed into the sea salt, which helps promote estrogen production. This mixture is traditionally named gomasio. When the beans are soft but still squeaky, transfer to a serving dish sprinkle gomasio over and drizzle with sesame oil.

KIDNEY TANTRA

SAY MY NAME

As discussed in the bonebroth and Jing section, stress is categorized into three forms, environmental, emotional, physical, and is extremely depleting for the body's Jing and sexual energy. When the body is in a state of stress, the sympathetic nervous system is active. Stomach digestion turns off, intestinal activity slows, fight and flight hormones such as adrenaline and cortisol are released, parts of the brain stop working, the vagina contracts whilst the bladder releases. The good news is that it is relatively easy to help the body switch to the parasympathetic nervous system where all parts of the brain are in use, heart rate slows, digestion, absorption and elimination of food is happening. This also allows the erection of the penis and the lubrication and opening of the vagina to take place. All you need to do is breathe.

Throughout the book, we discuss food being a source of Chi/energy for our body but so is the air that we breathe. Having control and awareness over our breath means we can manage our nervous system and our response to stressful situations. We can harness feelings, become emotionally flexible, and not be at the mercy of a relentless mind or an agitated nervous system.

Many practices blend body and breath such as Qi Gong, Yoga and Tai Chi. Here I share a couple of simple breathing exercises that I use.

1. Place your hands on your belly, just below the navel. Take some large breaths. As you breathe in, feel your hands rise and as you breathe out feel your hands fall as your belly decreases and the diaphragm pushes out the air. Focus especially on the out-breath. Breath out as long as possible, let the in-breath take care of itself. Do this at least ten times. Taking your attention along with your breath to the area just below the belly button or to your kidneys themselves. This works if I am in a meeting or if someone is shouting at me. It increases my sense of self and I don't feel so defensive. My boundaries are strengthened and I gain emotional distance from the situation and perspective that all this will pass.

2. Sweep your arms up overhead to gather the energy all around you as you breathe in. As you breathe out, bring down your palms over the front of your body, coming to rest at your lower Dan Tien Point (See page 45). Imagine energy, like water, flowing over your body. Do this ten times and feel your body restored and kidneys invigorated.

3. There are many ways to synchronize the breath and body movements, experiment and see what works for you. You may like to come up on your toes when breathing in and sink back into your heels when breathing out. Raising your arms with the movement up and letting them fall with the out-breath. The exercise is simple, be aware of your breath and move the body with it in effortless strokes, soft and flowing like the water of the kidneys.

EXERCISE WITH A PARTNER

The kidney and bladder energy is linked to the ears and the sense of hearing. In this practice, we will say our lovers name with reverence and divine love.

In day to day life very often we only say our partner's name if we want something or if we need them to listen. This is an exercise where nothing is required of them, they simply have to receive and hear their name spoken with love.

Sounds easy but it might take a little practice there's no harm in that, only sheer enjoyment. It need not be their given name, it can be a nickname or a pet name, anything that they agree to and associate with their self on the planet at this time.

When I first tried out this exercise it took bravery. I was fine with the stroking and massage but I did feel silly saying out loud my lover's name. I know that fear is the emotion of the kidney and its flip side is courage so I took a deep breath and began to softly speak his name. I found it so peaceful and intimate. Intensely private (until now) I felt the bond and understanding between us strengthen. When we swapped over the exercise and he spoke my name I felt cherished and loved. I felt he really cared for my well being and happiness. I felt truly witnessed.

This exercise is best done naked or at least from the waist up. So choose a warm soft space where you can lie your partner on their front and you have enough space to comfortably move up and down their back. A bed is an easy if obvious choice. Silence is best but if you would like background music make sure it is soft so you don't have to shout your lover's name. You can use oil and massage in sweeping strokes up and down the back or you can use dry fingers on the skin. I suggest using the bladder meridian that runs either side of the spine as it is the easiest for relaxing the body and helping it enter the parasympathetic nervous system. There are two meridians, the first is two fingers either side of the spine and the second is four fingers but you don't have to be exact. The entire back area unwinds tension and softens energy. There are no rules except the giver gives and the receiver receives. If you would like to make the experience extra special try using a long-stemmed rose. Let the velvet smooth petals gently brush against the skin with the occasional soft stroke of a sharp thorn. Say your partner's name softly. You can whisper it into their ear or breathe it into their back. Repeat it at a pace that is comfortable for you. Try not to join it with the rhythm of the strokes as this may send your partner off to sleep and what we are doing here is creating deep relaxing loving peace whilst remaining completely conscious.

Winter

Tread soft in a shakable
snowstorm
Padding in the soft snow of
a vacuum
Stand Stop Still
Anticipate the stalking
violence

With a stillness that
permeates
to lick the belly
where it rocks on the spine
Like silence it sits
A god with morals or malice
Just wry in the knowledge
of your Inevitable return

Kidney / Bladder
RECIPES

STRESS AND CARROTS

From a Chinese Medicine point of view, when the body undergoes a stressful reaction to an external experience, environmental, emotional or physical it enters a very Yang phase to enable it to survive anything from a car crash to a common cold. After the hot Yang activity, the body needs cooling, quiet Yin to bring the body back to balance. From a western point of view, this would equate to the pH scale of acid and alkaline. When responding to any of the 3 stressors the body becomes acidic. I discuss this briefly within the kidney bladder overview and recommend salty mineral-rich kidney foods that alkalise the body. Here, I want to show how easy it is to remain balanced from a pH point of view.

Tissues, cells and fluids generally maintain a balanced pH of 7.35-7.45. When the body perceives an invading pathogen or poison, when it needs extra energy to break down blockages, it becomes acidic which is Yang. This is a good thing; the body needs to become acidic sometimes to increase energy, vitality and flow. For example, when an athlete is in training they push their body to extremes and it can become acidic, if however, they stretch and maintain a diet full of the necessary alkalising salts they can easily bring it back to balance. It should be noted that blood rarely changes pH, here we are talking specifically fluids and the functioning of kidney and bladder.

If constantly acidic, the body will begin to attack itself, pulling alkalising minerals from the body stores of muscle, connective tissue, teeth, and eventually the bones and organs. A constantly acidic environment decreases oxygen levels at a cellular level, which disrupts cell growth and reproduction and can lead to heart disease, liver failure, tumour growth and possibly cancer. Before this drastic degenerative stage, symptoms such as inflammation, swelling, joint pain, bleeding gums, brittle nails, thinning hair, dry skin, liver congestion, yeast infections, erectile dysfunction and loss of libido are signals to make some changes.

We have discussed how to address emotional stress with the breathwork exercise for kidney/bladder and how to enable healing of physical traumatic stress by nourishing Jing. Now we address the environmental stress of the toxins we put in our body.

Food can heal us or make us sick. How much acid/alkaline food you eat will inevitably need to be balanced. I believe that loving yourself and loving your food is just as important as eating the "right" things. I drink occasional coffees, wine, gin and tonics. One of my favourite comfort foods is boiled eggs on fresh white rolls with plenty of butter. I make my informed choice; too much, too often and there is a consequence of kidney infections, constipation and weight gain.

Remember food is anything that "rots and ripens." Anything with chemical additives or preservatives is not counted as food. Sugar is considered a warming Yang food, extremely acid-forming and best avoided in the refined state. Things like fizzy drinks, sweets, pasta, white bread and cakes. Alcohol and coffee are also acid-forming along with dairy products. Anything eaten that is burnt can be perceived as a toxin, so no burnt toast but more importantly avoid oils that have become overheated, overused and damaged.

Sometimes foods, which seem acidic such as lemons and tomatoes, actually alkalise the body. The natural acids such as ascorbic acid or vitamin C are used by the body and only the alkaline minerals remain to be absorbed.

Most meat, fish and poultry tend to make the body acidic. By eating vegetables, herbs, spices, nuts, seeds and fruit the body remains balanced.

From a Chinese Medicine point of view all three types of stress, including the environmental toxins detailed in the Bonebroth and Jing section, deplete the kidney energy. When the kidney is weak it cannot support the liver, (See page 26) which is responsible for detoxification of all substances in the body. This means the toxins that we eat in food are not able to leave the body, causing weight gain, bloating, inflammation, joint pain, thrush, painful urination, itchy vaginal hood and many other symptoms.

By helping the kidney and liver we increase flow, reducing inflammation and pain. Lumps, bumps and swelling will reduce as we alkalise the body and increase movement of Chi and blood.

Green is the colour of food for the liver and green leafy vegetables, such as kale, broccoli, spinach, parsley and rocket are high in levels of calcium, magnesium, manganese, zinc and many more minerals. Together with root vegetables they are the most alkalising of vegetables. In the following recipe I have mixed them with lemons and barley grass powder, which is especially supportive for the kidney and reduces irritation and swelling in the body.

TURKISH MASHED CARROTS

Serves 4

500g carrots
1 level tbsp. cumin seeds
1 tsp. salt
Juice of 1 lemon
3 tbsp. olive oil
1 tsp. ground black pepper
1 level tbsp. sweet paprika and barley grass powder
2 or 3 large handfuls of baby spinach leaves

Top, tail and wash the carrots, chop them into bite-size pieces. Pop them into salted boiling water then lower the temperature to simmer for about 10-15 minutes. When soft, drain, and mash with a fork. The idea is not to make a puree but rather a chunky mash. While the carrots are simmering, fry cumin seeds for one minute in a dry frying pan, when the aroma is high but they haven't browned, tip them into a pestle and mortar with the salt. Grind together and transfer to a large bowl. Add to the cooked mashed carrots with the lemon juice, olive oil, black pepper, sweet paprika and barley grass powder.

If your digestion is weak you may choose to wilt the spinach in a frying pan with a couple of tablespoons of water before adding it to the carrots. However, I find the heat of the cooked carrots is enough to soften the baby spinach before eating. This dish goes especially well with Puy lentils, beetroot and goat cheese from the heart chapter.

TWO PATES

When Chi becomes cold or weak it can condense into phlegm and if not warmed or moved it can harden to form lumps, bumps, cysts and nodules. Chi is similar to the flow of water, when overheated it evaporates and doesn't have the same power or hydrating ability and when it becomes cold it resembles solid ice, unable to flow.

Fibroids and polycystic ovaries are two different manifestations of the lack of movement of Chi. Fibroids can mean extremely heavy menstruation, lower abdomen pain and even pain during sexual intercourse whereas polycystic ovaries inhibit menstruation, resulting in difficulty to conceive.

From a Chinese Medicine point of view, these conditions would be caused by poor kidney energy leading to a lack of flow in the liver. From the constructive and destructive Five Element System diagram in the Introduction of this book, you see that the spleen, if overactive or overfed, compromises the kidney. The flavour for the spleen is sweet. Too much sugar or too many carbohydrates, especially refined will weaken the kidneys. To prevent weakening kidney Chi it is best that the spleen is kept in balance and not overfed with simple sugars and overly sweet food such as chocolate, ice cream, biscuits and cake. Orange foods such as carrots and butternut squash are great for the spleen and so are comforting, fibre filled, complex carbohydrates found in beans and pulses.

Aduki beans are especially nourishing for the kidneys. Rather than opening a tin you can buy dried beans and soak them for eight hours. Boil the soaked beans with a strip of kombu seaweed for approximately an hour until the beans are soft. Strain, remove and discard the kombu. Keep the water the beans were cooked in and drink it warm for a super kidney strengthening tea. Don't add salt to the water when cooking lentils or beans as this causes the skins to toughen. Cashew nuts are packed with minerals, especially zinc and selenium, to assist fertility. They contain many B vitamins, which help metabolize proteins, as well as fats and carbohydrates to assist the spleen. Eat small amounts of nuts or and seeds every day to assist the liver. The natural oils support the liver's role in the smooth flow of blood. Too much of a good thing however, eating bowls of nuts or seeds will overload the organ, having the opposite effect. Eating approximately enough to fit in the palm of your hand is perfect.

Blood and Chi accumulate in the abdomen causing larger fibroids, painful periods and exacerbation of polycystic ovaries. The green flat leaf parsley, in this recipe, will help the gallbladder produce bile, break down fats in the liver and shift any blood stagnation. I think the more flat leaf parsley you can put in this recipe the better. It's an amazing herb, containing way more vitamin C than oranges, heaps of calcium and magnesium it even kills bacteria in the mouth and gums, preventing bad breath.

ADUKI BEAN AND CASHEW NUT PATE

Serves 4

- 1 can of Aduki beans
- 100g of cashews
- 1 medium red onion
- 50ml olive oil
- Pinch of cayenne pepper
- 1 tsp. sweet paprika
- 1 large handful flat-leaf parsley
- 2 cloves garlic
- 1 tbsp. tomato puree
- 1 tbsp. lemon juice

Rinse the beans and add to a food processor. If you prefer a smooth pate, soak the cashews overnight in 200ml of water, for crunchy pate, half an hour is fine. Combine the cashews with two tablespoons of the soaking cashew water to the beans. Pour in olive oil, cayenne pepper, paprika, tomato puree, lemon juice and blitz. Chop the garlic and flat-leaf parsley and add to the food processor.

Feel free to add ingredients like black olives or sundried tomatoes to this delicious vegetarian pate.

The following recipe works in the same way, supporting the spleen with the satisfying beans and sweet roasted garlic. The aubergine and lemon juice help the liver to move blood in the uterus and the salty seaweed feeds the kidney for Chi and flow.

WHITE BEAN DIP

Serves 4

1 tin butter beans or cannellini beans
1 roasted medium aubergine
1 bulb roasted garlic
3 tbsp. olive oil
Juice of 1 small lemon
1 tbsp. of Dillisk or Wakame Seaweed
1 tbsp. of finely chopped rosemary
Salt and pepper to taste

Roast the garlic first by cutting the top of each clove whilst it remains as a bulb. This sounds trickier than it is. Simply hold the stalk in the middle and leave the stalk in the center so that the bulb holds together. Place the bulbs on a roasting tray and drizzle generously with olive oil. Place into a preheated oven at 180°C for 30-40 minutes at until each clove begins to brown and one or two of the cloves pop up from out of their paper casing.

To roast the aubergine, pierce it all over using a sharp knife then wrap it in tin foil, place either on a baking tray or directly onto the oven shelf. Roast for about 40 minutes at 180°C, checking to see if they are ready by pulling back the foil and piercing with a sharp knife. When ready, the knife should pass through the aubergine like butter. When they are soft, unwrap from the tin foil, slice lengthways in half and using a spoon, scoop out the soft squidgy brown middle, leaving the purple skin behind. When you have your roasted garlic popped out from the papery casing and soft fleshy aubergine, drop them into a food processor with the rinsed beans, olive oil, lemon juice and finely chopped rosemary. Rehydrate the seaweed in a little water, chop and add with the rosemary, blitz all ingredients together. If the beans make the dip very sticky you can add a little water or a little more oil. This dip has a softer consistency than the previous pate and is fantastic with celery sticks but try it drizzled over warm new potatoes too.

I usually roast three garlic bulbs at the same time, they are great to keep in the fridge to add to tomato sauces, casseroles or even to spread on toast. If you roast extra aubergine you can store the extra flesh in a zip lock bag in the freezer to add to curries or stews later.

ALKALINE WATER

I wrote this recipe in my last book – ***Shiatsu & the Art of Conscious Cooking*** and it's one I recommend to most clients. I teach it again and again. It is the most consistent way of bringing alkaline minerals to the body, plus it strengthens the bladder, meaning you don't constantly get up in the middle of the night to use the loo. It is an alkalising drink that reduces inflammation and pain throughout the body especially in the urinary tract. Barley water can lessen swelling, puffiness and water retention. It can help clear the bacteria that causes urinary tract infections, vaginitis and prostatitis. If you have experienced stress, joint pain, sleeplessness, Christmas with the family or maybe burnt the candle at both ends, then make this drink. Stress and adrenaline-filled situations create acidic conditions. This drink can maintain the pH balance in the body, although you may have to address lifestyle issues and food choices to maintain Yin Yang balance.

BARLEY WATER

Serves 6

50g barley – pearl or pot barley
2 litres water
½ lemon
Pinch of sea salt
Pinch of dillisk seaweed (Optional)

Place the barley into a heavy-based saucepan with a good fitting lid. Pour in the water, add the half lemon and pinch of salt. Bring it to the boil and simmer for an hour, make sure the lid is on firmly. After an hour of a slow simmer, use a fine mesh sieve and strain the barley from the water. Using the back of a spoon push on the barley into the mesh to get as much of the white gloopy mixture into the water. This water can be kept in a jug or a bottle in the fridge for about 5 days. Shake or stir the barley water before use as the sediment will fall to the bottom. I usually make a batch from which I take a measure in the morning and in the afternoon. A measure for me would be 1/3 barley water, poured into a mug topped up with 2/3 hot water. You can use agave or honey to sweeten if you like. Its best to drink first thing in the morning, before eating to clear your system. Treat it like medicine because that's what it is.

Save the cooked barley to use in the following Avocado Salad or in the Chilli Con Barley recipe.

If you find the barley water gives you loose stools, you can dry roast it on the base of the pan first.

AVOCADO, BARLEY AND ARAME SALAD

Barley is a fantastic, underrated, underused ingredient. As described in the last recipe, it can soothe and help clear urinary tract infections, reduce inflammation and lessen the urge to pee often. This frequent urination can become common as we age, after childbirth or during cold winter months all of which weaken the kidney and bladder meridians. The realm of the kidney also governs the nervous system and production of hormones such as adrenaline and cortisol. For a healthy body that can thrive these hormones must be kept in balance. Prolonged, elevated cortisol levels can shut down the reproductive system, reduce testosterone, cause intense food cravings and interfere with T-cell production leading to a reduced immune system.

When I experience stressful times, often the glands in my neck swell, I develop earaches, my lower abdomen feels heavy or my lower back aches. These are all symptoms that the kidney/bladder meridian system is under pressure and if I don't pay attention, it can develop into severe headaches, fever, chills and a full-blown kidney infection. Barley is a highly alkalising ingredient that balances the acidity in the body caused by stress. In Chinese Medicine, there are internal and external causes of disease. Stress is an internal condition brought on by our own emotions, it is not an external pathogen invading to cause sickness but its symptoms can be just as debilitating, causing bleeding gums, arterial damage, inflammation and joint pain, yeast infections, fatigue, kidney stones, liver congestion, irritable bowel, infertility and a reduced immune system.

So, take care. Pay attention to how you feel and take responsibility for your symptoms. It is possible to address the cause of the problem, not just the symptom. Making and eating Barley will alleviate symptoms and strengthen the kidney but if the internal causes are not addressed then the situation may remain the same. Change has to come from within, there are no magic wands or magic ingredients but awareness and responsibility for one's own body are a great place to start.

All types of seaweeds can benefit thyroid and hormone production. They are all cooling in nature, acting as a diuretic, transforming phlegm and hard masses in the body such as cysts and goiters. As seaweeds are salty in flavour and deep blue/black in colour they all benefit the kidney and Endocrine system encompassing all glands and hormone-producing organs such as thyroid and ovaries. Arame is exceptionally high in its concentration of calcium and iodine. It is tougher than some other seaweeds and requires brief cooking rather than just rehydrating.

AVOCADO, BARLEY AND ARAME SALAD

Serves 4

300g barley (or brown rice barley mix half and half)
2 large handfuls of arame seaweed
2 avocados
Juice of half lemon
150g spinach
50g almonds
25g sunflower seeds
25g pumpkin seeds
Sea salt

Dressing

100g yogurt
Juice of one lemon
2 tbsp. olive oil
Salt and pepper to taste

Cook the barley and brown rice together in 700ml of water for about 45 minutes. If you have left-over barley from the barley water recipe, then just cook the brown rice. This recipe also works with just barley. I like to add brown rice for extra chewiness and texture. Add the arame seaweed to the barley or brown rice 10 minutes before the end of cooking by which time, all the ingredients will be ready together. Simply strain and leave to cool. The cooking liquor from the barley, rice and seaweed can be reserved and taken as a tea.

If you prefer to have slightly wilted spinach in your salad, then toss it into the barley and rice just after straining, whilst it is still warm. If you like your spinach raw and crunchy let the barley and rice cool before assembling the salad.

To create the dish, simply slice the soft avocado and toss it through the barley, rice and seaweed with the lemon juice, almonds, seeds and salt.

For the dressing, simply stir ingredients together gently and drizzle over the hearty, wholesome salad.

The thyroid gland requires iodine for normal function. However, in its Yin Yang irony, if you have already developed a thyroid problem, high concentration of iodine may aggravate the condition.

HUMMUS WITH SEAWEED

Most people are familiar with hummus – it's a sandwich staple and fantastic as a substitute for cheese. It's so versatile in its ingredients I decided to experiment and add seaweed. Chickpeas are traditionally used as a tonic for the stomach. They reduce dampness, candida and bloating. However, I have found some clients suffer from gas when eating beans and lentils. Adding seaweed helps the digestion and breakdown of peas, beans and lentils. In Japan, Kombu is cooked traditionally with beans to breakdown the pulses and make them more digestible. But it's not just kombu that can do this, all seaweeds have this property and its not just about softening beans. Seaweed has a quality that can dissolve bulges and bumps within the body such as goiter, ovarian cysts, breast lumps and lymph node swelling.

Seaweed can be easily incorporated into your food everyday. It can be sprinkled into stews or tossed into stir fry. As a simple guide, I have listed the common properties and then specific qualities of the most common seaweeds.

- Cooling nature
- Softens hard masses in the body and assists in reducing swelling
- Detoxifies
- Transforms phlegm
- Diuretic
- Alleviates liver stagnancy
- Benefits thyroid and blood
- Removes residues of radiation in the body

Dulse/Dillisk - Exceptionally concentrated in iodine and rich in manganese. Does not need to be soaked before use and can be eaten raw like crisps.
Recipes: Black Wood Ear Noodle Soup, Beet Marmalade.

Hijiki and Arame – High concentrates of calcium and iodine. Soak the small strips for 10-20 minutes before tossing in stir fry.
Recipes: Avocado, Barley and Arame Salad.

Kombu and Kelp – Very good at reducing swelling – goiters, arthritis, rheumatism, high blood pressure, prostate and ovarian problems, blood clots and anemia. Generally cooked with pulses.
Recipes: Two Pates.

Nori – High protein content and most easily digested. Rich in vitamin A, B1 and niacin, decreases cholesterol, treats painful urination. Comes in delicate sheets that can be eaten raw or toasted and sprinkled over salads.
Recipes: Tamari Kale Crisps.

Wakame – Good for purifying the blood and promoting healthy skin and hair. Pre-soak for a minute or two, chop and add to salads or buy pre-chopped and add to stews and quiches.
Recipes: Miso & Kudzu Soup, Seaweed and Scrambled Eggs.

Carrageen – Resolves phlegm, soothes and moistens the lungs and large intestine soothes peptic and duodenal ulcers, mild coagulant effect on the blood.
Recipes: Lemon Carrageen pots.

HUMMUS WITH SEAWEED

Serves 3/4

1 tin chickpeas
2 tsp. tahini
2-3 crushed garlic cloves
4 tbsp. olive oil
Water – amount depending on the desired consistency
Juice of a lemon
1 large handful pre-soaked wakame or dillisk
100g coriander
Salt and pepper to taste

Rinse and drain the chickpeas. Add them to a blender with tahini, garlic cloves, olive oil, lemon. Blend, adding water to create the desired consistency, whether that be crunchy coarse or smooth and silky. Meanwhile soak the seaweed in water, when soft, remove from the water and chop finely with the coriander adding to the mixture in the blender. When all ingredients are in give it a final whiz adding extra olive oil, salt and pepper to taste. Tip out into a bowl and serve with the drop scones from the lung/large intestine chapter.

When buying seaweed be mindful of where it come from. How is the water quality, the environmental impact of harvesting and the air miles it has acquired? Some good Irish suppliers of seaweed that I use from the Wild Atlantic Way can be found at www.connemaraseaweedcompany.ie, www.blathnamara.ie and www.wildirishseaweeds.com

SEAWEED SCRAMBLED EGGS

Serves 1

Wakame seaweed is easy to use and so good for building and purifying the blood. This recipe is especially good for anyone recovering from surgery or childbirth. If you have had a cesarian section that's a double whammy. It will also promote lactation and support your kidney energy which weakens during childbirth for women.

For men, depletion of kidney energy can happen through ejaculation, as semen contains many vital minerals such as magnesium, phosphorus, potassium, sodium vitamin B12 and zinc. Once released, the body draws on the reserves of these essential minerals to create more semen. Orgasm doesn't have to mean ejaculation and for fantastic reading on how this is possible, I recommend *Multi Orgasmic Man* by Mantak Chia.

Making a baby and producing semen both deplete the Jing. Precious fluids are lost when the gates of vitality are opened by both these actions. Eggs and seaweed restore and rebalance kidney Chi and Jing.

Millet soothes and builds spleen energy which is put under pressure during pregnancy and childbirth. The spleen controls insulin levels and the risk of developing gestational diabetes whilst the fetus is growing. Millet will feed the spleen and comfort the body during exhausting times.

50g millet
1 tbsp. wakame seaweed
100ml stock *(use either bone broth or good quality, MSG free vegetable bouillon)*
1 tbsp. sunflower oil
3 eggs beaten
2 roasted red peppers *(optional)*
Salt and pepper to taste

Place the millet, stock and seaweed into a medium sized saucepan to cook for about 20 minutes until the millet is soft and the stock has been absorbed. Next, take a frying pan, add the oil and begin to fry the roasted red peppers on a medium heat. When warmed through add the eggs and scramble. Scoop in the cooked millet and seaweed mixture to the eggs, adding salt and pepper to taste. A simple, supportive Saturday morning breakfast.

CHILLI AND PARMESAN POLENTA

Serves 6

Polenta, made from corn, is much underused in Ireland. People, here in this country, on the whole, love potatoes.. Potatoes are real comfort food, craved in times of stress or when sleep patterns are out of sync. In Chinese Medicine, they fortify the kidney Yin which soothes us in times of stress. But too much of a good Yin can cause excessive laziness and make us into real couch potatoes. Compared to the corn in polenta, the potato releases sugars far quicker into the body, meaning greater mood swings and energy slumps. So instead of mashed potatoes, try this delicious polenta dish. It's delicate, yet warming texture tonifies the kidneys and fortifies sexual energy. Its high B vitamin, and niacin content increases blood circulation to the brain making it less soporific than the dish of mashed potatoes. It assists in the production of the happy hormone, serotonin, giving us the feeling of contentment.

1500ml veg stock
250g polenta
1 tsp. salt
½ tsp. red or green chilli finely chopped
1 tbsp. chopped dillisk or wakame seaweed
60g parmesan
25g butter
Large handful of chopped coriander or parsley

In a heavy based, large pot, bring the stock to the boil; add the polenta, chillies, salt and seaweed flakes. Turn the heat down and stir constantly until it begins to thicken. Make sure you get your spoon right to the bottom as the polenta can sink and stick. Allow the polenta to bubble like soft lava for about 20 minutes stirring occasionally. At the very end stir in the grated parmesan, chopped parsley or coriander and butter. The chillies counteract the phlegm producing properties of the dairy and you should be left with a warming, kidney fortifying dollop of creamy mash, perfect as an accompaniment to the Chilli Con Barley.

CHILLI CON BARLEY

Serves 6

What to do with all the cooked barley from the Barley Water recipe? I'm always thinking up new ways to use cooked barley. Here I use it instead of meat to make a thick and tasty vegetarian chilli.

3 tbsp. organic sunflower oil
2 onions
3 cloves garlic
2 stalks celery
2 medium carrots
1 red pepper
2 tsp. ground coriander
1 tsp. cinnamon
1 tsp. cayenne pepper (to taste)
1 tsp. tomato puree
500ml vegetable stock
2 tin plum tomato
1 tin (400g) cooked black/kidney beans
Salt and pepper
200g pre-cooked barley
Handful fresh coriander
5g dark chocolate

In a large heavy based casserole pan, soften the onions in the oil on medium heat until they are golden yellow, then add the chopped celery, garlic, carrot, tomato puree, cayenne pepper, cinnamon and ground coriander. Let them all fry for a couple of minutes taking care that nothing burns or sticks to the pan. There should be a wonderful aroma at this point. Add the stock, kidney beans, tinned tomato, salt and pepper, bring to a boil and allow to simmer for fifteen minutes, at which point add the barley and cook for another ten minutes. If you find after adding the barley it is still very watery leave the lid off and keep stirring for another 5 minutes. All the vegetables should be cooked at this point so it's just a matter of finishing off by adding in the chunk of chocolate and fresh coriander.

Serve with the creamy chilli and parmesan polenta making sure your mojo is alive and thriving with satisfying food rather than sleepily smothered with lacklustre comfort food.

BLACK SESAME GRAPES

Serves 4

As mentioned in Bonebroth and Jing, as we pass through stages of life, hormonal shifts happen for both men and women. Many physical symptoms can manifest such as, hot flushes, drying skin, changes in sleep patterns and loss of sexual desire. Most of the time we accept these changes as the normal aging process however, it is possible to age and retain a full va va voom for all areas of life including a juicy, sexual appetite. Loss of libido can happen at any time of life. Often stress and pushing ourselves to succeed causes depletion of kidney energy and loss of libido. The following recipe builds kidney strength at any age however, lifestyle changes need to be made in conjunction with the food. Sexual energy needs conscious balance. In flow, sexual energy releases tension and stress and a healthy libido adds to the vibrancy of life. However when we become fixated on sex and especially orgasmic climax it can produce more problems than it solves. I would combine this recipe with the breathing exercises in the at the beginning of this chapter or the Circulation of Sexual energy in Yin Yang chapter. This will improve relaxation, flow and desire, rather than the grasping, needy craving of orgasmic success.

For best results, sesame seeds need to be taken regularly. 1 or 2 tsp. of black sesame seeds per day is best. Both the black and white sesame seeds are rich in vitamin E and calcium but the white focus in bringing moisture to the large intestine whereas the black seeds support the kidney, which in turn support the endocrine system and boosts core energy. They can tonify brain function and alleviate painful, weak or stiff joints. They build Yin fluids and reputedly stop greying hair. They repair hair loss and improve declining fertility. These are all symptoms of the aging process. I love that these little seeds increase fluids and lubrication. Let's stay vibrant and juicy by breathing deeply and taking time to add these little seeds to the diet.

In this recipe, I combine them with grapes which also fortify the body and its fluids. Traditionally grapes are given to convalescing hospital patients and in Spain, they are used at New Years to signify new life and new desires.

150g seedless grapes
1 tbsp. caster sugar
2 tbsp. black and white sesame seeds

Sprinkle a heaped tablespoon of caster sugar onto the base of a large non-stick frying pan on a medium high heat. As it begins to melt, scatter in the grapes. Shake the pan so that the sugar sticks to the grapes and toss in the 2 tablespoons of sesame seeds ensuring that they are picked up by the melting sugar. The sugar content of this dish is very high so they are not exactly the healthiest snack in the world but they are a delicate treat to tickle the taste buds and wet the desire. Perfect to use in the heart tantra exercise.

BENEVOLENT OATS

When I give Shiatsu, I almost always start with the bladder meridian. It runs either side of the spine, right down the back of the whole body. No matter what is going on, the bladder meridian is a good place to begin. It brings relaxation to the whole body. Muscles begin to melt and the mind begins to relax and receive.

The majority of the population subscribe to the Darwinian theory of evolution in which only the fittest survive to evolve and procreate. I believe at a deep level in our psyche this means there is a part of us that is always in defensive mode, ready to protect ourselves and defend what we have. Whilst this can be helpful in some situations, when used every day it becomes exhausting and depletes the kidney/bladder energy by introducing hormones such as cortisol into the bloodstream. When cortisol remains high for a prolonged period it has many detrimental effects on the body. It lowers and blocks the effects of testosterone, it inhibits the immune system, it can disrupt ovulation cycles and lead to erectile dysfunction. However, it doesn't have to be this way. We can choose to see the flip side, which is that human beings are fundamentally compassionate and will work together to ensure species survival. Instead of feeling threatened, feel supported by your fellow human. As you eat your oats, know that someone has grown, harvested and prepared them for you. Give thanks that they do that for you and know that in your day you too will support your fellow human. By practicing this mindful gratitude each day, we are acknowledging that we share the planet and its resources as a community, working together to support each other. To release from fear, and develop trust and support, the body becomes receptive and communicative, essential qualities for intimacy and arousal.

Buckwheat is not wheat or grain as it sounds, but rather the triangular seed of the Fagopyrum Esculentum plant which is related to rhubarb. It slowly lowers blood sugars and is beneficial to reduce inflammation of the blood vessels. It contains rutin, a mineral that helps lower blood pressure. Buckwheat is bitter in flavour relating it to benefits for the heart. When combined with Oats energy circulates whilst the nervous system and Shen remain calm. With a broad span of minerals, both ingredients support the kidney/bladder and build sexual energy. Oats with their slightly salty and sweet flavour build blood and bring heat to the digestive system, helping to clear toxins, including cholesterol from the large intestine.

OATMILK PANCAKES

Makes approx. 8 crêpes

200g oats
700ml milk
(or half water half milk, almond and brown rice milk also works well here)
2 eggs
200g buckwheat flour
Pinch of salt

Liquidize the oats, eggs and water so that it becomes a milky mixture. Pour into a bowl with the buckwheat flour and salt. Whisk the wet ingredients with the dry so there are no lumps remaining and leave to rest for at least half an hour. In a large non-stick pan melt a nob of butter and coat the pan with it. Pour a ladleful (approx. 50ml) of the prepared pancake mixture onto the pan tilting it so that it covers the base with a thin coating. These are a crepe style pancake rather than thick American pancake. When bubbles begin to form on the top of the batter in the pan, flip and cook for another couple of minutes. These are delicious with maple syrup and lemon juice but excel with a savoury filling. Try chopping a tomato, a couple of slices of hard cheese, grate a small clove of garlic and lots of flat-leaf parsley.

After you flip the pancake place the ingredients on one half of the crepe as it cooks so when it's done simply fold over the pancake to form a half moon, slide it out of the pan and onto the plate. This batter is easier to use when it is made the night before and left in the fridge to settle, simply whisk it to wake any sediment that is sitting at the bottom and add more water or milk if it has become too thick to pour.

BAKED PORRIDGE

Serves 6-8

As discussed in the oatmilk pancake recipe, oats are high in magnesium and help to calm the body and build sexual energy. They contain a nervine alkaloid called Avinine which, on a long-term basis, works to restore the nervous system. Oats are a popular breakfast food and this recipe is perfect for a weekend brunch. It's rich and sweet yet still full of soluble fibres to help remove cholesterol from the large intestine. In addition, oats are a great source of manganese, selenium, vitamin B1 and magnesium. They regulate hormones and the spontaneous sweating associated with fluctuating hormones.

Mixing the oats with pecans, which are full of pyridoxine (vitamin B6), further increases the usage of amino acids found in plant protein available in oats. In terms of Chinese Medicine this means pecans transform nutritional essence, which feed the kidneys, into usable energy. In this way, they reduce nervous tension and overproduction of hormones. You can substitute the pecans for walnuts if preferred. These further warm the kidney Yang and help prevent premature ejaculation.

BAKED PORRIDGE

2 ripe bananas
200g frozen raspberries
250g oats
50g walnut pieces
50g pecans pieces
1 tsp. baking powder
1 ½ tsp. cinnamon powder
½ tsp. fine sea salt
475ml almond or oat milk
60ml maple syrup
1 large free range egg
60g melted cooled butter
2 tsp. vanilla extract

In a large bowl mix the pecans/walnuts, cinnamon, baking powder and salt.

Take a pyrex or earthenware dish approximately 20cm x 20cm and butter it. Cut the banana into medallions and cover the bottom of the dish, sprinkling half the raspberries before layering over the oats, walnuts and pecans. Repeat layers reserving some of the berry mix for the top. In a jug beat together the milk, egg, butter, maple syrup and vanilla extract. Pour the milky mixture gently over the oats and place in the oven for approximately 30-45 minutes at 180°C. The oats will begin to dissolve into the juices of the fruit and milky mixture. When ready the breakfast pudding will look slightly golden, soft, spongy and smell sweet.

Recipe adapted from *Super Natural Every Day* by Heidi Swanson.

GREEN BEANS, BLACK EAR FUNGUS AND SESAME SALAD

Serves 4

For me, green beans have always been a sexy, cosmopolitan food. When I was 12 we went on our first family holiday to the south of France. The sun and the food were a revelation. Nicoise salad with its mix of olives, green beans and eggs seemed the most stylish food I'd ever seen. This elegance of green beans remained with me so I was delighted to discover just how good they are for the body.

Silicon is one of the most abundant elements on the planet's surface. Within the body, it assists calcium, growing and maintaining healthy dense bones. It increases collagen within bones aiding repair and flexibility for the whole skeletal system. A study at the Rayne Institute in the UK showed that the silicon in green beans was more easily absorbed by the body than that of any other vegetable. Silicon plays many roles in the body which link to the kidneys such as bone building, moistening membranes, and encouraging thick, healthy hair and nails. It also helps the large intestine remove aluminium from the body. In Chinese Medicine, green beans' slightly bitter flavour means that they also benefit the heart by decreasing the formation of plaque on artery walls, thereby assisting circulation and transportation of blood.

Black fungus, sometimes known as Black and White Fungus or WoodEar fungus reduces platelets in the blood stopping excessive clotting and just like the green beans, further aids blood flow which lowers blood pressure. They are black in colour and therefore fall under the domain of the kidney -Water element and are brilliant for bringing moisture to the body. Blood circulation and wetness are essential elements for arousal for both men and women so even if the black fungus doesn't seem to be an appetising ingredient for you just think of the health and pleasure benefits. Sexually this increases lubrication for women and erectile function for men.

500g green beans
Handful of black fungus
1 tbsp. of white sesame seeds
1 tbsp. of black sesame seeds
Pinch of sea salt
1 tbsp. of sesame oil
1 tbsp. of rice vinegar
1 tbsp. of tamari

To make it easier and quicker to trim, hold a bunch of the green beans in your hand and tap them stalk side down on to the chopping board. Once they are level, lay them down and chop off the woody stalks. Fill a saucepan with half a litre of water and add the black fungus. Bring the water to the boil and steam the beans over black fungus filled water for approximately 5 minutes depending on the thickness of your bean and how squeaky you like them.

While the fungus and beans are cooking, prepare the dressing by whisking remaining ingredients together in a bowl, tossing them over the drained, warm beans and fungus. This salad is delicious cold but when served warm, the aromas are fabulous.

The black fungus, I find, is better bought small and already chopped. Larger pieces of fungus require longer soaking, cooking and chopping. Also, black fungus can rehydrate to scary proportions so just buy it ready chopped and cook it for ten minutes in the water you are using to steam your beans. It doesn't have much flavour and is used to add texture, colour and stupendous health benefits to stir fries and salads in Asian cuisine.

WARM BROCCOLI, GREEN BEAN AND MISO

Serves 4

Silicon, found in green beans, strengthens bones and repairs all cells throughout the body. From a Chinese Medicine point of view together with sesame seeds, they nourish blood and generate bodily fluids. Miso is outstanding at supporting the kidneys and supplementing the Chi. If you have been running on adrenaline and need a tonic to counteract those strung out days, this is the dish for you. Think of energy as a currency – where will you spend your money? If it all gets spent on work, what is left for play? Are you overdrawn, spent up and worn out? This driven behaviour drains the kidney energy. As discussed in the overview, the kidney is about survival and procreation. If the adrenals are always engaged in survival there is nothing left for procreation. Miso, which is salty in flavour, will feed and support the kidneys making sure that we have enough creative energy to feel like engaging sexually with ourselves and with others.

300g broccoli
150g green beans
3 tbsp. toasted sesame seeds

Dressing

2 tbls. Tahini paste
1 tbls. lemon juice
1 tbls. miso paste dissolved in 25ml water
100ml sesame oil
1 clove crushed garlic
2 tsp. Tamari soy sauce
½ tbls. honey
Pinch of gomasio

Cut the broccoli into small florets and place in a steamer over boiling, salted water. After 5 minutes add the trimmed green beans and steam for another 3 minutes. If you prefer your vegetables softer, steam a little longer. Meanwhile, make the dressing by dissolving the miso in 25ml hot water from a recently boiled kettle. Make sure the water is not too hot as miso is full of live probiotic cultures which are fantastic for the intestine. Cooking the miso will kill these cultures.

Next, mix into the miso, tahini, lemon juice, garlic, sesame oil, tamari and honey. If you find the dressing too salty you can omit the gomasio or sprinkle it on later as a condiment. When the vegetables are soft but firm take them out of the steamer and toss them in the dressing which should be thick enough to stick to the broccoli and beans.

POACHED EGGS WITH ASPARAGUS

Serves 2

This is a perfect breakfast when you want to spend the day in bed. It is beautiful to the eye and delicate to the palate. Exactly what you need when you want special time with yourself or your lover. Whilst both Yin in quality, these foods benefit the kidneys in slightly different ways. Eggs are a symbol of fertility and rebirth, with high levels of vitamin B6, B5 and B12, they help balance hormones and produce healthy testosterone, vital for sexual function in men and women.

"Asparagus, stirs up lust in man and woman."

Nicholas Culpeper -
English herbalist 17th century

Asparagus is a fantastic, if not slightly odourful, diuretic. It contains potassium, fiber, vitamins B6, A and C, thiamin and folic acid. It helps clear arteries of cholesterol and plaque build up aiding movement of blood and Chi. It is used to ease menstrual pain and to promote fertility. Asparagus also boosts histamine production, which is helpful for the ability to reach orgasm in both men and women. However, before rushing off to fill your basket, be aware that if taken in excess, asparagus can irritate the kidneys, so keep an eye on that Yin Yang balance.

1 bunch of asparagus
2 eggs
1 tsp. vinegar
1 tbsp. finely grated parmesan cheese
1 knob of butter
½ Gomasio
Fresh ground black pepper

In a medium sized saucepan bring salted water to a boil over medium-high heat. Wash and trim the woody ends of the asparagus placing them in a steamer above the boiling water for 2-3 minutes until bright green, tender but crisp. Transfer the asparagus to a plate; place the knob of butter on them to melt, keeping them warm whilst you add the vinegar to the hot water in the saucepan. Reducing the heat to its minimum setting and using a spoon, stir the water to create a whirlpool. Crack the eggs carefully into the centre of the whirlpool and cook gently for 4 minutes. Using a slotted spoon remove the eggs, making sure all the water is drained, place on top of the asparagus. Sprinkle the gomasio, pepper and cheese over the plate and take it back to enjoy in bed.

LOVE LUBE

In Chinese Medicine, lack of fluid in the body is a Yin problem. The decline of vaginal lubrication in women and semen in men is seen as a decline in Jing stored in the kidneys. This can happen as we age and especially following menopause or andropause. Whilst lubes are great at substituting fluids for intercourse, it's best to avoid a problem rather than fix one. As the classic texts say "it's too late to forge weapons when war has already begun".

Yin and Yang deficiency can be addressed with changes in lifestyle and supplemented with food however, your essence is a precious substance and cannot be replenished. Eating black sesame seeds, royal jelly, bone broths, seaweed and algae such as Chlorella and Spirulina will all help kidney Yin. Too much ejaculation, coffee, pushing the body and mind too far, will damage it.

Take care with what you choose to insert into the vagina. Lotions and potions can upset the pH of the vagina leading to all sorts of unwanted problems such as bacterial vaginosis and other yeast infections like Candida. Adding essential oils such as tea tree is also not a good idea as this can cause internal scarring. However both ingredients can be added to the recipe if you are using as an external body massage oil.

As this lubricant is made from only natural based ingredients you could eat it, but why would you. It's so good for your skin it makes a great massage lotion. It can be applied in and around the vagina safely before, during and after intercourse to help ease discomfort. It's fabulous for lingam massage too. A word of warning though, oils can break down latex, making your condoms ineffective, so be sure and be safe.

50 ml sweet almond oil
2 large tbsp. beeswax

Place the sweet almond oil and beeswax in a ceramic bowl over a saucepan of boiling water until the two have melted. Allow the mixture to cool and harden slightly then whisk or use a stick blender to whip together until its light and fluffy. Use a spatula to transfer the lovely lube into a sterilized glass jar. If the lube is cold it may be difficult to play with. So leave it near a radiator before applying . Or use slowly with patience and long strokes so that the body's own heat melts the waxy oil

Extra Added Bonus Practice

Food is not the only source of pleasure and health for the nervous system. Massage and touch work wonders for the neural networks of the body. Relaxing the body, encouraging it to release emotional and physical stiffness and pain increases well-being and health. Use the Love Lube to massage the penis and vagina directly. If you aren't going to use the oil internally you may like to omit the beeswax and just use sweet almond oil with perhaps a few drops of Lavender or Rose essential oil. Massage can be done alone or with a partner. The aim here is not to orgasm although it may be a highly pleasurable and erotic experience, instead to relax and just receive the touch. If you are massaging a partner make sure you have connected with them. Ask them if there is anything they would like and importantly, anywhere and in any way they would NOT like to be touched. This can be a deeply relaxing and nourishing experience for the giver as well as the recipient. As the receiver, resist the urge to participate, simply lie back and receive. In this way, you can pay attention to the sensations without needing to respond.

Begin by massaging the feet, the calves and inner thighs. Bring the hands and fingers up to massage the pubic bone and CV2 (page 65) gently with small circular motions moving down to the perineum with gentle strokes. If there is any tension simply hold the area until it warms and softens, again, small circular motion may help to ignite nerves and get the blood flowing. Find CV1 which is the point between the anus and the scrotum or labia and gently massage and press into this magical spot. Move upwards to the labia and scrotum sack, loosening and lubricating the skin. You can use more oil and work your way to the penis or vagina and clitoris. Allowing warm oil to drip onto the head of the penis you can then stroke from head down shaft to base and return. Try using one hand to encircle the base of the penis whilst the other hand strokes. If you find yourself coming to climax simply move the hands back to the perineum or the pubic bone. You also might try squeezing the head of the penis very gently to arrest the flow of Chi. Paying close attention to the breath is also important. Slow it down if the body becomes overexcited. This is about releasing and relaxing not ejaculating.

For the woman to receive, allow warm oil to flow around the clitoris, labia, vulva and vaginal opening, Gently stroking and massaging the whole area, paying close attention that your partner is not resisting or in pain. Trauma and tension can be stored deeply in this sensitive area so less is more, remember whilst this can be deeply sensual, it is being offered as a therapeutic massage not an element of foreplay. Don't underestimate the power of this practice, be prepared to stop and hold the whole body if necessary as emotions arise for release. If your partner is receptive you can gently squeeze and even tap the head of the clitoris. Vary the intensity by moving the area being massaged. Bring the hands from the genitals and gently sweep around to the anus allowing all the pelvic nerves to be incorporated and stimulated. At the end of the massage simply sit or lie in silence for a time. It is likely that the mind and body of both giver and receiver will be in a deeply meditative, heightened state. Allow your body's to just be, accepting all the physical sensations.

BROWN RICE AND LIME LETTUCE WRAPS

Brown rice in Chinese Medicine traditionally benefits the Yin and has a calming effect on the body. It strengthens the spleen which when out of balance, adversely affects the kidney. Modern nutritional research shows brown rice to have beneficial effects for the whole nervous system because of its high levels of B vitamins and manganese. It prevents over-stimulation of the nervous system and reduces involuntary spasms, twitching and cramps. As a whole grain it has a wealth of minerals that support the kidney and keep nerves healthy. For libido, erectile function and orgasm the Pelvic nerve and the Pudendal nerve need to be firing correctly. These nerves have both motor and sensory functions for the clitoris and the penis. They connect with the central nervous system, sending sensory information up the spinal cord, to the brain and back to the sexual organs. Nerves need to be kept healthy so that chemical and electrical information can be passed, use food that strengthens connections and smooths communication.

2 garlic cloves, peeled
1-inch segment of fresh ginger, peeled
100ml coconut milk
Pinch fine grain sea salt
100g cashew nuts
200g precooked brown rice
1 tsp. tamari
1 tbsp. freshly squeezed lime juice
1 small cucumber,
1 small carrot, grated
Large handful of chopped flat-leaf parsley and/or coriander
10 - 12 whole lettuce leaves *(romaine, little gems, etc.)*
Juice of a fresh lime
Drizzle of sesame oil

Using a pestle and mortar, smash the garlic and ginger into a paste. Add this to 50ml of the coconut milk and heat over a medium flame. Stir in the salt and the Cashews. Allow ingredients to infuse for a couple of minutes then add the precooked brown rice and heat through. Meanwhile mix the remaining coconut milk, lime, tamari and add to the heating rice. When all heated through transfer to a large serving dish and toss in the cucumber, grated carrot and herbs, adding a final squeeze of a lime. To serve, fill each washed and dried lettuce leaf with the lime infused coconut rice and drizzle over with sesame oil.

WARM CASHEW MILK WITH ASHWAGANDHA

When Jing is low libido diminishes. As discussed at the beginning of this chapter, Jing can weaken for several reasons most notably pushing on through exhaustion, living in fear, anxiety or putting our bodies through stress , bad diet and poor lifestyle choices. Foods can help strengthen Jing, but it works best when accompanied by a lifestyle change. Jing can reduce with age so don't wait to take care of it. Frequent rest, relaxation, sleep patterns, balanced diet, physical activity, and a healthy connection with your sexual energy, can ensure we live a hearty, fertile, sexually active, long life.

Ashwagandha is a potent traditional medicinal herb used for thousands of years to increase strength and potency. In this way it is fantastic for increasing libido and sexual energy. It is sometimes described as the Indian Ginseng. Traditionally, the powder is taken every evening with warm milk and honey before bed for healthy sleep patterns and a strong reproductive system. I have incorporated cashews into the recipe as they have a very high zinc content.

Zinc is a mineral essential for helping the body produce testosterone, a hormone critical in regulation both men and women's libido and fertility. Research has found that zinc can improve sperm strength. As a mineral, it falls under the domain of the kidneys and will support their essence and your sexual activity.

75g cashew nuts
4 dates
200ml water
1 tsp. Ashwagandha root powder
1/4 tsp. Cinnamon powder
Agave syrup or honey to taste

Soak the cashews and the dates in water for four hours or overnight if possible, strain and rinse. Pop the nuts and dates in a blender with the 200ml of water that was used for soaking and blitz until smooth. If you want a completely smooth mixture you can use a fine mesh strainer to pass the liquid through. Otherwise, pour the liquid in a saucepan over a medium heat. Whisk briskly the Ashwagandha and Cinnamon into the milk and warm through for approximately 10 minutes. Take off the heat and allow to cool slightly before drinking, then slide straight into bed.

SALTY, CRISPY, CRUNCHY

When I was pregnant with twins my craving was for Bovril™ on toast. I couldn't get enough of the black salty paste. Now in relation to my knowledge of Shiatsu & Traditional Chinese Medicine I know I was craving salty foods to strengthen the kidney/bladder. I was making two babies and they turned out to be two big babies at 6lb 2oz and 6lb 3oz each. Think of all my energy that went into making all that flesh, blood and tissues for two babies. All the minerals that went from my body to theirs, making skeletons, flesh and organs. That took a lot of my own Jing, minerals from my bones and spleen energy to make blood to feed all three of us.

There's an old wives saying that goes "gain a child, lose a tooth". It could be that they are referring to the minerals and the very essence that is drawn from the woman's body, to grow new life for nine months inside her. The skeletal system and Jing both fall under the domain of the kidney/bladder and that intense salt craving tells us that we need to feed that meridian system during gestation. Some pregnant women have been known to crave non-foodstuff such as chalk, soil and coal. This condition known as Pica which, according to the Journal of American Dietetic Association, may be connected to an iron deficiency. Andrei Rebarber, MD, associate director of the division of maternal-fetal medicine at NYU Medical Center in New York has speculated "that it represents some nutrient that the mother may be lacking... And the crave is the body's way of asking for what it needs". In the same way that I craved Bovril™, the body will tell us what it is lacking. Now with the knowledge of Chinese Medicine I understand that I could have found healthier alternatives. Rather than reaching for the Bovril™, bacon, or super salty crisps or things that aren't actually food such as coal and dirt, I suggest mineral-rich salty food such as seaweed, miso, gomasio, bonebroth, tamari, oysters and feta cheese to feed the deep essence of the body.

Even after the baby has been born, kidney energy, Jing and mineral depletion can have many knock-on effects such as osteoporosis, dental problems, depression, prolapse and the disappearance of libido. For men symptoms are similar when they ejaculate excessively, have a poor diet and do not replenish minerals lost in the sperm

Low libido following childbirth is common. Low levels of estrogen, progesterone, lack of sleep and emotional fatigue can all play a part. Sometimes the Vagina can be drier and there can be a fear of penetration following the birth. All of these symptoms are addressed by feeding the Yin and supporting the kidney/bladder. Food may not be the complete solution, addressing emotional changes in the relationship and physical changes in the body often require a toolbox of solutions. These include counselling, massage, acupressure points, time, rest and most importantly sleep. Enter the quiet winter of kidney for restoration so the libido can rise again like the new shoots in spring.

TAMARI KALE CRISPS

Serves 6

500g kale

Dressing

1 tbsp. tamari
2 tbsp. sesame seeds
1 tbsp. milled seaweed
2 sheets Nori
1 tbsp. organic sunflower oil

Preheat the oven to 180°C. Rip the leafy kale from the stalk and tear into smaller pieces and wash. Mix the tamari, seeds, milled seaweed and oil and set aside. Pop the nori sheets in the preheated oven for 1 minute. This should crisp up the seaweed so you can crumble it into the dressing. Toss the washed kale through the dressing and spread it out onto two large baking trays. Bake for 10 minutes then shuffle and toss it around the baking tray so that it crisps and browns easily. Bake for a further 10 minutes until crispy, salty, and delicious.

Traditionally, Tamari is a Japanese equivalent of Soy Sauce. I use it because usually it is fermented for longer, contains no wheat and gluten, tends to be lower in sodium and has fewer additives than it's Chinese counterpart. However it is still high in sodium and is made from soy beans which are frequently from a genetically modified source. Keep your Yin Yang balance, eat a little of what you fancy but don't eat a trayful. Easily done though as these little crisps are delicious and moreish.

ACUPRESSURE POINTS

KIDNEY 1 – BUBBLING SPRING

Descends the Chi, brings the energy down. Focus on this point for premature ejaculation. Reducing hot flashes and impotency.

Found on the sole of the foot between the 2nd and 3rd metatarsal bones. Flex the toes upward and find the depression for the thumb to press.

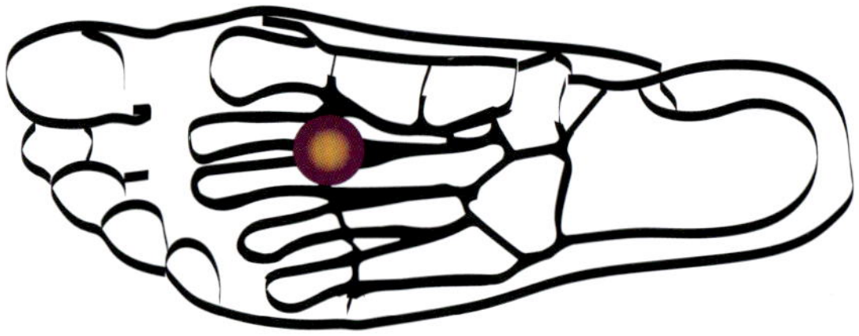

KIDNEY 3 – GREAT RAVINE

Invigorates kidneys, regulating menstruation and mood swings. Relieves sexual tension and fatigue.

Find the point on the inside of the foot between the ankle bone and achilles tendon.

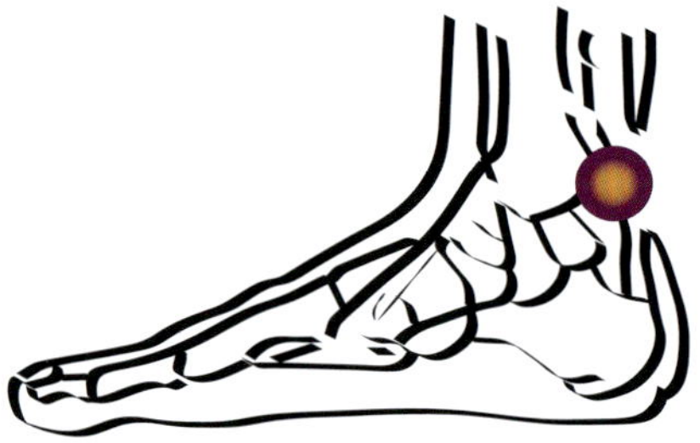

KIDNEY 6 – SHINING SEA

Nourishes the Yin and all body fluids, moistening dryness. Grounds the body when there is restlessness even when exhausted. Manages night sweats.

Find the point by pressing under the ankle bone on the inside of foot in-between the tendons.

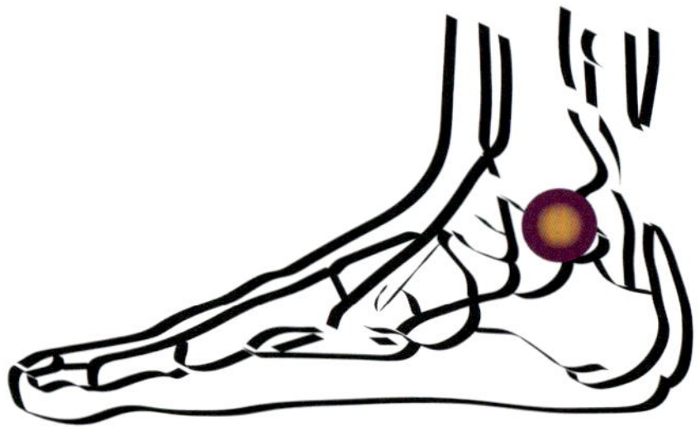

KIDNEY 7 – RETURNING CURRENT

Tonifies Yang clearing heat from the body reducing hot flashes.

Find the point on the inside lower leg, three fingers width up from kidney 3.

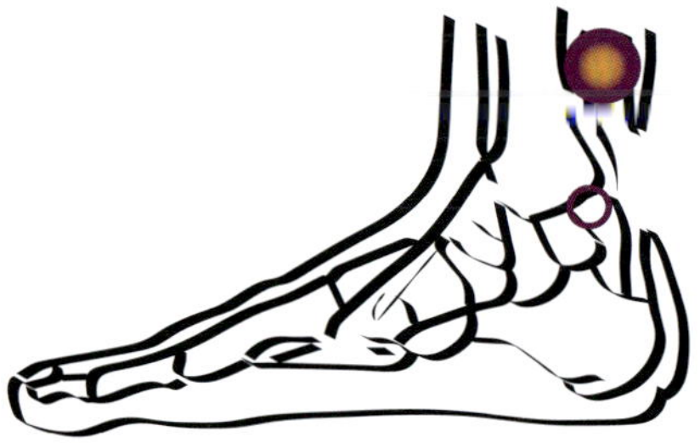

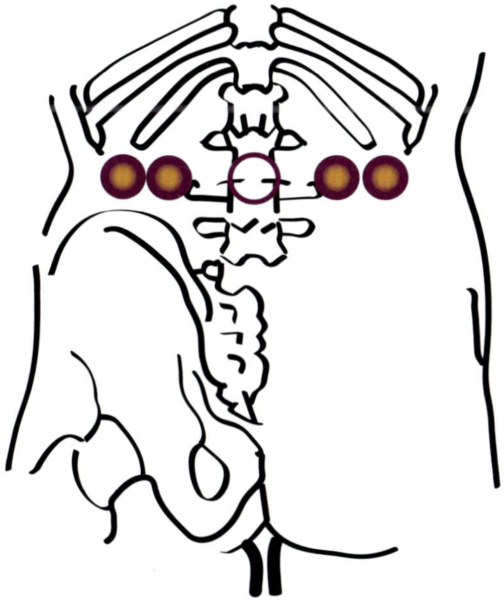

BLADDER 23 - SEA OF VITALITY AND BLADDER 52 – WILL POWER ROOM

Do not press hard if you have weak, crumbling disks of a fractured or broken back.

Nourishes Jing and restores lower burner energy following childbirth. Aids all sexual/reproductive problems including impotency and premature ejaculation. Increases vaginal and semenal fluids.

Locate Mingmen (see page 63) by resting your hands on your hips, thumbs pointing forwards, where the fingers meet upon the spine is Ming Men (L2). Two fingers laterally from Ming Men is Bl 23, four fingers from Ming men is Bl 52.

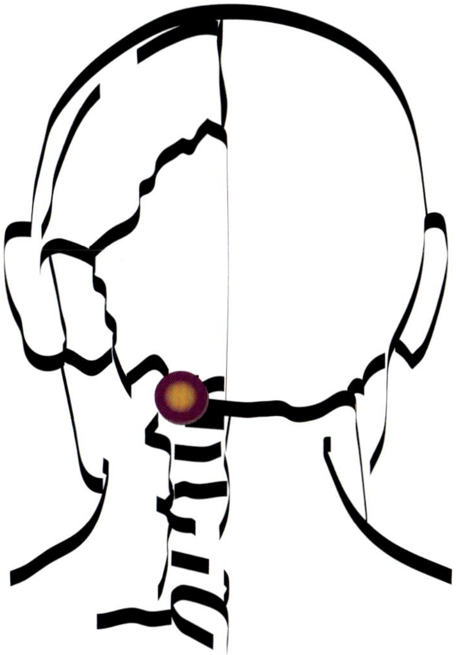

BLADDER 10 – HEAVENLY PILLAR

Realigns the spine, relieves stress and exhaustion.

First find the hollow at the base of the skull and the hairline, then move one thumbwidth down and two thumbwidth's out from the spine.

Chapter 3

LIVER / GALLBLADDER

Shall I tell you how easy it is
to fall in love with you
About why you have so
many female friends
About why we flock to you,
to speak with you, to listen
to you and to care for you
Because you are genuine,
you hold your own space
and you keep a good counsel
You don't look to take
anything
But are open hearted to
receive
You know how to take care
You move softly and speak
gently with thoughtful
consideration
Yet you are solid and truthful
I know you could hold me
Really hold me as I uncurl
and unfurl to stretch out
languid legs in gentle
relaxation
Whispered thoughts upon
a driftless sea of your clear
blue eyes

OVERVIEW
POWERFUL CREATIVE FUN

From old religions that use eggs as symbols of fertility, to the new testament where Christ dies and is born again, Easter and the time of Spring is the time for regeneration and new birth.

Fantastically, the liver is the only organ in the body that has the ability to regrow, it is paired with its Yang partner, the gallbladder, to the time of Spring.

Bulbs and flowers that have hidden dormant over the winter, burst forth with vibrant colour. Bees fly to the new blooms signalling fertilisation, pollination and new life. The emerging sunshine illuminates all the dirt and cobwebs that have hidden in the shadows of winter and we are filled with the urge to spring clean, within and without. There's talk of detox, of a Lenten fast and Ramadan. Our diet begins to change from stews and casseroles to lighter soups and salads. New fruits and vegetables appear like rhubarb, plums, the first greens of spinach, rocket and beetroot tops. It's a time when we want to clear out, clean up and get ready for that rising sap. It's the rising energy of creating and starting new projects which requires vision and foresight.

The liver loves clarity, clear seeing and finding a way around obstacles. It loves flexibility, suppleness and smooth flow. It is in charge of ligaments and tendons in the body. Sometimes when our chosen path is blocked, when things don't go as we had planned, it can cause us to feel frustrated and angry. This emotion can become locked within the muscles and create tension stiffness.

Shopping does this for me, it is not my favourite activity, especially with three children in tow. There was a time when my twelve-year-olds were transitioning from boys to teenagers and proving very difficult to find clothes that fit. Boys clothes were too small but men's clothes too big. But for an upcoming special occasion, we had to persevere and complete our quest to find smart clothes. The boys were bored and unruly, I was frustrated and cross. Didn't they understand I didn't want to be there either? I lost my temper on more than one occasion. Especially when Sam, the twins younger brother, put a waste-paper basket on his head in the middle of TKmax and pretended to be a lamp. All very funny in hindsight and with perspective but at that emotionally charged moment, rage inducing. When I woke in the morning my neck and left shoulder had become stiff and painful. The Yang emotion of the anger and frustration had become tension, stuck solid Yin in my shoulder. Emotions left unchecked cause physical blocks and diseases in the body.

Spring is the time for regrowth and creativity seen in the new shoots and green pushing through. Sometimes the regrowth can get stuck or blocked by plant pots or rocks above. But unlike me, faced with a shopping centre and three unruly boys, new growth is flexible and finds a way around immovable objects. At the time, I lost perspective, I let my anger take over and to enforce how badly they had behaved, and I carried on being angry. Its not ok to for the boys to try shoes on that are way to big for them so they look like clowns, its not ok to throw shoes at each other and its not ok to get distracted by toy shops when jumpers and shoes are the focus so I will say no, set boundaries and enforce consequences. But I don't have to be a furious, hair pulled, put upon, screaming harridan of a mother just to prove a point. It's not good for me, my liver nor my kids to see nothing but red. I became my emotion and lost perspective and from that dangerous place, where people and things can get irreparably broken and hurt. Emotions are not who you are, they don't bring power or strength, they are just a way of expressing how you feel. Try to look from different angles and see the funny side. My kids are hilarious and they won't be kids for long. The lightness of laughter can relieve the tension of the body and the frustration of the liver.

Laughter doesn't come easy when you are tired and the liver is overworked with rich food, medication, toxins and alcohol so look for the support you need and use food to flow.

It is important to take the emotional and physical together, sometimes the emotions create physical symptoms and sometimes the physical body can create an emotional state, so create a positive supportive state rather than a vicious self-destructive cycle. The liver is responsible for filtering, detoxifying and nourishing the blood. If our diet is constantly rich, full of fats, sugars, chemicals and denatured substances, the liver and gallbladder will become overworked, hot and unable to function properly leading to a clouded mind, tension headaches, muscle tension, stiffness and cramps in the body.

It is relatively easy to eat for the liver without going on any mad detox diets. Eat simply, plenty of fresh fruit and vegetables including raw salads and dark green leaves. Oily fish with lemon dressings keep everything smooth, flowing and flexible. On an emotional level be clear about what you want in your life, what turns you on, what fires you up. Create a vision for yourself of how you want to see love in your life – is it healthy family relationships, more sex, less sex, better sex, loving sex, sexy play, to live in comfort, to experience joy – what does that look like for you? What do you say yes to and what do you say no to? When you have that clarity you will find that you have that internal flow. External obstacles such as family members, jobs, money, which seem to block your path to the loving, juicy life you want to lead, become opportunities for greater joy, rather than frustrations. With a healthy liver and gallbladder, you will find it easier to negotiate blocks. Sometimes a powerful angry NO is necessary but using it constantly it can rip apart relationships and is not a foundation for love, with ourselves or others.

Don't build a wall to isolate yourself and don't keep banging your head against it thinking you are not heard. Instead, walk around the wall, find another path, know that alternatives are always possible for your flexible self.

Physically the liver is in charge of the smooth flow of blood and energetically, is in charge of the smooth flow of emotions.

Just because you have conscious sex, drink green juice, eat porridge and sit on a meditation cushion for hours does not mean you won't experience negative emotions. However, when balanced physically and emotionally, you are more able to take responsibility for emotions, feeling them, and transforming them instead of acting upon them.

By acting them out we often transfer the negative sensations on to people around us and they end up feeling hurt, angry or sad.

I was taught that's it's not good to feel angry, it's not good to feel upset, abandoned, vindictive or jealous. It's best to feel happy and benevolent, serene and calm. To be a good person, one has to be distanced from passionate emotions. Especially in the case of some religions, to attain enlightenment, means to renounce feeling sexual energy or sexual relations. In the case of Chinese Medicine, this is the furthest from the truth. We have to balance worldly emotions with spiritual thoughts. We have to embrace dark and light, Yin and Yang. When we are brave and truthful about how we feel, when we examine uncomfortable feelings, then we are less likely to act on them and more likely to transform them. Being honest means unwanted emotions become springboards for new situations.

When I was 24, I was a fire-juggler. I juggled in clubs and busked on the streets. I was pretty good but the best guy I ever saw was Devil Stix Pete. He was amazing. Not many people used devil stix in 1992 so I was excited to meet him and learn from him at a juggling convention in Manchester. As part of the gathering, there was an open mic evening for jugglers in a small circus tent. It was painful to watch some of the acts as the audience jeered and heckled the young jugglers but next up was Devil Stix Pete. He came on to dead, menacing silence and the silence continued as he began his tricks. Nothing too impressive was happening, just regular devil stix stuff but then he began to take off his clothes. A murmur began around the tent as he took more and more of his clothes, whilst still juggling, until he was completely naked. To a complete stunned silence and still juggling, he said, "Heckle me now you bastards" the place erupted into a standing ovation, with roars of laughter, applause and admiration. Using the negativity of the audience he had created a memorable and life-changing event for me. He had stripped himself bare, no defences, just simple straight forward juggling and absolute bravery and commitment to who he was. This naked authenticity was powerful.

By being honest with our emotions rather than contracting and reacting with fear, a raw essential vigour exists within us, powerful, creative and free.

Spring

Break the teeth of the
seraphimgrin
Because guarded by
the fushia mist
Is the hidden snarl of
its anger

It spooks me now
Shrieking and swirling
Insane
Crack through the sugar
coating and find it
bursting to rot

Ripping and tearing at the
leather belly
With its razor point claws
Exposed the pink veined
solid
Squelching mulch that
vomits seeds

LIVER TANTRA
I SEE YOU, I SEE ME

Because the liver channel opens into the eyes, this is the organ to connect with any shame, disgust and self-loathing; letting it go, expanding our acceptance and deep love for ourselves. This meditation works on the judgments we make of ourselves and others that prevent our experience of love and being loved. Use it with the Loving compassion meditation in heart protector/triple heater chapter to build self-worth and confidence.

When we enter a sexual relationship with another we offer them an experience of interacting with our physical body and energy, so how we feel about our own body directly impacts upon how open, receptive and loving we can be with another human being.

Sometimes we measure capacity to receive love against how much we weigh on the scale, how many wrinkles surround our eyes or how much our arms wobble. "I'll attract the perfect partner when my hair grows a bit longer" or "I can't date at the moment, I need to lose a little weight," "If only my tummy was a little flatter, if only my breasts were a little bigger, if only I had better pecs, bigger muscles, whiter teeth, if only I was taller..." Is it true, can we be absolutely sure that this is the case? Of course not, and these beliefs are shaky ground on which to build a relationship. When the beauty fades will we be unlovable? Of course not, Love doesn't come from those external beliefs, it comes from a deep satisfaction and love for ourselves. Unless we develop a real loving relationship with this amazing body and spirit of ours, which is unbelievably complex and intelligent no matter it's size, shape, or pigmentation, we may always look outside ourselves for the elusive entry card to happiness when all the time, the invitation was within through self-acceptance.

That isn't to say that you can't change, if you want to get slimmer/tighter/richer, by all means, work away, with the understanding that the result won't bring you love and happiness, the joy is on the path along the way. Cultivate loving feelings about yourself and you will know exactly how to get slimmer/tighter/richer and it will be a joy to do so rather than a chore.

The act of sex itself with its release in orgasm becomes addictive. We can constantly search for satisfaction through climax. ***We stack up Tinder matches and bedpost notches as proof and validation of how desirable we are. No matter how many men or women we take to bed, the numbers do not change how we feel about ourselves.*** Just like chocolate, there's nothing wrong with having lots of sexual partners but if, like chocolate, you are using them to meet a deep emotional need, in the end, you will only make yourself sick. Start by accepting and caring for your entire self, then you can assess your needs honestly and with love.

You can enter this practice at any level but I recommend the first time you do it, start at stage one. Once you are comfortable you can use any part of this practice any time especially when you notice a negative judgment arising.

STAGE 1

Find a photograph of you as a baby or a child. As a baby you knew you were loveable, you didn't judge yourself, you simply received love and gave love, unconditionally. When looking at the photo, feel the unconditional love you feel for that child or infant, pour it over the image, realising and feeling that it is you. Receive that love.

STAGE 2

Sit or stand quietly, fully clothed in front of a mirror. Scan your body from the top of your head to the base of your feet to see where any tension is being held. Release the tension, relax and breathe. Allow your arms to fall loosely by your side.

Starting at the top of your head, allow your eyes to wander down slowly over your body, taking in every part.

See your hair, perhaps its short/ long/ straight/ curly.

Feel the judgment you make and apologize to yourself and to your hair. Use the ho'oponopono phrase on page 206, I'm sorry, Please forgive me, Thank you, I love you if it is helpful.

Find something that you really appreciate about it. Perhaps the colour, that it grows quickly, or that it's soft to touch and thank the hair for that quality and what it brings to you.

Continue down the body, breathing and seeing; the eyes, the nose, the neck, the shoulders, the chest, the belly, the thighs, etc. and watch were any negative judgments arise around those body parts. When they do, feel the assessment, apologize and find a positive aspect that generates appreciation.

STAGE 3

Repeat stage 2 but this time naked in front of a full-length mirror.

Allow your eyes to scan over your flesh, pausing when you feel shame or critical assessment.

Don't be surprised if you have to do this exercise over and over again. In western culture we are bombarded by cultural stereotypes of what is acceptable and normal for the body so we may have to remind ourselves, frequently of our utterly loveable uniqueness.

This exercise is extremely powerful when practiced with a partner, clothed or unclothed. Simply sit in front of each other and look without judgment. Be present, don't allow your mind to wander, return to your partner. You can look in their eyes, at their hair, their shoulders, chest, torso, genitals, knees, toes, take it all in, just look and allow yourself to be seen at the same time.

For example my belly would be the area I'm always trying to make look smaller, whether that's through food, exercise or magic pants, so...I sit and see my belly, sometimes I use my hands to feel my belly, squishing its soft wobbliness and I say sorry belly for making it a constant problem. Sorry for sometimes believing if only it were gone I would be attractive and desirable. I'd have a literary agent, a loving boyfriend, a better wardrobe and generally be more comfortable in my own skin. I am really sorry for that – you are not the problem.

I really appreciate that you, squidgy belly, remind me of my own softness, that I'm not perfect, that I don't get everything right and I don't get everything finished by the end of the day but I am huggable and very loveable.

I love that my kids cuddle into my belly's softness and I love that it reminds me it was where they grew inside me, nurtured and loved, surrounded by my belly with its huge capacity for massive growth as my 5ft frame carried 6lb twins boys in their own amniotic sacs.

Liver / Gallbladder
RECIPES

UMEBOSHI PLUM

It can be difficult to ask your partner for what you want. Many couples don't talk intimately about sex. It's just something that happens or doesn't happen in their relationship. It can get stale, boring and unsatisfying. Perhaps one partner is more sexual than the other. Perhaps one partner just wants the physical act and the other wants an emotional connection. All these things are possible in a relationship, the important thing is that you communicate your needs. Perhaps you need touch, a massage, a hug, or any regular, physical connection that isn't sexual. Perhaps you would like things from your partner, an increased libido, cunnilingus or rope-play. Talking to each other is the place to begin.

Expressing yourself and telling another person what you need can be difficult. When you share your innermost needs you are being open and vulnerable. But if you want to share your physical body with another it is essential that you share your emotional body also. Self-expression takes courage, it also takes practice. The place to start is with yourself. How often do you create a situation where you can express yourself? Do you dance, do you paint, do you keep a journal? Even the clothes we choose, the way in which we arrange our home or have our hair cut is a physical expression of who we are. So practice creating time and space to emotionally express who you are. How do you feel? How would you like to feel? What are your dreams? What do you like to do? What makes you feel good?

When you can answer these questions for yourself, then you can have the same conversation with your partner. Talk about what you like now and what you would like in the future. Have an intimate discussion about sex without having sex and do it regularly. If you aren't in a relationship, even better, now is the time to think and explore who you are and what you like. Practice self-pleasure so you have an idea of what works for you. Try new things, see what you like and don't like. Keep a journal and write a page every day. It doesn't matter about what, just write how you feel, how things are for you. Of course, a partner brings new things to the table, the bedroom, or wherever you fancy. They may do things you may have never imagined but it's important that you don't expect the other to do all the work. You have to show up, express yourself and be an active participant with a truthful voice.

The liver in Chinese Medicine is responsible for speech and self-expression. There is a condition called plum pit throat where the neck and throat swell, meaning swallowing and talking can become difficult. Western Medicine can't explain why this happens and views it as psychosomatic but Chinese Medicine says that the conditions stems from a blockage in the liver channel and therefore self-expression. Anything sour in flavour will help clear the liver and ease the feeling something stuck in the throat but the ingredient I share here has extra special liver properties; Umeboshi plum.

This is a small salted pickled plum which has both sour and salty flavour and has been used for centuries in Japan as a restorative tonic. It was famously eaten by Samurai warriors who were depleted after battle. It is a powerful antiseptic used for killing harmful bacteria, stomach virus's and as a natural remedy for food poising. It is supremely alkaline, perfect for balancing acid-forming foods such as alcohol, sugar, meat and dairy thereby preventing heartburn and acid reflux. I place it here for the mumefral it contains which aids the liver in cleansing the blood and the Adiponectin found within the pickle which stimulates insulin and metabolisation of fats. Chemicals found in diabetes medication enhance Adiponectin in the blood and tissues in the body. Again it works on both the spleen and liver, harmonizing and balancing: allowing flow, physically and emotionally.

Combine this amazing ingredient with sprouts and it's total support for the liver. Mung beans have been used for thousands of years in Chinese Medicine. They help the liver excrete heavy metals, pesticides and poisons. When germinated the medicinal and nutritional benefits increase. The high levels of proteins, amino acids, oligosaccharides and polyphenols regulate fat metabolisation, decrease inflammation and increase detoxification.

MUNG BEAN AND ALFALFA SPROUT SALAD WITH UMEBOSHI PLUM DRESSING

Side dish serves 4

100g mung bean or alfalfa sprouts
1 red onion
10 cherry tomatoes
1 fried or roasted aubergine
100g feta cheese

Dressing

Juice of 1 lemon
60ml rice or cider vinegar
50ml olive oil
1 tbsp. umeboshi vinegar
1 tbsp. sesame oil
1 tsp. dijon mustard
Large handful of fresh coriander

To make the salad, chop the aubergine into small chunks, toss in olive oil and fry on a high heat for two minutes. As they begin to brown turn down to a low heat and cook slowly until they are golden brown and soft. If roasting its the same procedure but pop on a roasting tray instead of a frying pan and into the oven for 30-40 minutes at 180°C. Tip onto kitchen paper which will absorb the excess oil and allow to cool. Meanwhile slice the red onion into fine half moons, wash through the mung bean or alfalfa sprouts and chop the cherry tomatoes in half. Pop all the ingredients in a large bowl so you can toss through the dressing and finish by crumbling over the feta cheese.

The sour flavour is also great for distracting the body from sugar cravings so suck on the pit when you fancy something sweet. You can have too much of a good thing though, so eating whole jars of these plums at once can weaken the liver. I would recommend taking a nibble or a quarter plum every day and eating no more than 1-2 plums per week.

Sometimes the plums come with nasty additives and preservatives so use organic Umeboshi. You can find it in health food stores and is an easy, versatile ingredient. Spread the paste it on toast for a fabulous flavour punch, even smear in on corn on the cob instead of butter. I add a teaspoon to casseroles and stews to give a hearty, depth of flavour.[12]

SPECIAL UMEBOSHI SAUCE

Side dish to serve 4

60ml rice vinegar
60ml tamari
40ml sesame oil
2 tsp. maple syrup
1 level tsp. umeboshi paste
Sprinkle of black sesame seeds and gomasio

Umeboshi is such an amazing ingredient I couldn't just leave it at one recipe so here is another using the paste. This sauce is superb as a dressing for any vegetable especially broccoli, kale or leafy greens. It is also brilliant tossed through a just finished stir-fry. For this recipe shred half a head of savoy cabbage and steam for five minutes. Two minutes before the cabbage is ready add couple of handfuls of sugar snap peas, steaming together until tender. When ready, remove from the steamer, drain any excess water and place in a bowl. Combine the ingredients for the sauce in a jug, pouring over the warm vegetables and toss through.

12 https://healthfully.com/277687-health-benefits-of-japanese-ume-plum-concentrate.html

CHRYSANTHEMUM

For a cell to stay healthy and function in the body it must have nutrients delivered and waste taken away. This is one of the many functions of the liver. It transforms food into energy our cells use, takes up the waste products and releases them from the body. The liver is also involved with digestion, especially in the breakdown of fats. However, if the liver is overloaded, detoxifying the body, it cannot effectively conduct the conversion and release of energy. The result is weight gain, especially around the midsection, energy swings, chronic fatigue, frustration and depression. None of these things support pleasure or the libido.

Why is the liver overworked?

- Over-eating and drinking alcohol.
- Eating foods with preservatives and additives.
- Absorbing hormones and toxins from our external environment.
- Hormone Imbalance.
- Taking medication including over-the-counter painkillers.
- Colon is not functioning properly - waste cannot leave the body and re-enters the bloodstream for the liver to re-process.

As we approach menopause or andropause for men, you may find that you gain weight around the middle while your legs and arms stay skinny. This is a classic symptom that the liver needs support. The good news is that the liver is the only organ in the body that can regrow so there is an opportunity to make a change where the liver is concerned. Unfortunately, most people struggle with change. I urge you not to wait until a condition becomes chronic before loving your body. Forced change makes life seem dour but I promise you as you clean up your liver you will feel new creativity, zest for life and a rise in sexual energy.

As you begin to clean the liver, the body begins to release toxins. Some toxins are water soluble and can be carried away by drinking plenty of water. Others are fat soluble and for that, the gallbladder needs to be working well; producing bile to break down fats. Chrysanthemum tea all by itself will not solve your meno-pot belly but being aware of all the factors below will.

A few simple tips:

Pick one or two days a week where you only consume a minimum amount of plant based foods. No wheat, no dairy, no meat, drink only water.

Check your cleaning products in the kitchen and the bathroom, take a look at your shampoo and skincare products. Pick one product a month that you replace with an organic, petrochemical free product.

Make sure you get enough sleep and try to lie flat for a rest during the day as much as possible. When the body is horizontal blood circulation slows and allows the liver to be stored and replenished. As soon as you get up - do some light exercise, tai Chi or yoga stretching to make sure the blood moves well around the body.

Avoid over the counter medications and get your long term medications checked for dosage.

Look at emotional issues that may stagnate the liver such as anger and frustration. Be flexible and creative with possible alternative scenarios for situations.

Eat plenty of green leafy vegetables and Chlorella to assist with bile production and fat breakdown.

Milk thistle and Chinese Gentian are powerful herbs to clear the liver. If you are going to undertake a fast to cure a chronic condition, I would recommend doing this under the supervision of a healthcare professional.

Chrysanthemum flowers arrived in Japan during the 8th century where they are truly loved. They became part of the royal seal pictured as a single flower with 16 petals. They also appear on the front of the Japanese passport and the 50 yen coin. Chrysanthemum tea has long been used in Traditional Chinese Medicine to cool the blood and aid flow through the liver. It is not advised to take during pregnancy as it may stimulate the uterus. This drink is so popular it is available, ready-made in cartons but I would recommend buying the dried flowers and making it at home as many prepared drinks have added sugar.

CHRYSANTHEMUM TEA

Serves 2

Buy dried Chrysanthemum flowers in packets, from an Asian supermarket, check to be sure they do not contain sugar or additives. Add 1 or 2 tablespoons to a teapot with 1 litre of water and allow to brew for 5-10 minutes. I use a teapot that has an integral sieve because fishing out the flowers can be tricky with a regular teapot. After you have finished the first pot you can add more water. It will be weaker in colour and taste but still pleasant and effective.

CHRYSANTHEMUM BROCCOLI

Serves 6

In this recipe, the broccoli uses its **glucosinolates** to stimulate detox activity in cells. It also contains a phytonutrient called **kaempferol** which lessens allergic reactions to food and therefore lowers inflammation. In Chinese Medicine it has a cooling nature and it's green colour supports the liver and gallbladder.

1 head of broccoli
3 tbsp. dried Chrysanthemum flowers

Dressing

2 tbsp. tamari
2 tbsp. of sesame oil
2 tbsp. of lemon juice
½ tsp. honey
Tamari to taste

Add salted water to a steamer pan and bring to a boil. Break the broccoli into small florets and chop the stalk into bite-size pieces. Add the flowers to the boiling water and place the broccoli in the steamer section above, cover with a lid, turn down to a simmer and let the broccoli steam for about 7 minutes. While the broccoli is steaming make the dressing by adding all ingredients to a jug or bowl and mix with a fork. Pour over the steamed broccoli when soft, discarding the water and flowers.

POACHED EGG WITH GRILLED MACKEREL

As men age, they enter the andropause, (male menopause), Testosterone levels fall, causing symptoms such as low sex drive and poor energy levels. There may be difficulties getting and maintaining erections also emotional changes such as depression, irritability and mood swings. The physical body may lose muscle and gain fat. Men can also suffer hot flashes, palpitations and anxiety. So just like the last recipe, we need to protect their liver from becoming congested and fatty.

Here are some good rules to help strengthen the liver:

Liver likes oils but doesn't like fats. Plenty of oily fish, avocado, nuts and seeds.

Green colour. Plenty of green leafy veg full of vitamin E, magnesium, calcium and zinc will help with muscle tone including that of the penis and vagina by stimulating blood and Chi flow. This also includes crucerferous vegetables such as broccoli and Brussels sprouts.

Sour flavour. Alcohol has that sour underlying flavour and cravings for certain flavours will often give us a hint as to what organ needs attention. Instead of blindly satiating a craving, fulfil your needs with other sour foods such as umeboshi plum, lemons, limes, cider vinegar, kimchi, pickles, rhubarb, sauerkraut, These boost metabolism, enabling energy levels to rise.

Emotion. Self-expression or frustration? You choose. Alcohol can lower inhibitions and give a sense of freedom but taken in excessive quantities it damages the liver causing feelings of anger and irritability. So take a look at why you drink. Is it boredom, is it to become someone else? Does it give you courage to be the best dancer, the best writer, the best lover? In the long term alcohol can really mess with your hormones. So be brave and be yourself.

This next recipe is full of Jing ingredients to slow the bodies aging process and essential fatty acids to help retain muscle mass and ligament flexibility. Eggs have a bit of a bad reputation. Is it ok to eat one a week or one a day? Opinions vary. Too many eggs have been linked to Non Alcoholic Fatty Liver Disease. Moderation in all things is key. Eggs are rarely the sole cause of NAFLD, rather look at the complete diet. Is it full of refined carbohydrates, sugar, processed foods and very little vegetables?. Here is a perfect Saturday Brunch to set you up for a day of dancing, painting, poetry and self-expressive, self love.

POACHED EGG WITH GRILLED MACKEREL

Serves 1

- 2 eggs
- 300ml water
- 2 tsp. vinegar
- 1 or 2 fillets of mackerel
- 2 tbsp. olive oil
- Juice of 1 lemon
- Salt and pepper to taste
- 2 tsp. black sesame seeds
- 1 tsp. milled seaweed (optional)

Line a tray with baking paper and place the fish skin side down, flesh side up. Drizzle over the olive oil and squeeze the lemon juice over the flesh. Sprinkle with salt and pepper to taste and pop under the grill at medium heat to cook for about 10 minutes. No need to touch it, no need to turn it. Meanwhile, on top of the hob bring a pan of water to a boil. Reduce the heat to its minimum setting, add the vinegar, and using a spoon, stir the water to create a whirlpool.

Crack the eggs carefully into the centre of the vortex and cook for 4 minutes. Very fresh eggs are the easiest for poaching as the whites come together easily. Also using eggs at room temperature helps the process. Using a slotted spoon gently remove the eggs. To make sure all the water is drained you can place on kitchen paper or towel before transferring to the plate. At this point, the fish should be brown and a little crispy on top whilst the flesh has changed from pinky brown to flaky beige. If you aren't sure, push down with a knife of fork into the middle of the fish, it should flake and come apart easily. Place next to the eggs and sprinkle the sesame seeds and milled seaweed on the eggs for a full-on Jing feast, accompany this with a delicious green tea, which reduces liver inflammation and stimulates circulation and you are good to go; let the Chi flow.

NETTLE TEA

A common problem for men as they age is an enlarged Prostate (BPH benign prostatic hyperplasia). This can have many uncomfortable symptoms such as frequent, urgent and dribbling urination. It can also prevent complete urination and left untreated can lead to cancer. Keeping kidney and bladder strong is essential for this condition, as is reducing toxicity in the body. Saw Palmetto Berry is used in Chinese Medicine to regulate hormonal activity, reducing oestrogen and increasing testosterone. So too is the Nettle plant, which is great for detoxing the liver, reducing bladder infections and promoting urination. You can buy tinctures and supplements of Saw Palmetto and Nettle but picking and making your own nettles for tea is easy and effective. Because of their hormonal effect, nettle tea is contraindicated for children and during pregnancy.

Nettles are best picked in spring and early summer when the leaves and stems are fresh and soft. Later in the season they become dry, woody and have been known to cause stomach problems. The hairs produce stinging and itching - never eat them raw. Use gloves to pick off the top six inches of the plant, usually meaning you have two or three pairs of leaves. You can use the leaves fresh or dry them by tying them together and hanging upside down until dehydrated. Store them in paper bags or jars. Don't cut up the leaves as large pieces will keep much of the essential oil and flavour. When picking nettles choose an area that is free from pesticides.

1 cup of fresh nettles
2-3 cups of near boiling water

Place the nettles in the water, simmer very gently for 2-3 minutes. If you want a stronger flavour cook for longer or if you prefer weaker, add more water. Remove from the heat, strain the nettles from the water and pour the liquid into a mug to drink. This tea can have very strong health benefits so start slowly, drinking one maybe two mugs per day and enjoy. Nettles are used in Chinese Medicine as a potent clearer of the emotional liver which when blocked we can feel frustrated, stuck and quick to anger. So increase the stream, go with the flow, and reduce pressure on the prostate.

BLOOD FLOWING BEETROOT

In the constructive cycle in the Five Elements System Diagram on page 26, you can see that the liver is the mother of the heart. It supports it and gives it health and vigour. In western terms, we understand that the liver detoxifies and cleans the blood so that the heart can pump and circulate it around the body. If the liver isn't functioning properly by removing exhausted blood cells and other metabolic wastes from the blood, this will impact the heart. At a physical level, if the liver is swollen or congested it can impede venous blood flow returning to the heart causing palpitations and dizziness.

This recipe supports both the liver with its sour flavour and the heart with its bright red antioxidant beetroot. The liver also supports the second branch of the heart, the triple heater.

Triple heater's function is to keep lines of communication open with all three burners/energy centres in the body. If messages become impaired or blocked, the body can experiences fluctuations in temperature or pain that moves inexplicably, around the body. When this happens, the triple heater sends fluids or Chi to cool, heat or harmonize the body. However, if the liver is congested, the triple heater flounders, message systems become scrambled, temperatures fluctuate, sleep patterns are all over the place and the body can feel anxious and panicky. What we seek is harmonious conversation within the body. By feeding the liver and supporting the heart/triple heater we can assimilate and integrate change, affecting clear communication within the body rather than medicating random chaotic symptoms. It's a lot to ask of beetroot but it's a start. Being conscious of the food we choose and it's consequences is a first step to loving ourselves more.

BEET MARMALADE

Serves 4

- 2 tbsp. sunflower oil
- 1 red onion
- 1 tsp. sea salt
- 5 garlic cloves
- 1 tbsp. wakame or chopped dillisk seaweed
- 2 or 3 medium beetroots, peeled and chopped into matchsticks
- 100ml water
- 3 tbsp. balsamic vinegar
- 1 tbsp. mirin
- 2 tbsp. olive oil
- Black pepper
- 1-2 tbsp. of black and white sesame seeds

Heat the sunflower oil in a large pan with a lid as you will need that later. Fry the onions gently for about 10 minutes until they are transparent and beginning to caramelize. Sprinkle over the sea salt and add the garlic cloves. Allow to soften for a couple of minutes before stirring in the beetroot and the seaweed. Fry all ingredients together for a couple of minutes add the water and cover. On low heat simmer the mixture between five to ten minutes, until the beetroot is almost soft. Pour over the olive oil, balsamic vinegar and mirin bringing it to a soft bubbly boil for a couple of minutes. Uncover and allow the mixture to evaporate slightly so you are left with moist, stickyish beetroot. To finish, sprinkle black pepper to taste and the sesame seeds as a textural Jing flourish to this tangy-sweet dish.

This recipe was adapted from the gorgeous “At Home in the Whole Food Kitchen” by Amy Chaplin.

COOL FOOD

Hot Flashes are one of the most notorious and debilitating symptoms of menopause. They can wake you at night, stop you sleeping, create exhaustion and sweaty situations in the supermarket. Sometimes this exacerbates anxiety that can occur at menopause as the body behaves unpredictably, changing temperature, moods and emotions without any rhyme or reason. As discussed previously, with it's predominantly sour flavour and astringent properties, alcohol impacts the liver. If you are sensitive during menopause, one glass of wine can trigger these seemingly random symptoms.

A good tonic to assist the liver is milk thistle. This herbal remedy can be taken as tincture or in tablets. It's antioxidant, anti-inflammatory and has antiviral properties. It promotes liver and gallbladder function reducing, environmental toxins, cholesterol and excess hormones. As the liver and gallbladder process substances such as alcohol, fatty food, excess sugar, highly refined foods, additives and preservatives they can become damaged and inflamed and unable to function correctly. Taking milk thistle on its own however, is not enough to prevent these conditions. Combining them with a good diet for the liver which has plenty of greens together with sour flavoured food will help the smooth running of the liver and less unexpected flashes.

This next recipe does all this and more. The sweet fennel will support the spleen, the almonds and feta cheese will feed the Jing. The rawness of the salad combined with the tangy lemon dressing and green herbs will activate the liver and gallbladder.

SHAVED FENNEL SALAD

Serves 4

1 medium-large courgette, sliced into paper thin coins
2 small fennel bulbs, trimmed and shaved paper-thin
Handful loosely chopped fresh dill or tarragon
80ml fresh lemon juice
80ml extra virgin olive oil
Fine grain sea salt
5 or 6 generous handfuls rocket
60g chopped almonds
60g feta cheese

Using a mandolin, slice the courgette into paper thin coins and the fennel into transparent slices. Take great care with this implement as it is easy to add paper-thin slices of thumb to the salad. I say with experience, always use the guard. Allow the veggies to marinate in the lemon, oil, herb and salt mixture while you wash the rocket and lay it as a bed for the fennel and courgette. Finally, sprinkle over the almonds and crumble the feta for a perfect accompaniment to the baked aubergines also in this chapter.

AUBERGINE TWO WAYS

When Chi (energy) doesn't flow it accumulates and creates dampness. If allowed to develop this dampness concentrates to become fluid and with further stagnation can condense into solids, forming all sorts of lumps and bumps, cysts and tumours. It likes to accumulate around joints and make them hot as it tries to move the Chi. Or, as the Chi and blood flow become lessened, joints become cold and frozen. This is seen most obviously in cases of arthritis, gout, bursitis, tendonitis, tennis elbow and frozen shoulder. Here though, we are talking about sexual conditions and specifically endometriosis, where womb tissue (endometrium) is found growing in other parts of the body such as ovaries, fallopian tubes, bladder or bowel. This can cause pain during or after sexual intercourse. Penetration and other sexual activity can pull and stretch the endometrial tissue especially if it has grown behind the vagina or lower uterus.

Even though this condition slightly differs from the arthritic conditions caused by lack of Chi flow it is still treated as blood stagnation in the pelvis. Avoid spleen depleting sugary foods plus cold damp foods such as ice cream, dairy and bananas. Focus on foods that warm and move blood in the uterus area such as ginger, garlic and good warming lentil stews with cinnamon, clove, cardamon, coriander, cumin. All blood nourishing foods such as oils, eggs, bone broth, spirulina and seaweed, will aid warmth in the uterus. This can prove beneficial when trying to conceive. Incorporate the liver, green, sour foods and the blood should flow smoothly. One of the best ingredients I know to move blood stasis in the uterus is aubergine. There are many ways to cook this wonderful ingredient and here I share a few favourites.

A simple way to use them is to pierce them as you would a potato, wrap them in tin foil and bake in the oven for 50 minutes. When the insides are as soft as butter when skewered with a knife, remove from the foil, cut the top off, slice in half and remove the soft flesh. Often I put this in a strong plastic bag, and straight into the freezer, removing and adding it to stews and curries when I want a rich and creamy dish without any dairy. Despite their rich lushness they don't clog arteries or stop blood flowing.

Here are two of my favourite recipes from my time spent living in Israel and traveling Egypt.

BABA GANOUSH

Serves 4

3 medium aubergine
3 medium cloves garlic, minced
2 tbsp. juice from 1 lemon or more to taste
3 tbsp. tahini
80ml extra-virgin olive oil, plus more for serving
120g chopped flat leaf parsley
Salt and Pepper to taste

Roast the aubergines as detailed on page 143, scooping out the flesh, mixing in a blender with the lemon juice, tahini, olive oil, flat leaf parsley, salt and pepper. I like to gently fry the garlic in the olive oil, on a very low heat to add a smoky flavour to the dip. Be careful not to burn the oil or the garlic as the dip will taste bitter. Add garlic and oil to the other ingredients and liquidise. Serve in a shallow dish sprinkling over finely chopped, flat leaf parsley and drizzling with more olive oil. You can also shake over some smoked paprika if desired, it looks good and adds a depth of flavour.

WARM BAKED AUBERGINE WITH YOGURT AND CUMIN

Serves 4

2 medium-sized aubergines
Olive oil for brushing

Dressing

100ml Greek yogurt
1 tsp. extra virgin olive oil
1-2 cloves garlic, finely minced
A couple of dashes ground cumin
Sea salt and freshly cracked black pepper, to taste
Seeds of 1 pomegranate

This is so simple yet it makes a delicious vegetarian centre-piece for a Sunday roast or festive occasion. Simply cut the aubergines in half, brush the flesh with olive oil and add a drizzle to the roasting pan. Place them, flesh side down on the pan and roast for 20 minutes at 180°C. Remove from the oven, turn the aubergine, so that they are flesh side up, and carry on cooking. If you turn them whilst they are still fairly solid, they won't come apart. After 40-50 minutes, when they are buttery soft all the way through remove them from the tray.

For the dressing simply mix the greek yogurt with the olive oil, minced garlic, salt and pepper. When the aubergines are cooked, spoon over the creamy dressing and sprinkle over the ground cumin and pomegranate seeds. If you can dry roast and grind your own cumin seeds it makes all the difference.

FETA AND ROASTED CARROT SALAD

Serves 4

Polycystic Ovaries contain harmless follicle sacs in which eggs develop but are not released. This means ovulation does not happen, causing irregular or no menstruation, and difficulty in conceiving. It can also give symptoms of excessive hair growth on face, chest, back or buttocks whilst at the same time thinning hair on the scalp. Between 30-60% of women with polycystic ovarian syndrome (PCOS) are also overweight and it can lead to type 2 Diabetes.

Within Western and Chinese Medicine Diabetes falls under the domain of the spleen/pancreas and its control and production of Insulin. However, in Chinese Medicine, the spleen/pancreas also absorbs nutrients from food and is in charge of creating blood. It is responsible for bodily fluids, transforming them and transporting them around the body. When the spleen is overworked and deficient through eating too many refined sugars and sweet foods there will be an accumulation of fluids especially in the lower burner, giving symptoms of cramping pain, candida, constipation, bloating, weight gain and polycystic ovaries.

So then why is this recipe in the liver chapter and not the spleen? The liver is responsible for blood flow in the lower burner and the metabolisation of stored energy. It produces digestive enzymes, which assist the stomach and spleen in their job of transforming and transporting Chi and fluids. A good place to start moving blood and fluid build up through the pelvic area, is by working on the liver. I have found it essential to develop a beneficial partnership between the spleen and the liver, so I love recipes that work on both organs. The large amounts of green leaves and lemon juice will stimulate the gallbladder and liver. Roasted carrots, which are orange and sweet in flavour, are a perfect ingredient to nourish the spleen. Lack of ovulation would relate to a root cause of kidney deficiency, feed this with flat leaf parsley, feta cheese and the sprinkling of gomasio with milled seaweed over the finished dish.

500g organic carrots
2 tbls olive oil
200g feta cheese
200g baby spinach leaves
100g rocket
2 large handfuls of roughly chopped flat leaf parsley

Dressing

2 tbsp. olive oil
Juice of 1 lemon
2 tsp. of ground cumin
1 tsp. ground black pepper
a Sprinkle of gomasio and milled dried
Seaweed (optional)

Roast the carrots in the olive oil in a preheated oven at 180°C for 40 minutes.

Toss them in the oil occasionally and move to the top shelf to help the edges brown and caramelize. While the carrots are roasting, wash, dry and mix the leaves, laying them in a bowl.

For the dressing, it is worth dry roasting the cumin seeds in a frying pan and pulverizing with a pestle and mortar. Add these to the other dressing ingredients and mix. Don't whisk too fiercely or the olive oil will become bitter. Drizzle the dressing over the leaves, scattering the roasted carrots and crumbling the feta on top. Serve immediately, reserving some of the dressing, or making more, for those that like it extra tangy.

APPLE AND RHUBARB CRUMBLE

Serves 6

This recipe also balances the stomach/spleen and liver/gallbladder with its mix of sour fruit and sweet topped crumble. Because of its high fruit content it may not clear dampness in the lower burner as quickly as the green leaves with lemony dressing in the last recipe but the inclusion of the much underused fruit, rhubarb, more than makes up for it. In Chinese Herbal Medicine, rhubarb is used frequently in its dried state, mixed with other ingredients, to balance and tonify the whole digestive system. It works directly on the large intestine, reducing inflammation and autoimmune disorders. It is a brilliant natural laxative and a potent blood cleanser, helping to clear a fatty liver. The high amounts of absorbable calcium can strengthen bones.

This crumble is sweet, and succulent the ultimate comfort food. Take care not to eat the whole dish in one sitting as it serves six.

2 or 3 cooking apples
1 bunch of rhubarb
8 de-stoned plums
50ml maple syrup
50ml apple juice

Crumble topping

50g coconut flour
50g rice flour
50g pumpkin seeds
50g sunflower Seeds
50g porridge oats
50g coconut Sugar
50g butter
2tsp. ground cinnamon

Prepare the rhubarb by cutting it into small chunks, place in a bowl and pour over boiling water. While it is are softening, peel, core and chop the cooking apples into bite-size pieces, mix together with the plums which have been de-stoned and halved. After 10 minutes, the soaking the rhubarb should be soft, strain and combine with the other fruit.

To prepare the crumble, mix dry ingredients in a bowl and rub in the butter until the mixture resembles wet sand. Prepare a pyrex dish approx 20cm by 20cm the fruit should sit on the bottom comfortably, not too layered and not too many gaps. Splash the maple syrup and apple juice over the fruit and sprinkle the sandy crumble mix over the fruit. Don't worry if you can see bits of the fruit peeking through this will help make the crumble juicy, sweet and delicious. Bake in a preheated oven 180°C for 40-50 minutes. You may be able to see the fruit bubbling through the crumble and the apples will be soft when it is ready. Serve hot or cold with a little natural yogurt or vegan ice cream for a real treat. Regular full fat ice cream will just clog the liver which is exactly the opposite of what this dessert/breakfast is all about.

GETTING JUICY

As mentioned in the Bone-broth and Jing recipe, hormonal changes in the body happen in seven-year cycles for women, eight for men and are under the domain of kidney Yin. Following menopause or andropause, the epithelium, a thin tissue covering the outer layer of a body's hollow structures including lining the respiratory tract, uterine tubes, uterus, alimentary canal, intestinal wall and other hollow structures, begins to thin. This can cause frequent urination or urinary tract infections in men. In women, this can also thin the walls of the vagina causing uncomfortable, sometimes painful sexual intercourse. If we aren't careful how much we swing our Yang or how brightly our fire burns, the decline in the moistening and lubricating kidney Yin can happen at any age and internal pain during sexual intercourse can happen at any time. Protecting Jing along with kidney Yin foods can aid moistening secretions, slow the aging process, and build thinning vaginal walls.

Stimulants such as coffee, tea and recreational drugs can deplete kidney Yin as they keep us going long after we should have stopped. Overdoing alcohol and over the counter medication can deplete the liver Yin. Both the kidney and liver Yin bring cooling fluids to the body. They nourish, lubricate and are essential for smooth juicy sex. Even antihistamines and paracetamol can weaken the liver and dry us out. So eat foods that nourish kidney and liver to keep the body hydrated. Avoid heating and drying the body through smoking. Rather eat deep leafy greens that build blood and Yin fluid such as spinach, chard, rocket, dandelion greens, spirulina and seaweed. Barley and millet are grains that are mildly cooling and great for the kidney Yin. Don't be tempted to completely chill the system with too many salads and too much raw food as we don't want to put the fire out completely. I know sounds contradictory but **it's really about finding out how your own Yin Yang turns and what's working for you to keep you in balance.** How are you Goldilocks? Not too hot, not too cold, just right – everyone likes their porridge differently.

This next recipe is fantastic for building blood and helping liver and kidney Yin. You can toss in some hydrated chopped seaweed to further cool and moisten the membranes of the body. Only the noodles are cooked in this dish, the pesto type sauce is prepared separately and added to cooked and cooling noodles ensuring this dish isn't difficult to digest because it's not completely raw. Flaxseed is rich in phytoestrogens which can help increase oestrogen levels which decrease during menopause. It's full of Omega-3 fatty acids which further help strengthen liver function thereby helping reduce cholesterol.

It's important to keep blood and fluids moving through the genitals so make sure you have regular sexual stimulation. This doesn't have to be done by someone else, feel completely free to make things happen for yourself. Even in a coffee shop on a Sunday morning, take your attention down to the chair you are sitting on an imagine sitting on a hot water bottle, that the warm is penetrating upwards through your body which is soft, relaxed and full of blood. Where your attention goes blood will flow. Far too often we are in our head so take things down south, low, slow and sexy, with no expectation than feeling like a juicy human being.

HERBY LIME NOODLES WITH CASHEWS

Serves 2

2 very large handfuls of Corriander
2 very large handful of flat leaf parsley
50ml olive oil
50ml flax oil
Juice of 2 limes
Pinch sea salt
1 bundle buckwheat noodles
50g toasted cashews
Sprinkle black and white sesame seeds

Prepare a saucepan with 2 litres of salted boiling water, drop the buckwheat noodles and simmer them, with the lid off, so the noodles roll and separate in the water for ten minutes. Meanwhile in a liquidizer, blitz the coriander, flat leaf parsley, olive oil, flax oil, salt and the lime juice. Roughly chop the cashews and the rehydrated dillisk. When the noodles are cooked toss through the lime pesto mix followed by the chopped cashews and seaweed. Garnish with the sesame seeds and serve.

If you want to keep it really raw then use spiralized courgettes in place of the buckwheat noodles.

THREE COLOUR NOODLES

Serves 2

Where to put this recipe? The salty seaweed in the recipe helps to drain dampness, reduces soft masses and generally falls under the realm of kidney/bladder. The Buckwheat and Seaweeds are great sources of easily absorbable protein and are great at building blood and helping the heart. However, I am putting it here because of the colours. The green of the scallions, the orange of the carrot and the white of the noodles remind me of the Irish flag which is everywhere for St. Patrick's day 17th March. This, for me, marks the time when I feel spring is sprung despite the unpredictable, changeable weather. I have spent the National Holiday lazing in parks, in a t-shirt, listening to a monster céilí in the sunshine. I have also spent it bundled up with hundreds of others, like penguins against the snow, waiting for the parade to begin on O'Connell Street. No matter the weather there are always daffodils and alcohol in abundance, both of which point to the liver. The green/yellow of daffodils are the colours of spring, the time of liver/gallbladder and the sour flavour of alcohol works directly upon the liver. After the winter we can feel sluggish and stodgy. This simple and quick-to-prepare recipe wakes the liver with its tangy flavour. It clears stagnation helping to move blood, improving circulation and flexibility for the whole body.

All seaweeds are good for the blood and wakame seaweed contains high levels of vitamins; calcium, magnesium and iodine which build blood strength. As an effective diuretic, it reduces water from the blood and therefore reduces blood pressure. Often wakame comes dried and ready cut, but for this recipe, I recommend the long, uncut variety as it blends together well with the noodles and brings extra texture to the dish.

I have used tamari instead of soy Sauce as its fermentation can bring vitamin B12 and other amino acids to the body, which further builds blood. Finally, the vitamin C in the raw carrots aids the absorption of minerals, especially iron into the blood.

1 handful wakame seaweed
1 bundle noodles
1 clove garlic, minced
25ml rice vinegar
50ml tamari sauce
3 tbsp. dark sesame oil
2 tbsp. sesame seeds
2 carrots
4 spring onions

Soak the seaweed in a little water for ten minutes to rehydrate. Bring a large saucepan of salted water to the boil and add the noodles. Noodles should take 3-5 minutes depending on the brand. Thick Udon noodles work well in this recipe.

Meanwhile, chop the spring onions into thin lengths and use a potato peeler to shave thin lengths of carrot. Mix these into the minced garlic, rice vinegar, tamari and sesame oil, which have already been blended in a large bowl. Strain the cooked noodles and add to the bowl along with the lengths of hydrated wakame. Combine all the ingredients, sprinkle in the sesame seeds and chow down.

BLACK OLIVE AND LEMON COURGETTI

Serves 2

This recipe is full of get up and go, the raw courgettes provide the enzymes to spring the liver into action, assist digestion and the metabolisation of stored energy. The dressing is stimulatingly sour, awakening your taste buds and helping detox the liver. In this way, life has vitality and optimism. Your body is not a heavy burden that you are dragging around, rather it is invigorated with the excitement of spring. If your liver is in balance, instead of problems being barriers that thwart your plans, they become opportunities for new ideas, new ways of thinking, and new ways of being. Life is full of relationships, and they don't always go the way you planned. Not just relationships with people but with food, work, our bodies, homes, and nature. So rather than getting angry by things not going your way, see everything is an opportunity for love. Leap in! Be flexible with the unpredictable rather than frustrated. The liver is all about the energy of spring, the sap can rise and new shoots find ways around obstacles if this organ is not overburdened by a fatty rich diet. So keep it clean, keep it green.

2 spiralized courgettes

Dressing

100g black olives
80g basil leaves
80-120g flat leaf parsley
Tbsps. thyme leaves
5 tbsps. extra virgin olive oil
Juice of 1 lemon

Spiralize the courgettes. If you don't have a spiralizer you can always use a potato peeler and slice thin slivers, then roughly chop lengthways.

For the sauce, you can pop everything in a blender and blitz but I like to hand chop with my cleaver. This keeps the flavours separate and distinct with different zesty bursts in each mouthful. Mix the chopped ingredients with a fork, tossing and mixing in the courgettes to finish.

ANCHOVY PESTO

When we fall in love we can be swept away on the addictive happy hormones, endorphins and oxytocin. All well and good when we getting what we want, in the form of text messages, dinner, and desired attention but tantrum producing when phone calls aren't returned and things aren't going our way. Insecurity runs riot as the heart is open and defences are down. Unfortunately, security can't come from outside.

> **"Fulfil me, make me happy, make me feel safe, tell me who I am. The world cannot give you those things and when you no longer have such expectations all self-created suffering comes to an end".**
>
> Ekhart Tolle

Fortunately or unfortunately depending on your viewpoint, my head is turned and my heart opens easily. With the advent of internet dating, opportunities abound. If anyone has engaged with Tinder ™ , Plenty of Fish™ or similar websites, you may have found, like I have, a roller-coaster of emotions as people simply disappear or declare undying lust for your profile picture. I have been lost in whirlpools of despair and excitement so I found giving myself space was essential. I needed to notice the clouds as I ran around the park, see the wonderful colours of the flowers as they burst open in my garden, laugh with my children as the youngest drew Popeye muscles on his arms and a six pack on his tummy with indelible black marker. With this space I could gain perspective and no longer only having eyes for my smartphone screen. I was able to see again how much wonder there is in the world and how many opportunities there are, to exercise this muscle of love and generate my own endorphins. I wasn't reliant on other peoples likes, swipes or matches.

To help with this perspective I ate a lot of this delicious recipe which is great for stimulating the liver, detoxing the body, clearing emotional frustration and helping the to see things more clearly.

Remember the liver loves oils but hates saturated fats. These clog the liver and prevent flow, which causes tension in the muscles, frustration and infuriation in the mind. All the chlorophyll filled greens help the gallbladder produce bile and support the liver metabolize fats. So swipe right and make sure you don't lose yourself to on-screen love.

200ml extra-virgin olive oil
120g flat leaf parsley
150g drained capers
1 tbsp. oregano leaves, fresh or dried
1 tbsp. cider vinegar
1 pinch red chilli flakes
5 drained anchovy filets
(substitute sundried tomatoes if vegetarian)
2 minced cloves garlic or handful of washed wild garlic
Salt and freshly ground black pepper

Blitz all the ingredients together in a food processor and pour over spaghetti, courgetti, spread on wraps or drizzle over grilled fish.

RELISH THE PEPPER

In the Asian Slaw recipe of the next heart protector/ triple heater chapter, I discuss how the production of scar tissue following inflammation caused by injury, obstructs flow in many areas of the body and specifically the penis. For women, adhesions caused by scar tissue in the pelvic area can cause a multitude of problems such as heavy menstruation, bloating, pelvic pain and even infertility. Endometriosis, when uterine tissue lining the womb migrates, to other places in the pelvis or anywhere in the body, can cause pain during intercourse as the adhesions are pushed and pulled. Who wants that! So again avoiding alcohol and sugar will prevent inflammation. Eating green, sour, oily foods that support the liver will increase flexibility and elasticity for the connective tissue of the body.

Free radicals are cells that have unpaired electrons. They balance themselves by taking a negatively charged electron from another cell. They occur naturally as the body metabolises food and oxygen and aren't usually a problem. However, when under the pressure from the three stressors, environmental, emotional and physical, the production of free radicals increases. High levels of free radicals damage collagen, meaning cell membranes and connective tissue becomes rigid and inflexible, blood and Chi find it harder to flow causing obstruction, discomfort and pain. Antioxidants balance these free radicals by giving them negative electrons thus maintaining the bodies Yin Yang.

Red, heart foods are packed full of antioxidants and so are the liver, green, sour foods. This recipe is stuffed full of both. It goes perfectly with oily fish such as mackerel or sardines, whose oils aid the stretching and twisting needed for lubrication and flexibility, inside and out.

Plants and animals, in life, are supple and succulent: In death, withered and dry.

Chapter 76 Tao Te Ching

PEPPER RELISH

Serves 4

3 garlic cloves
3 fresh red chillies
4 tomatoes
1 red onion chopped
1 large red pepper
Handful fresh flat leaf parsley
Juice of 1 lemon
Salt and pepper to taste

Apart from the red pepper, pop all the ingredients into a food processor and blend. You may need to add a couple of tablespoons of water or high-quality olive oil to help it blend. Meanwhile, de-seed the pepper and chop very finely, adding it to the blended ingredients. Leave all ingredients to marinade and merge together for at least an hour before eating or spooning over steamed courgettes, green beans or grilled fish.

There is no better lover
Than a cool breeze on
a hot day
As it strokes my calves
And flutters against
my thighs
Cool along my lips
As I lie here naked
knees apart
sun heating me
where normally remains
dark and hidden

it is seen and beats with
blood and warmth
relaxing and opening
to allow the sun to be
swallowed
to enter

ACUPRESSURE POINTS

LIVER 3 – GREAT RUSHING

Descends Chi clearing anxiety, headaches, dizziness and insomnia caused by fluctuating hormones. Helps clear dampness from the body which causes swelling, stagnation and lethargy. Reduces excessive or continuous sweating. Eases sexual frustration, depression and genital pain.

Find the point in the hollow between the first and second toe just above the knuckle of the big toe.

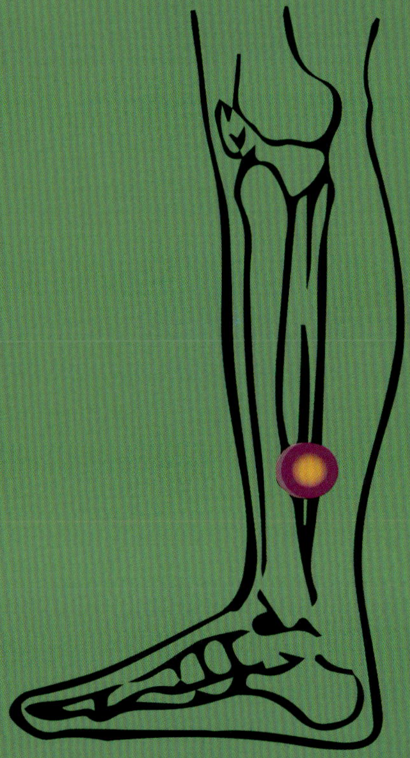

LIVER 5 – GOURD DITCH

Clears acute cystitis, urinary tract infections and helps relieve painful urination. Supports self expression, clearing obstructions to say what you want and how you feel.

Find the point one third up the inside of the leg, approximately one hand span.

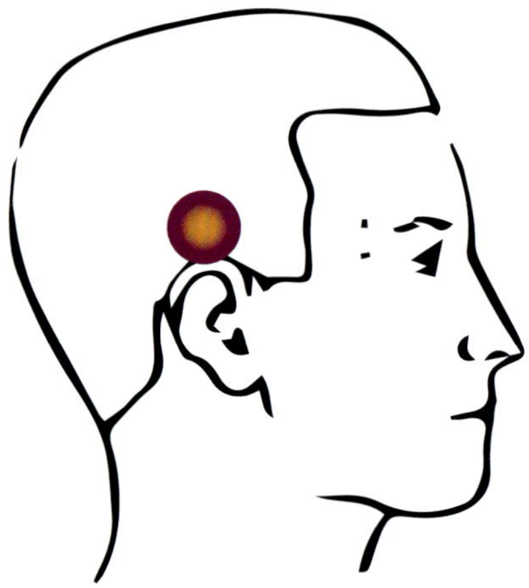

GALLBLADDER 9 – PENETRATING HEAVEN

Reduces muscular spasms and contractions, releases and relaxes the body. Great for migraines, detox headaches and anxiety when letting go of addictive behaviours.

Find the point one thumb width above the apex of the ear and move into the depression behind that toward the back of the head.

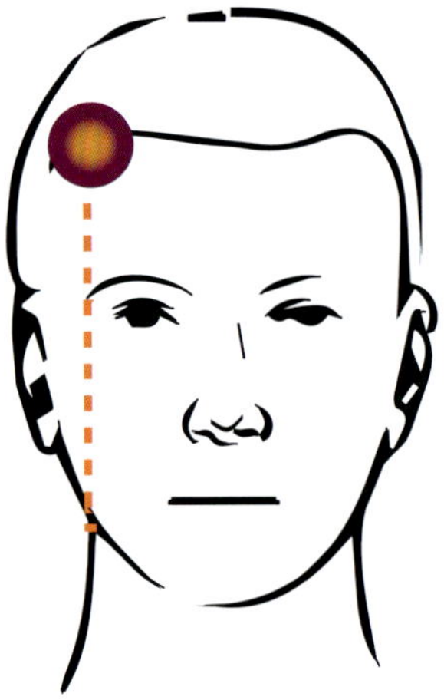

GALLBLADDER 13 – MIND ROOT

Helps distribute jing to the mind meaning that the mind is clear. Reduces obsessive thoughts, constant worry and paranoia especially when paired with Conception Vessel 4.

Find the point one thumb width back from where a line from the outside of the eye would meet the hair line.

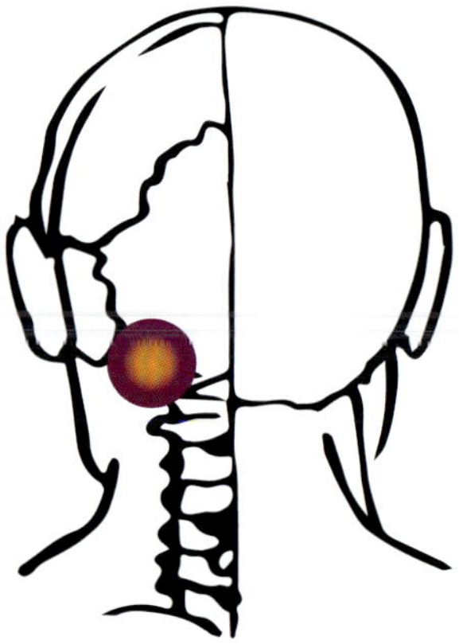

GALLBLADDER 20 – WINDPOOL

Reduces hot flashes and irritability, descends Chi and harmonizes kidney and liver.

Find the point in the hollow at the outside of the occipital ridge where the sternomastoid and trapezius muscles begin.

GALLBLADDER 21 – SHOULDER WELL

Removes pain and stiffness in neck and shoulder. Not to be used during pregnancy as has a strong effect on uterus including aiding healing following post partum haemorrhage, retention of placenta, miscarriage and swift duration of labour.

Find the point at the very top of the trapezius muscle, usually indicated by maximum tenderness.

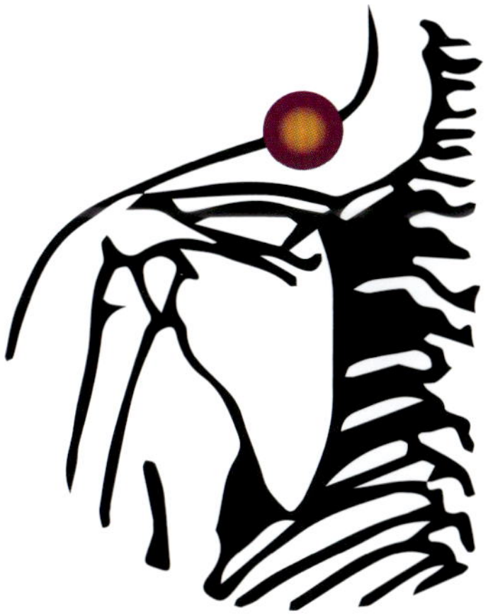

GALLBLADDER 41 – FALLING TEARS

Removes damp heat from genital and breast area which can cause thrush, candida, cystitis, urethritis and left to accumulate it can form cysts and fibroids

Find this point by running a line from between the fourth and fifth toe toward the ankle. Immediately after the tendon there will be a significant depression in which to press.

Summertime Evenings

Dusk fell as a dreamsoft
lady
Sifting her gossamer with
dandelion heads
Heavy and soft the dew-
drenched music
For the couple who silently
danced

He held her soft within his
arms and with her small
child hand she touched his
chin
“When I grow up I want a
man just like Daddy”
But ahh said the wind with
the beath of a kiss
“There’s no-one who’s just
quite like him.”

Chapter 4
HEART PROTECTOR / TRIPLE HEATER

Mine to you

He is asleep, examine him in
his fetal shape
Features so fine, dints made
with loving thumbs
Hair swept back leaving his
forehead bare
No lines, thoughts or wrinkles

The eyebrows soft to shape
Form a mold for the eye
A delicate kohl smudged line

I watch you dream
Your pupils reacting and
downy lashes fluttering
Your nose I know is cold as
I've felt it's nudge caress me
Leaving skin tingling with
sensation

I want to lick the line where
the two lips meet
So that your mouth will open
and you'll take me in
Warm and wet, over and over
again

OVERVIEW
SENSE OF SELF IN AN ENGAGING WORLD

In life, there is no state of perfection. It's constantly changing; an evolving loop that swings through Yin and Yang. Loving times, happy times, sad times; The flow of life doesn't distinguish between good and bad. Perfect health and contentment is to be aware and accepting of exactly where you are in this moment. However, ***we need resilience and equanimity to manage the ups and downs. It is the heart protector and triple heater meridians that navigate and manage the loops of change that life throws at us.***

In western medicine, the heart protector can be associated with the Pericardium muscle that surrounds the heart. It does what it says on the tin – it protects the heart from anything emotionally hard to handle. It's known as the "king's bodyguard." It manages grief from the lungs, fear from the kidneys, addictions from the spleen and anger from the liver so the heart can sit serenely as an Emperor, connecting with the Divine, to love, to higher consciousness and the beauty of the universe. The heart stays deep inside doing all the really important, love stuff whilst the heart protector manages the day-to-day connections in life, dealing with family, work colleagues, cancelled trains and boyfriends forgetting your birthday. All these external life events we don't have control over but the heart protector manages and controls our response.

The triple heater assists the heart Protector by ensuring energy movement is connected and smooth between all the organs. It is the "Minister of Dykes and Dredges" maintaining smooth flow of solids, fluids and energy throughout the body. This meridian can also be linked to the fascia of the body, which protects the organs and joints of the body from external harm and wraps nerves and blood vessels as they pass between muscles. It covers the whole body and touches every organ. The fascia itself contains nerve endings and it has been proposed in western medicine that it works as a sixth sense, sensitive and responsive to chemicals, interactions and signals from the external environment. So just like the heart protector, it manages our internal response to external situations.

It also works in conjunction with the kidney meridian in transporting prenatal Chi, Jing, to each of the body's organs by assisting in maintaining the nervous system and hydration of the body. Sometimes called the Triple burner, it regulates the three energy centres or burners illustrated on the next page.

This meridian and its function of internal communication is essential for hormonal regulation, which is at the core of physical sexual health and intercourse.

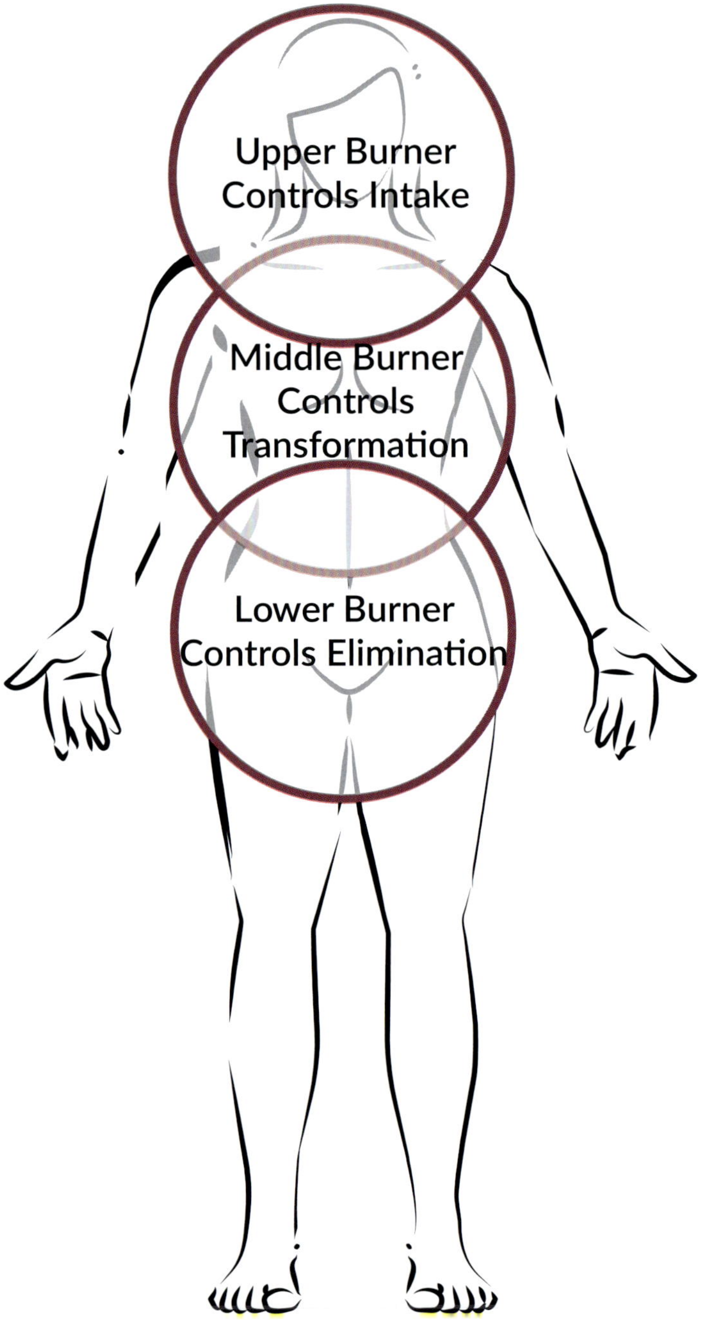

Together the heart protector and triple heater energy systems decide how best to manage external situations and defend the body. Once they find a way that is comfortable and that works they don't like to change. Some of these neural pathways of managing the world are formed very early; they can be learned behaviours passed down through generations or culturally absorbed reactions to uncomfortable situations. They keep the status quo and perpetuate patterns in the hope that everything will stay the same. Unfortunately, that is never true. The universal truth in Chinese Medicine is that everything is energy, therefore is constantly changing.

If our responses remain the same we don't grow, we don't flourish and can even become dissatisfied and unhappy with what we have. We don't open up to the possibilities of even greater love than we imagined.

It is not easy for the mind to accept that nothing is permanent, that everything is groundless. There is no security in that feeling and it is uncomfortable. It feels easier to focus on keeping money in the bank and a partner by your side. To buy more stuff to prove we are secure, solid and successful. However, if we can relax when we realise that things might not be as solid as we think, then it helps to make changes to those neurological pathways and knee jerk reactions. It's usually within a familial setting that social negotiating patterns are learned. It is no surprise that the ones closest to us usually trigger our most intense emotions and press our sensitive buttons.

But if you imagined them lying sick, possibly dying somewhere all the irritations of the past would disappear, you'd hold their hand, you'd look into their eyes, deeply connecting with them and tell them that they are loved and valuable.

Only when we see life as unstable and fleeting can we value its true beauty and the wonderful loving relationships it creates. By being unafraid of the uncomfortable groundlessness of change, taking a breath and paying attention to our responses we can support these two meridians in creating new answers to old patterns. It takes courage to know that the soft heart will still be protected and safe if it's open to possibilities and new territories.

Relationships are an integral part of being human. For the kidneys, which determine our basic instincts in stressful situations, it's all about fight or flight. Do we stay or do we go? But for the heart protector and triple heater there is a third way, how do we reach out to ask for help, support and love. How do we connect?

Often, in established relationships, curiosity can wane, less care and attention is given to generating romantic, loving feelings. The relationship is taken for granted or we can feel unseen and superfluous. The physical body can also let us down, sexual energy drops, responsive arousal weakens and libido is no longer the rampant consumer it once was. Relationships and our bodies change but if we are committed to loving ourselves, change can be embraced. Downturns and problems can be used to further communication and connection with our partner and ourselves. The triple heater will want to stay in a pattern it's used to and the heart protector will want to defend. This is a moment to replace the worn path of reaction with innate intelligence, trusting that your heart and your love don't need to be defended. The pleasure and relief of instant reaction to a situation doesn't help in the long term, it merely perpetuates the situation. It's like a child scratching chicken-pox, it brings immediate release but in the long term, it makes the condition worse.

Take a moment, breathe and endure the discomfort and fear of taking a new path. Choosing something new when you don't know the end result takes courage. It requires an open heart and softness, both with yourself and others.

Mouth to cover my mouth
Taste of anothers
Gasps of breath short in
my ear
Sweat upon the skin to be
licked by me

HEART PROTECTOR TANTRA
BREAST AND TESTICULAR MASSAGE

Touching the sexual areas of our body is something we don't do often enough, whether it is for health or pleasure, ***It's time to let go of the idea that connecting to our sexual or arousal energy is something shameful.*** When I was growing up, being good didn't involve being sexual. It was naughty or bad if I touched myself. When I took my clothes off to feel free and the sun on my skin, as I frequently did as a six-year-old girl, it was deemed as encouraging inappropriate sexual behaviour. So I shut that glorious little girl down for many years. Unfortunately this attitude left me conflicted and confused regarding feeling deliciously alive and sexual. Now, after untangling the disarray of my formative understanding of sexual energy, pleasure and my beautiful body, I own my energy more than ever. It's a light that has to shine. Sometimes it attracts unwanted attention but my inner sense of self means that I am free to say yes or no to what comes my way. I am not using anyone and they are not using me.

My body, my energy, my health is mine and my responsibility.

It is essential that we understand we are spiritual and sexual beings. We have both the Chi of Earth and the Chi of Heaven. ***If we don't connect, flow and recycle our sexual energy it can create physical health problems or emotional, psychological difficulties.*** As we have seen in the some religions, repressed sexual energy can manifest as deviant behaviour. Using someone else to meet our own needs is not healthy, for either the abuser or abused. Between consenting adults, exploration of arousal energy, physical stimulation and pleasure gratification is an exciting and enjoyable part of being human. However, be aware of your boundaries and those of others. Openness, communication, trust and vulnerability are key to healthy sexual relationships and it begins with yourself. Be honest with your body and how you feel. Explore your own body. Find what you like and what feels good without shame and embarrassment. Embracing the sexual being that you are, doesn't mean you have intercourse with lots of people all the time. It doesn't mean you will suddenly become a different person but rather you have access to the whole of you, nothing repressed, nothing denied. You can then use the energy that creates life, creates worlds to bring vitality and health to your own being.

This massage includes touching our sexual organs however, this is not a pleasure stimulating massage, this is a massage to move the Chi throughout your endocrine system. As most of the endocrine hormone-producing glands are inside your body we are going to use the ones outside, the mammary glands and the testes. If we connect with the whole glandular system while using these specific glands, it is possible to move Chi throughout the channels. This regulates flow, moving any blockages and build up of Chi, phlegm or blood that cause problems if allowed to stagnate, such as breast cysts, fibroids, irregular or heavy menstruation, and prostrate problems that cause erectile dysfunction.

It is the kidney and bladder that govern this system of glands but it is in this chapter because the Triple heater is all about communication, making sure all parts within the three burners are talking to each other. It is also important that you correspond with your own body. How often do you get out of bed and start straight into the day? Do you stop, stretch and see how you feel? As you get out of the shower, do you love your body, giving attention to the bits that feel good not just rubbing the ankle that hurts or checking that your big toenail is ok? It's time to take time, to feel how your body feels. *By activating the mammary glands or testes we bring attention and energy to the complete glandular system. It is really important that we do this regularly. It makes a tangible, physical difference to our sexual health and well being.*

First things first

Rather than seeing a picture in a book or on a screen and conceptually knowing, feel where the organs are in your body. What is most important here is that you feel inside your body and connect with the whole glandular system.

To find your ovaries – place your thumbs in your belly button and bring your index fingers together to form a triangle. Where your little fingers fall is roughly where your ovaries are.

To find your adrenals place your hands on your hips with your thumbs facing forwards, where your fingers fall is approximately your kidneys and above these, either side of the spine, are the adrenals. Give that area a rub now and see if you feel a little more relaxed.

To find your pancreas bring your hands to the front of the body and on the left side under the ribcage is your spleen/pancreas. You can press in and bend forward to give it a good massage and squeeze.

Next are your mammary glands. Place your fingers on your nipples and circle or squeeze. Include the whole breast. Make sure you know what they feel like so you are aware if any new lumps and bumps appear. Forty percent of diagnosed breast cancers are detected by women who feel a lump.[13]

The Thymus is behind the breast bone on the central line of the body and the butterfly shaped Thyroid sits low at the throat on the front of the wind pipe Giving the breastbone a thump is often used to clear indigestion of the feeling of something being stuck. It's used to reduce anxiety and panic in Chinese Medicine so don't be afraid to press into or tap that whole area. CV 17 on page 66 is a great point, between the nipples on the breastbone, to connect with the Thymus and Thyroid.

The Pituitary gland is between the eyebrows, on the forehead and the Pineal is deep with the centre of the brain. Close your eyes and connect, feel your whole brain filling with light from the inside out.

MASSAGE FOR WOMEN

After giving birth the best way to tighten the uterus is to put the baby on the breast. Whilst a mother is breastfeeding she is less likely to begin ovulating and menstruating. When involved in foreplay, the

---

13 https://www.nationalbreastcancer.org/breast-self-exam

breasts can be a way to stimulate arousal energy and lubricate the vagina before intercourse. This shows the breasts and the mammary glands have a direct physical correlation to the ovaries, uterus and hormonal system so why not use them?

Once you have connected with the glandular system and you are aware of where everything is, the breast massage is easy. To begin, place the hands on the breasts, squeezing the nipples and massaging the flesh. Feel the connection to the ovaries and the uterus. What we are looking for is to feel sexual energy not build arousal energy. It's fine if you become aroused but really we are just bringing attention and moving Chi in the breasts. Starting in the centre, around the nipple, make circles with an upward and outward motion. Do this 36 times, making circles upwards and outwards. Often I burp when doing this and this is perfectly normal, just the Chi moving. After 36 up and out circles, move the fingers and hands, in and down for 9 circles. ***Go at your own pace using firm but gentle strokes, seeing and feeling a connection from the top of your head within the Pineal gland right down into your Ovaries. You can do this practice clothed or naked.*** I find it easy to do after a shower when I'm already oiling my body. Finding a regular time to do it each day so, it becomes part of a routine. The Chi will flow and where Chi energy flows, blood goes bringing oxygen, nutrients and lubrication.

MASSAGE FOR MEN

It's equally important for men to have a connection with their body, to know what feels normal and when something has changed. Playing with your balls and pulling your penis is a health practice, not something to be done hidden away, alone in a darkened room. Too often touching our own bodies and especially genitals is seen as dirty and taboo. We have been taught that intimate touching is only for sexual pleasure and masturbation but it's really time to let go of that thinking. This practice is not a weird sexual fetish. Early detection of lumps and bumps in your scrotum could save your life. Accumulation of energy, phlegm and blood in the genital area can cause problems for the prostate and the kidneys. Correct blood flow around the testes is essential for temperature control. Overheating of the testes often leads to low sperm production. Impaired blood flow also inhibits hormone production and may cause erectile dysfunction.

The practice is similar to that for women but begins by placing your legs apart and bending your knees slightly so that the sacs hang and you can find the testes within them without pulling or snagging the skin. Firstly warm your hands, cold will make the scrotum shrink back into the body and for massage, you will want them to hang loosely away from the body. You can begin by massaging and pressing the fleshy skin around the groin, pubic bone and perineum. If you are practicing skin to skin, oil helps to prevent pulling or rubbing. But it's also possible to do this massage clothed, although the type of underwear or trousers you wear will impact accessibility and movement.

With warm hands, separate the testicles gently and pump each sac gently. Then move up to the base of the testicle and make small circular motions, then very gently pull, squeeze and release the sack. Hold up the penis towards the ceiling so that it's not in the way and tap each testis lightly with the middle finger. ***Using both hands roll the testis through your fingers as if they were delicate eggs.*** It's important to go at your own pace with your own pressure. Finally hold your penis and scrotum, circled with your thumb and forefinger and gently pull them forward whilst pulling back with your pelvic muscles. Pull to the right and pull to the left. All the time using your pelvic muscles in the opposite direction. This pulling of the penis should be done nine or thirty- six times, just like the breast massage. Whilst pulling on the penis it's important to connect with all the endocrine glands. Feel the stimulation from the penis surging up the internal body, lighting up the pineal gland in the centre of your brain. Feel it radiate out and down through the middle of the eyebrows, the throat, the chest, under the ribcage. Feel the glands expanding throughout your chest down to your lower back where your adrenals are nourished and calm. After pulling the penis move your hands to your adrenals or the breast area and circulate the energy there. Even though as a man you don't have mammary glands, there are still a lot of meridians running through the area around the nipple so massaging and circling here will help keep Chi flowing, improve sexual energy and overall life force.

To finish the practice for both men and women you can circle your kidneys with your palms or light fists then slide them around the girdle of the waist to store the energy in the lower Dantien point two fingers below the belly button at CV6 on page 45.

"You deserve a lover who takes away the lies and brings you hope, coffee, and poetry."

– Frida Kahlo

LOVING, KINDNESS, MEDITATION
AND THE THREE ENERGY CENTRES

Emotionally the heart protector smooths and balances incoming information and experiences from the world so that the Emperor heart is not shocked by any sudden changes. The triple heater ensures any physical, emotional or hormonal change, flows smoothly between the ***three centres of the body; the physical sexual centre driven by the kidneys, the embracing emotional energy of the heart and the spiritual, thinking of the mind.***

This meditation practice aids smooth flow of energy, creating positive mental and emotional pathways to aid connection, warmth, ease and movement between the three energy centres. This practice is also meant to cultivate compassion, gratitude and patience empowering us to take the lead in steering our relationships toward healing and thriving.

Some texts in Chinese Medicine link the triple heater and the heart protector to the Hypothalamus, the ancient part of the brain which guides reactions within us that are instinctual and prehistoric. Unconsciously, guided by this deep internal gland within the brain, the stimulation of the nervous system tells us to flee from danger. It gives us unbidden rising sexual impulses to push the body to procreate to ensure the survival of the species. It encourages the mouth to salivate and digestion to begin when smelling frying onions or baking bread. These two meridians, linked to this gland, deal with our interactions with the world. They like things to feel reliable and secure, they like the basics; are you

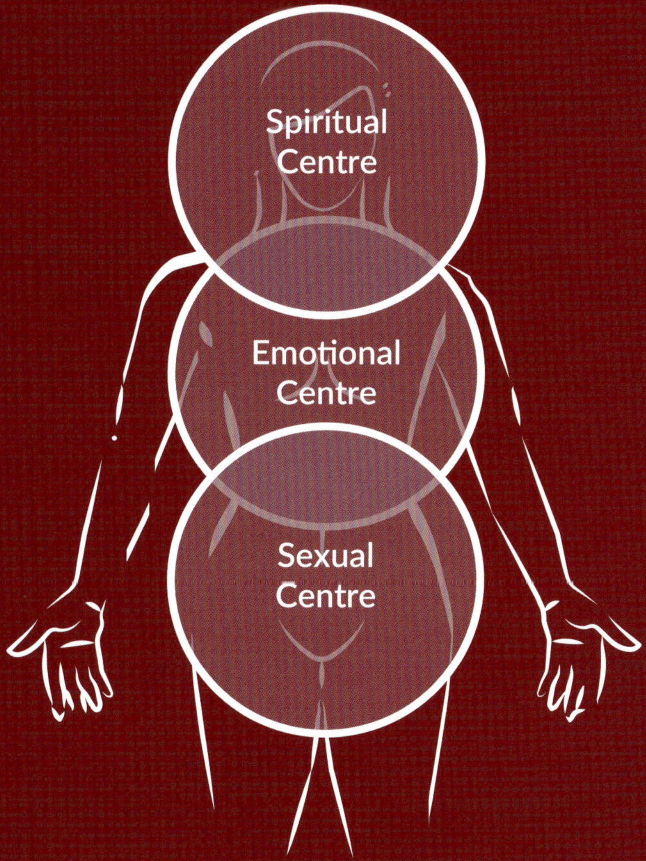

safe, do you have shelter, food, clean water, clothing and the means to survive? When things change this can disrupt these meridians. Unfortunately, we can only be sure of one thing ... That things will change. Parents will die, families will change, houses, jobs, money, partners all come and go. The only thing that remains constant is ourselves.

The relationship we have with ourselves gives us our foundation of being. Our emotional knowledge that we will survive relies on our self esteem, that we can meet our own needs.

If our self-esteem is low and we rely on others to provide a sense of security, then our inner compass is skewed.

We look for others to buoy us up, to secure us in an ever-changing world. This means making decisions from a place of insecurity, which is never the best situation to say yes or no. I suggest using this practice to strengthen your own self-love. It's called a practice because you have to do it all the time, sometimes the session will go better than others. Sometimes you will finish the exercise feeling great and ready to love the world and sometimes not so much. But it's important to practice, there's no getting it wrong, no getting it right, you just have to do it, practice it, over and over.

THE PRACTICE

1. Begin by sitting a quiet space. You can lie down but I have found it's easier to fall asleep like this, especially as this practice is done with your eyes closed. Sit comfortably with your spine as straight as possible and make sure you are warm. Take a few breaths to clear your thoughts, to let them go like clouds across a blue sky. Just park any problems; tell your mind you are going to take a break from thinking about any pressing issues for five minutes, you can think about them again after the practice. After calming the mind and feeling yourself sitting in the room, call to mind someone you really love. With your eyes closed, in your mind's eye, see them sitting in-front of you. Generate a feeling of love in your middle burner, your heart space. Make it a tangible feeling. Perhaps it's warm, perhaps it's soft and then feel that tangible love pour out of your body and over the person in front of you. Feel them bathed in your love. I like to imagine it as treacle. I loved the children's story of the jug that poured never-ending treacle over the boy's toast but it wouldn't stop until it filled the village so that is the image I use to make manifest the intangible feeling of love. There is a version of the story that uses porridge and whilst porridge is great for your kidneys I much prefer treacle to pour all over them. Just to remind you, this is not real life, it's an image in your mind's eye and a feeling in your heart. In my mind's eye, they love receiving all this wonderfully warm, sticky, treacly love.

2. Now call to mind someone you encounter but you don't really know. For instance the postman, a neighbour you wave to, a checkout assistant in the supermarket, it doesn't matter who, as you cover them also in the warm treacle of love. It is important to keep the feeling of love active in your own body. Perhaps you feel your chest soften, your shoulders drop or you lips loosen; keep that love flowing.

3. Next replace the person with someone you don't like, someone you avoid, someone with whom you may be having a disagreement. Someone who has disappointed you, or hurt you. Don't get caught in the story, keep the love flowing. If they start to talk to you in your mind's eye just ignore and keep pouring. There's enough distance between you that you just keep generating the love without getting caught in any drama. This is your process, your healing, your love, be in control, keep sending the love.

4. Then, see yourself sitting in front of you and in the same way, send the love. Feel it coming from you and pouring over the you, sitting facing. Sometimes this part makes me cry and that's ok but don't get caught in a story of how sad or uncared for you are, just keep loving, no differently than at the start, you deserve it.

5. As that image falls away after ten or so breaths, hold the world in-front of you. There is enough love generated by you that you can send it out to all living things, including the planet itself. Your heart is that big, your love is that powerful and you can make a difference. Finish the practice by repeating three times, ***"May I be happy, may I be well. May all beings be happy, may all beings be well"*** and let the images fall away.

Love does not diminish when shared it only grows. No matter whether you believe a person deserves love or not, whether you feel loveable or not, it is the sharing of love that is important. When you experience the giving of love, unconditionally, it relaxes the body and grows the self-esteem. It increases the feeling of well-being and supports the two meridians that manage change. When others seem to be succeeding whilst you feel like you are sinking, be happy for them and know that you too deserve this same love and success. It can be hard if you feel in pain, lost, abused or forgotten.

This practice stops us comparing ourselves to others, it builds our self worth from the inside.

It gives us our ground, our security when all else seems to be crumbling. We always have something to give and what we have, what we are, is always valuable.

"And the day came
when the risk to remain
tight in a bud was more
painful than the risk it took
to blossom."

- *Anais Nin*

Heart Protector / Triple Heater RECIPES

SAGE TEA IN THE SEA OF CHANGE

The triple heater comes under great pressure during times of great change. As I talked about in the cycles of Jing at the beginning of the kidney and bladder chapter, physical and hormonal changes happen every 7 years for women and 8 for men. How we manage these changes can affect the smooth running of the triple heater. Some of the symptoms of an unbalanced triple heater are fluctuation in temperature, increase in skin sensitivity, palpitations, dizziness and insomnia. These are also symptoms that can occur during perimenopause, usually 42 onwards and menopause which occurs at the general age of 49 in women. Men will also have changes in hormones such as reduction in testosterone usually from the age of 48 onwards.

In Chinese Medicine the triple heater would be linked to the, only recently medically recognized, fascia. The fascia is mainly made up of layers of collagen and elastin which operate like a gel covering all bones, muscles nerves, organs in the body. It connects them with a springy spiders web of sliding, gliding twisting elastic, promoting connection and communication throughout the body. Over time toxins can build up in the fascia impairing movement and neural connectivity. At prominent times in the 7-year cycle, its important to make sure our bodies have not accumulated substances which prevent flow of energy, blood or the tensile elasticity of the fascia.

Detoxifying the blood and the ground substance within the fascia aids triple heater and it's internal flexible communication.

Heart foods tend to be red in colour, bitter in flavour and full of antioxidants. These will also have benefits for keeping the triple heater running smoothly. Although not red in colour Sage leaves like most herbs have a bitter flavour and are rich in antioxidants such as apigenin, luteolin and diosmetin. They also contain rosmarinic acid which has anti- inflammatory properties. Sage has been used for thousands of years in many cultures and traditions to keep the body healthy. In Chinese Medicine, Sage leaves are used to increase Chi and strengthen immunity. They increase blood flow thereby regulating periods, decreasing cramps and most importantly regulating the internal thermostat, which can fluctuate wildly at the time of menopause causing instant, unexpected full body sweats.

This recipe is made by infusing Sage leaves in hot water as a tea to further detoxify and hydrate the body. Massage, Shiatsu and yoga practices will help stretch out the fascia, ease flow and regulate temperature, digestion, heart rate and elimination. The body may return to its well-worn pattern unless we initiate a personal change in diet, patterns of thought and ways of responding.

SAGE TEA

Serves 1 - 2

7-10 sage leaves
150-200ml hot water
Teapot or large mug

Sage grows easily in the garden and weathers well through snow and frost, coming back with a lovely purple flower that bees love. To make your cuppa, cut a stem and remove a handful of leaves, give them a quick wash and pop into the teapot filled with boiling water. Leave to infuse for 5-10 minutes and drink. If the sweats are extreme and drinking hot drinks can trigger them, allow the tea to cool before drinking. Add honey if you need but the taste is mild and pleasant especially as a summer cooler with a few edible borage flowers on top.

STUFFED SQUASH

**"When my father died we put him
in the ground
When my father died it was like a whole library
burned down"**

Laurie Anderson

I share with you the thing that broke my heart, that was my father dying. I was 17 and in the midst of a life that didn't fit me. I was a rebellious, confused, obnoxious, drunk, little girl – lost, terrified and desperately sad. That was before he died. After he died I had an excuse to carry on being all those things. People just looked, they watched, they said, "ahh poor girl, her father just died." I remember the night my mum told my brother and I how he died, I felt the pain in my chest, like my heart was being ripped open, slashed apart as if it were the chest was cracking and splitting from a large quake. That pain, the grief was like nothing I have ever felt since. I howled, screamed my cries in an unstoppable, keening flood. He was my idol and I adored him. He wouldn't be there anymore and I was out of my mind and out of my body, with grief.

For over 30 years that grief stayed with me. I learned to function day to day so I kept it at bay but it was always there, just beneath the surface. It took a lot of organisation to keep the grief hidden so I could function. As I grew up, I took on too much work, ran too many projects, all to divert my mind and emotions from the maelstrom swelling beneath the surface. I had it in a box, wrapped up at the back of my mind but if a memory unexpectedly cropped up with a smell or a song I would be instantly inconsolable. Even as the years passed, if someone asked about him, tears welled up and I became a vulnerable mess, unable to function, unable to run a busy house as a single mum. So, I didn't allow the pain and the grief, they were too uncontrollable and I didn't have space for them in my busy life.

Finally, I had had enough of being alone, of choosing thoroughly inappropriate and incompatible boyfriends. By no fault of their own they weren't available or capable of supporting me, either physically, emotionally, or financially with love. I had chosen partners with whom I was never going to be able to completely let go with. To be seen and supported in all my incapable, messy, debilitating sadness. I remained safe if I picked partners who were thoroughly inappropriate. They enabled me to stay the same, safe in the isolation. More often than not I was attracted to people who needed a bottomless pit of emotional, financial or physical support themselves. Their needs distracted me from my own which meant I was never vulnerable because I was in control.

In my 40's I decided to seek a professional therapist to help me open up to the grief of losing my father. I explored my relationship with him, warts and all, but most of all I began to let go. I gave in to the swelling waves of deep emotional agony, smashed down the boulders that I had put up as protection. I was raw, vulnerable and broken but I also felt soft and lovable. Slowly and gently I picked myself up and nurtured that delicate, fluid, new me. I learned that I was able to cope, I went shopping, cooked dinner, put the kids to bed, gave Shiatsu treatments but now I knew that no matter how much I experienced grief, I would survive.

This realization brought about freedom to actually love, without defences or fear. When we deeply connect with another it is inevitable we will lose them. There is no stopping death and loss. I know one day I will lose my new found lover and one day my children will lose me. Touching that deep pain and catastrophic loss of my father broke down my defences and I am more able to love without armour or superficiality. I can show my vulnerability and sadness without the terror of loss.

"Grief and love are forever intertwined. Grief is the terrible reminder of the depths of our love and like love, grief is non-negotiable."

Nick Cave

The world can be desperately unfair. Tsunamis, war, drought, famine, all bring grief on a daily basis. Through the sorrow, and the injustice, keep your heart open, circulating and in connection with the possibility of change and love. This recipe can't right the wrongs in the world but it can support you so that you don't harden your heart to the grief and sadness of loss.

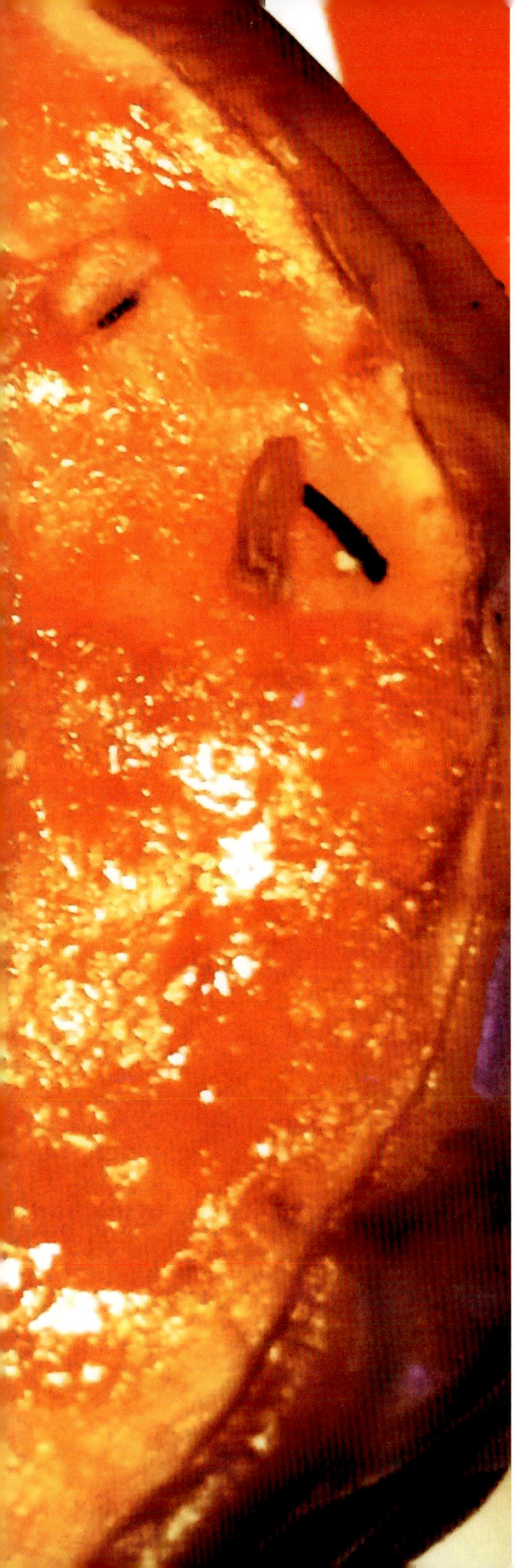

STUFFED SQUASH

Serves 3

Base of 3 medium butternut squash
250g cooked rice
2 tbsp. sunflower oil
2 or 3 leeks
4 tbsp. crème fraiche
2 tsp. Dijon mustard
½ tsp. cayenne pepper
150g strong hard cheese,
(mature cheddar, pecorino or manchego)
2 tbsp. of thyme leaves
2 large handfuls of chopped flat leaf parsley
Salt and black pepper to taste.
1 mozzarella ball

Cut the top off the butternut squash leaving the bulbous base. Scoop out the seeds and set aside. Prepare the filling by gently frying the leeks in oil until they are soft and transparent. Take off the heat and mix the cooked leeks with cooked rice, crème fraiche, Dijon mustard, hard cheese, herbs, salt and pepper. Stuff the mixture into the cavity of the squashes, place on a baking tray, top with a mozzarella disk and bake for 40-50 minutes at 180°C. To test if thoroughly cooked, slide a knife through the side of the squash. It should slide in and out like butter when ready.

Butternut squash and rice will assist the stomach and spleen meridians, giving the body comfort and support. The cheese and crème fraiche can put the lung and large intestine meridians under pressure meaning they may clog with mucus but the mustard and cayenne pepper are warming and clearing so this should balance things out. The herbs will benefit all areas of the body but especially the heart and the heart's protective meridians, making sure we do not lose the capacity for connection by overprotection.

SPECIAL LETTUCE SALAD

In Chinese Medicine, the heart responds and loves the way food looks. Therefore prepare and serve food with care, even if it's only you at the table. Your spirit will thank you for it. By taking care of ourselves we show the outside world how we wish to be treated. A simple gesture of lighting a candle or saying thanks over our food can bring more joy to life. This salad has a predominantly bitter flavour, which clears and supports the joyful heart and it's watchful secondary channels of the heart protector and triple heater.

Growing your own food is psychologically and physiologically beneficial for the heart. Even in small spaces, vegetables such as radish, beetroot and lettuce can grow easily. Beetroot will appear in other recipes for opening the blood vessels and building heart blood, here we use radish and bitter green leaves which can grow in window boxes or small planters in your garden. Picking and eating straight from the ground is optimizes all nutrients from your food and at a sensual level, there is great satisfaction in eating something you have grown yourself.

Flowers added to a salad turn a simple bowl of leaves into a work of art with great intensity and colour. Calendula and Nastursians grow like weeds in my garden and even the ungreenest of fingers can encourage life from these seeds. Chive heads with their purple potency can be harvested by simply buying chives in a pot, leaving it somewhere sunny and waiting for the indigo heads to appear. Simply pick the petals and sprinkle them over any dish such as rice, pasta or a green leafy salad, to add vibrancy to dinner and your heart.

The radish, pink on the outside for the heart and white on the inside for the large intestine, has a pungency and heat which encourages flow and energy whilst the bitter lettuce ensures that this energy doesn't overflow. Sexually, this means the energy is up and moving whilst at the same time it is controlled and centred within the body meaning premature ejaculation is less likely to surprise us.

Salad

2 heads of Gem lettuce
1 head of curly leaf lettuce such as lolla rossa or lambs lettuce
150 g watercress and rocket or 1 red endive or chicory
3 scallions with optional sprinkle of chives and chive flowers
Approx. 20 radishes

Dressing

6/7 finely chopped sundried tomatoes
2 tbsp. capers finely chopped
1 garlic clove crushed
1 ½ tbsp. lemon juice
1 ½ tbsp. olive oil
1 tbsp. rapeseed oil
Salt and black pepper

A salad spinner has become an piece of kitchen kit. I resisted for a long time because it is bulky and difficult to store, but there's nothing worse than a soggy sandwich, damp from undried lettuce leaves. A €5 investment in a simple salad spinner improves the quality of all summer leaves and herbs. When you prepare all the leaves it will seem like mountains but once the dressing hits the salad shrinks to about half its size.

Begin by washing the leaves in the salad spinner and empty into large mixing bowl. Finely slice the scallions and radish, popping them in with the leaves. Assemble the dressing and toss in the leaves, scallions, radishes and chive flowers just before serving and enjoy.

SUPER GREEN PESTO

The word "foreplay" is interesting; it suggests to me some kind of preamble, a prelude to the main event. As if it were a support act, just like the trailers to a film, enjoyable and entertaining but not essential to the main feature. This unfortunate word choice, I believe, diminishes its sexual role and potential for lasting pleasure.

I grew up surrounded by a culture in which men had to do a few things before they could have sex. They had to buy flowers, to say nice things, buy a few drinks or pay for dinner; they had to stroke and engage with a woman's body in ways that weren't necessary for their own arousal. A man had to perform a few perfunctory roles before the main penetrative event. As a woman, you withheld intercourse, as a gift to be earned through the male chore of foreplay. These fit with the common baseball analogy used as a road map to sex; 1st base = kissing, 2nd base = breasts, 3rd base = clitoral stimulation until you could make your home run and have full intercourse.

I suggest that there is no road map because there is no destination. Intercourse, penetration and orgasm are not a goal. I am suggesting that the whole of life can be viewed as foreplay. How you treat each other through daily life will stimulate sexual responsiveness not just the hunt for the clitoris. Be relaxed and open with your partner. Have conversations about sex; don't just have sex. Have conversations about how you are feeling and what you need. Support your partner by considering them in everyday thoughts and actions. What can you do to make them feel good? This support means that you will build deep trust with one another. This trust enables leisurely spontaneity. There is no need for second-guessing, this person wants only to support you, bring you happiness and ultimately pleasure. This certainty of pleasure means that you can wait without anxiety. No grasping, no grabbing, no frenetic crazy lusting after a moment that is yet to come. Rather you are in the moment, enjoying it for what it is. It might be full of frenzied, hectic activity, you might be completely fired up and crazy with desire for each other but the sympathetic, flight or fight nervous system is not turned on. There's a joy in being completely at home in your body, enjoying every lip-smacking sensation without using responses as a means to an end.

Being completely in the moment and savouring every second may mean sexual interaction lasts longer. Orgasms themselves have been shown to last longer and be more intense when the body is relaxed when you are not racing towards the orgasm. For one person orgasm may be elusive and another it may come quickly. Rather than focusing on that moment of pleasure, take your time and enter a deep state of relaxation that is the parasympathetic nervous system. Enjoy your body as it relaxes with the attention of another person stroking, touching, gazing and loving you. There's no need to perform, simply love and be loved.

The kidney and bladder are in charge of the nervous system, foods rich in minerals such as zinc, magnesium, calcium and potassium will help the body's nervous system relax. In a sexually stimulated situation however lots of organs are involved. The heart rate rises and blood flow increases to all parts of the body. This recipe links heart with kidney and liver. The green of the leaves stimulate the liver into detoxifying the blood so it is easily transported. The bitter herbs aid circulation in the heart of clean blood whilst the kidney minerals maintain flow within the nervous system. It is the triple heater that helps all this communication. This is a recipe to keep you at home in your heart, reducing any anxiety you may have around intimacy. Be easy on yourself and be honest. Enjoy the pleasure your body can give you without demands or performance expectation.

SUPERGREEN PESTO

100g basil
50g spinach
50g rocket
100g flat leaf parsley
100g cashew nuts or pine nuts
100g grated grand padano cheese
100ml olive oil
Salt and pepper to taste

This pesto is fantastic spread on a wrap or smothered on white fish before baking. It's also a great way to eat your greens. There is not need to cook this pesto, instead, toss it through the pasta after it is cooked.

Place all ingredients in a food processor and blitz. You may have to add the herbs and leaves gradually depending on the size of your machine. Add more oil if you want to change the consistency or keep it longer in the fridge. This recipe is also useful if your greens are wilting as you can pop the chopped greens, smothered in oil, in an ice cube tray, in the freezer and use when needed.

ROASTED BRUSSELS SPROUTS

"Ejaculation of the male seed ..... is a wasteful loss of an extremely precious treasure"
Mantak Chia

On a physical level in Chinese Medicine, it is important that a man does not ejaculate too often. As he ages, for health benefits, he should ejaculate less and less. So that over the age of 48 he should ejaculate only once every 3 weeks. Ejaculation is not the same as reaching orgasm in Chinese Medicine. It is possible to separate the two so that as a man you can reach states of extreme pleasure without ejaculating.[14]

In the last recipe I talked about staying relaxed and not searching for climax but sometimes it's hard to avoid. It can take us by surprise, literally coming over us unexpectedly and too quickly. This is a recipe to guard against losing that seed and essential energy, making sure it doesn't leak out unintentionally weakening our Jing and essential vitality.

As a woman in Chinese Medicine I am supposed to be multi-orgasmic, meaning I can carry on being aroused again and again, experiencing climax after climax. Unfortunately, I don't think there is a one fits all rule and we have to find our own way with our own body. I find that I sometimes climax quicker than I would like and unfortunately, when I'm done, I'm done. I have been known to fall fast asleep almost instantaneously, with my partner still inside me following orgasm. To lengthen my lovemaking and pleasure time I use the techniques within the Circulation of Sexual Energy in the Yin Yang chapter, by drawing the energy up the spine and down the front. I sometimes stop moving altogether and I spend time looking at or simply holding my partner. I focus on his body rather than mine, stroking his hair, his neck, or lightly kissing, returning to the pleasurable plateau so I can reach a peak and rebound, rather than falling off the edge.

As a woman, it's not detrimental to my health to orgasm but it can send the energy outwards. If I can, I prefer to hold this energy and circulate it internally rather than release it. The feeling is more pleasurable and I feel more connected to my partner as we breathe together. As I circulate the energy, up, down and around the body, my body begins to vibrate and I feel tingling all over not just the shooting rush of energy that happens at orgasm. For a man, ejaculating during orgasm can literally leave him spent; it can drain his energy and leave him prone to energy depletion, serious health conditions and premature aging. So for both men and women, move positions if you feel yourself close to climax. Open your eyes and be fully present. Take time to just slow things down and breath. Talk to your partner, this doesn't kill the mood, but rather reduces the anxiety, promotes the heart to open and calms the nervous system. Focus your attention on your breath and feel your body relax. Practicing non-ejaculation does not decrease pleasure in-fact it can increase sensation and prolong sexual activity. Both men and women can

14 For more information and specific techniques please search out Multi-Orgasmic Man or Multi Orgasmic Woman by Mantak Chia.

become Sexual Kung Fu masters by controlling the Chi and circulating energy flow.

Sperm in Chinese Medicine is a treasure, it is made from the bodies Jing that I talk about in the kidney and bladder chapter and is difficult to replace once lost. Female Jing is depleted through heavy menstruation, pregnancy and childbirth. Minerals such as Magnesium, Zinc and Calcium support kidney energy and Jing. They are also major components in sperm and play a huge role in sexual health. Physically they benefit the parasympathetic nervous system, help the body to relax and can help slow the urge to climax. These minerals are found in many foods such as nuts, seeds, leafy greens, oysters, shellfish, beans and peas.

Brussels sprouts are high in Jing supporting, relaxing minerals. As a cruciferous vegetable, they contain high levels of glucosinolates, which reduce inflammation in the body, especially in the cardiovascular system, which together with high levels of vitamin C, help to reverse blood vessel damage. This supports the Chinese Medicine view that because of their bitter flavour they benefit the heart and circulation. Easy flow of blood will enable arousal for both male and female. The blood vessels that feed the vagina and penis are small and easily damaged through stress and over-consumption of sugars, so balance this with this cholesterol-lowering, inflammation soothing, omega 3, mineral-packed vegetable. It's not easy to make this much-maligned food attractive, but this novel recipe may help you see brussels sprouts as sexy food.

ROASTED BRUSSELS SPROUTS

Serves 3

1 lb brussels sprouts
2 tbsp. olive oil
Pinch of sea salt
Sprinkle of black pepper
1 lemon
100g parmesan / grand padano cheese
(optional)

Cut across the root of the sprout so that the damaged, outer leaves fall away. Then cut the sprout in half, lengthways so that the root is cut in half. Place them dry onto a baking tray and into a pre-heated oven at 180°C. After 20 minutes, take them out of the oven and toss them in the olive oil, salt and pepper. Squeeze the lemon juice over top and give them a shuffle on the tray. Place them back in the oven for another 20 minutes. They should crisp up nicely and brown on the edges. As an optional extra you can add a yin flavour to the Yang sprout by grating over grand padano or parmesan cheese. Super strong and punchy in flavour this is an excellent addition to a meal of roasted red peppers and soft, chewy brown rice.

RETURN TO HEALTH WITH ANGELIKA ROOT

To transform sexual energy into bodily Chi we must engage all three Dantien, energy centres. The lower Dantien located below the navel encompassing the sexual energy centre and the genitals. The heart centre, named the crimson palace, where Chi is transformed to Shen and where our consciousness is housed, and the upper Dantien, the centre of the brain where it's possible to find the emptiness and calm of the universe. The Circulation of Sexual Energy in the Yin Yang chapter engages all these three centres, drawing the energy up the spine to the top of the head and rippling it over the front of the body to return to the lower Dantien. So be in your body don't over think things, allow the mind to be open and spontaneous. Be relaxed and surrender so that your heart is open and carefree. This requires every day, attentive, foreplay for the development of trust as discussed in the Brussels Sprout recipe.

Circulation means energy is transformed into healthy life-giving Chi, not by a mind controlled by the ego, but by a heart, trusting and open to the possibilities of a spontaneous universe. Don't intellectualize the practice, be patient and limitlessly love where you are and who you are.

Sexual energy is extremely powerful. It is the energy of creation. All around us in the natural world are the results of the expression of sexual energy. However, in the human world, we are overusing natural resources because we have overpopulated it. Sexual energy can be extremely healing and powerful for our body but if we ejaculate too often or make too many babies we become depleted and sick. Learning how to recycle sexual energy rather than losing it can benefit every aspect of your life, the way you act, the way you think and the way you love.

This practice is not limited to within a partnership, feeling excited and moving sexual energy around your body is a habit we should all practice, for and with ourselves. Being truly embodied means being our authentic self and Sex is sometimes one of the only places we can escape the overthinking mind and be led by the body. I would advocate being sexual with ourselves or others as a way to be in the body and keeping it healthy. However, this does not mean ejaculation and orgasm, which sends the energy outside the body, but rather circulating the sexual energy around the body as an elixir of health to bathe bones and regenerate cells.

"This is a total orgasm of body and soul. The flow of sex energy alone cannot complete this circle; love must be present. The mind must participate in sex with a totally attentive feeling. This circle of energy cannot connect if a man only joins his penis with a woman's vagina without loving her with his heart. A true orgasm occurs when both man and woman continue to pulsate together. Their sexual energy completes a full circuit between their two magnetic poles, charging each of them more fully than before. This circle is the Tan, the black and white teardrop symbols of yin and Yang flowing into each other in perfect circular harmony."

Mantak Chia – Taoist Secrets of Love; Cultivating Male Sexual Energy

Much as I love the quote opposite, don't limit the cosmic experience to you and a partner, or a partner of the opposite sex. It is also possible for couples of the same gender to complete the energy circuit as they draw the energy up the back and down the front. Here I invite you experience this with yourself daily. Understand that you are both Yin and Yang. Mother Earth within the lower Dantien and Father Sky in the mind of the upper Dantien. These are the two poles the energy flows between, radiating in your crimson palace, your heart space of the middle Dantien. You have the capacity to circulate energy, vibrate; pulsate and resonate with the whole universe. This requires compassion for yourself and self-love. Feel soft and vulnerable, be guided by your heart Dantien, treat yourself with utmost care and respect on a daily basis. Only in through this foreplay will the body relax, diminish fears and begin to trust that you have your best interests at heart. When you can do this for yourself, your life energy is transformed into a higher love and the universe is limitless.

The triple heater helps the three energy centres communicate and a healthy heart protector supports the smooth interaction with the external environment, promoting both security and vulnerability. The bitter aromatic flavour of Angelica Root, otherwise known as Dang gui within this recipe works directly on the heart and heart protector Meridians. It also strengthens the sexual energy in the lower Dantien, warming and moving energy and blood in the abdominal cavity. Often used to regulate menstruation in women, Dang gui can also tonify and strengthen blood for men. This combined with bone broth is essential for replacing lost energy after heavy monthly bleeds, childbirth or excessive ejaculation. However, there's no use in shutting the stable door after the horse has bolted so rather use this recipe to support sexual energy and jing as there is no replacing it, once Jing is gone, it's gone. When there's none left, we die.

RETURN TO HEALTH SOUP

Serves 2 or a very hungry one

2 or 3 de-skinned organic and free range chicken thighs
2-3 litres of bone broth
Pinch of salt
1 inch of fresh ginger cut into slivers
2 medium sized pieces of Dang gui
(Angelika root)
3-4 cloves of minced garlic
1 tbsp. of Chinese red dates or goji berries *(optional)*
2 medium carrots cut into strips
1 stick of celery cut into strips
Miso paste and finely sliced scallions

In a large pot combine the chicken, bone broth and salt. Bring to a boil, skimming off any foam or fat. Add the ginger, garlic, dang gui, goji berries and simmer using a firm fitting lid, for at least an hour and a half. Ten minutes before the end add the carrot and celery. Just before serving take 100 ml of the broth and dissolve in the miso paste to desired taste, add this back to the soup, which is now off the heat and sprinkle on the scallions to garnish.

TOUCHING GOD WITH PEA HERB RISOTTO

Orgasms produce opioids in the brain. For a while after climax, we are at peace with the world. Interestingly, a research study[15] by Janniko Georgioadis in 2006 showed, through MRI scans, that the parts of the brain responsible for self-awareness, self-regulation and inhibition are still and quiet during orgasm, which may explain the feelings of deep peace and oneness.

It's important, however, not to focus on the attainment of orgasm as a primary goal of lovemaking with ourselves and/or others. If orgasm becomes the target it adds expectation and stress to the body which, in my experience, is in opposition to feelings of ecstasy and bliss. Almost a catch 22, you have to be relaxed and uninhibited to achieve orgasm and feel surrender and peace, one fuels the other. So which comes first?

For me, intimacy comes with a strong feeling of surrender. Even kissing a lover means making myself vulnerable, surrendering to them, offering my lips and tongue, communicating who I am and how I feel without words. Rather than only using the physical peak of orgasm, I am suggesting that there is a possibility for surrender with every deep connection, from looking into someone's eyes to penetration or self-pleasure. I am suggesting that any form of intimacy which gives space to be spontaneous in pleasurable reactions or requests means surrendering. I let go of myself, who I think I am, who I should be and how I should act. This relinquishment of ego means I have the ability to feel deeply connected with all beings and all creation.

In some traditions this surrender of self means touching God, the Divine, the Spirit of creation that run through all the "ten thousand earthly things".[16] Why wait to have this out of body experience only through orgasm. Experience it on a moment by moment level by opening your heart and surrendering, deeply connecting with all that surrounds you.

Perhaps you have had your heart broken and you don't feel safe enough to surrender to another? Then begin with yourself. Give yourself a break, accept who you are in this present moment, surrender to what is and love yourself.

This recipe is all about loving yourself. There's nothing to do here apart from stirring the rice and adding the ingredients. Take your time with the pleasure of this food. Feel your stomach softening and your heart opening with this deeply comforting, love-inducing dish.

15 https://bscs.umcg.nl/en/people/janniko-georgiadis/
16 The Tao - Lao Tzu

PEA AND FENNEL RISOTTO

Serves 2

2 tbsp. sunflower oil
2 tbsp. butter
1 onion, finely diced
1 large bulb fennel, diced
3 cloves garlic, minced
300g arborio rice
1300ml vegetable stock or miso
250g frozen peas or fresh peas
Juice of a lemon
60g grated parmesan cheese
120g chopped fresh parsley

Heat the oil in a large heavy based saucepan. When the oil is hot add the onions and soften them on medium heat for five minutes. Slice the fennel along the line of the vegetable and add with the garlic and half of the parsley to the onions, softly frying for another five minutes. Add the rice, stir this for a few minutes so that all the grains are coated with buttery juices. Meanwhile, heat the vegetable stock in a separate saucepan and keep it at a gentle simmer. Add 100ml of the heated stock to the cooking rice stirring constantly until the rice has absorbed it. Then continue adding 100ml at a time after each has been absorbed. After 15 minutes pop in the peas, which should cook in the rice until the remaining stock has been completely absorbed leaving a creamy sauce in which the soft peas and rice sit. Stir in the remaining parsley, parmesan, lemon juice and salt to taste.

COCONUT PANCAKES WITH SWEET SAUCE

Serves 4 (hungry people)

Most sensory pleasures such as eating, drinking, kissing, stroking, licking, talking, and laughing release the endorphins, oxytocin, serotonin and dopamine and as discussed previously, during an orgasm, the lateral orbitofrontal cortex, the region of the brain behind the left eye controlling behaviour, shuts down.

The brain, during orgasm, is said to look much like the brain of a person taking heroin, according to a study[17] published in the Journal of Neuroscience. All these feel-good chemicals produced by the brain can be addictive and therefore the actions that create them feed the addictive cycle. Chemical rewards produced in the brain following sex, chocolate or wine can lead us to focus on the stimulus rather than having a life which is resplendent with an pleasure-producing bounty.

The spleen is related to the mother, enabling support, comfort and nourishment from within. It is the season of late summer when sweet orange/red coloured vegetables are abundant, we start to draw inwards as days shorten and the temperature begins to drop.

Both the fruit and the pancakes feed the spleen with sweetness and a touch of bitterness to open the heart. The peaches and raspberries in the pancake recipe are orange and red in colour and bourne of summer benefiting the heart. The inclusion of coconut is bitter in flavour which also feeds the heart.

---

17 http://www.jneurosci.org/content/23/27/9185.full

COCONUT PANCAKES

50g plain/all purpose flour
50g rice flour
1tsp. ground cumin
½ tsp. ground turmeric
Pinch cayenne
60g fresh coriander
Salt
1 egg
200ml coconut milk
Splash of water if batter becomes too thick *(optional)*

Sweet Sauce

50g butter
75ml maple syrup
4 peaches or 2 mangos
200g raspberries

This is a strange combination as the pancakes are super savoury and the sauce super sweet but it works like a curry with chutney. Mix the dry ingredients in a bowl. In a separate bowl, beat the egg into the coconut milk. Then mix the dry into the wet ingredients with a whisk. If it's too thick add a splash of water. Drop spoonfuls of the batter onto a heated pan greased with a thin coating of half sunflower oil, half butter. These pancakes cook quickly and small bubble dots will appear when they are ready to be flipped. They only take a minute or so for each side.

To make the sauce cut the peaches or mango into chunks and add them to the butter heating in a frying pan. Cook on a medium heat for 5 minutes. Add the maple syrup and cook for 5 minutes more.

Dollop the sweet sauce on the savoury pancakes and serve with creamy natural yogurt.

POMEGRANATE AND CARAMELIZED ONION BULGAR WHEAT SALAD

Serves 4

In the Middle East, pomegranates have long been associated with fertility probably because of their abundance of seeds. They have a bitter-sweet flavour and with their red juicy berries, fall under the realm of heart and heart protector in Chinese Medicine. Health in both these meridians means good circulation and easy flow. The fruit contains high doses of vitamin C that ensures blood vessels are strong and circulation vigorous, keeping us "in the pink" as it were. They also contain different types of antioxidant and bioactive polyphenols, which help detoxify the blood ensuring easy distribution. This increase in blood flow from Pomegranates has been shown in some studies as a natural remedy for erectile dysfunction increasing blood flow to all those small capillaries in the genitals for both males and females.

A study by Queen Margaret University[18] in Edinburgh found that consumption of pure pomegranate juice significantly increased salivary testosterone levels. Elevated testosterone can mean increased sexual desire and increased libido. This juicy symbol of female fertility helps everyone get aroused and excited. In this salad recipe, every mouthful offers a different sensation from the sweet

---

18 https://www.researchgate.net/publication/275716515_Pomegranate_juice_intake_enhances_salivary_testosterone_levels_and_improves_mood_and_well_being_in_healthy_men_and_women

popping juice of the pomegranate to the crunch of the pistachio and the soft ,smooth apricot. This is a perfect salad to arouse the senses whilst taking the time to savour, suck and chew each morsel.

200g cooked bulgar wheat
400ml salted boiling water or stock
2 tbsp. coconut or sunflower oil
3 red onions
2 tbsp. Pomegranate molasses
100g apricots
150g of pistachio nuts
1 Pomegranate seeds
Handful of fresh chopped flat leaf parsley
Handful of Fresh chopped mint
Salt and pepper

Bulgar wheat is such a forgiving grain to cook, don't worry about having too much water, you can always cook it off at the end or drain it. It is not to be confused with couscous as it is a wholegrain which hasn't been stripped of its bran or wheat germ.

To cook, add the boiling water or stock to the bulgar and let it gently simmer for 10 minutes with the lid on. Then leave it, with the lid on but the heat off, for a further 10 minutes in which time the bulgar should have absorbed the remaining water. In the mean-time heat the oil and add the onions to fry on high for a couple of minutes before turning the heat down to a very low sizzle. Leave the onions to caramelize for at least 10-20 minutes before stirring in the Pomegranate molasses. Add the sweet sticky onions to the cooked bulgar wheat and the finely chopped apricots, pistachios, parsley and mint. De-seed the pomegranate by scoring around the top like a little hat and cutting down each of the six raised segments on the side. Pull the hat off and gently pull apart the segments. The very bitter white pith which separates the six segments, will come away easily from the jewelled red juicy pomegranate arils as you slowly prise them apart. Add in the juicy pomegranate fruit and mix all the ingredients well to make a vibrantly coloured, scintillating salad.

CALM IT WITH PINEAPPLE

Through my Shiatsu practice, I have found that after suffering trauma or stress, clients may develop thought patterns and behaviours that put the body's sympathetic nervous system on high alert. A person may feel under constant threat, constant danger, that the world is a bad, malevolent and dangerous place. The body with its muscles and its energetic pathways contract, preventing openness and flow. The overprotection impedes healing and eventually, under constant threat, real or imagined, the body creates an acidic environment and begins to attack itself. Chronic conditions develop such as fatigue, Fibromyalgia, Trigeminal neuralgia, Arthritis, Lupis, or autoimmune diseases. Inflammation and pain are never conducive to feeling juicy, alive and ecstatic. It can lead to erectile dysfunction, vaginitis, candida and decreased fertility.

Emotionally, it's important to address this by calming the nervous system. Begin by doing something you love, a walk on the beach, read a book, fall asleep on the sofa, catch up with friends or take 5 minutes to look at the sky. Whatever it is, do it consciously for yourself. You are worth it. Regularly practice the Loving Kindness Meditation in this book or use a variation of it to build feelings of self-worth.

Another tactic to relive stress is to synchronize your breath with movement. This can be anything from yoga sequences to simply raising your arms on your in-breath, dropping them on the out-breath. This will help the fight or flight sympathetic nervous system transfer to the rest and restore parasympathetic nervous system.

Then we have food. For centuries pineapple has been used in Central and South America to treat inflammation and indigestion. It has a unique protein-digesting enzyme, bromelain, which minimizes the body's inflammatory response system -reducing swelling and pain, especially around joints. This dish is packed with vitamin C, to help the body repair and regenerate and incorporating mint as a natural digestive - cooling and soothing the gastrointestinal system. From a Chinese Medicine point of view, Pineapple clears heat and dampness, assisting movement and flow. Together with mint, it tonifies the Yin, which helps the body chill out and relax.

PINEAPPLE SALAD

Serves 4

1 pineapple, fresh, cut into chunks
2 tbsp. maple syrup
2 tsp. lime zest, freshly grated
1 tbsp. fresh lime juice
1 tsp. ginger root
2 tbsp. mint leaves

Remove the skin of the pineapple, top, bottom and core, cutting the pineapple into chunks. Measure the maple syrup into a large mixing bowl and grate in the lime zest plus the ginger. In a separate bowl squeeze the lime juice and add it together with the finely chopped the mint. Whisk together to make a dressing and pour over the pineapple.

Toss the dressing in with the pineapple chunks and allow to infuse for 10 minutes before eating. Be careful! This is so delicious you may want to eat the whole lot at once but this may cause inflammation in the lips and tongue. Food can be your medicine or your poison; it's all about the dosage.

VALENTINE MOUSSE

This dessert is perfect for lovers or those special days to express a bit of love. Super easy to make and as healthy as a salad. I've named it after Saint Valentine as something special to make for the day of the heart.

During the lead up to 14th of February we are bombarded by the media, shops, family and friends, as to what we have planned for Valentine's night. Everybody has an idea on how love should be made manifest and sometimes all that love gets funnelled into just one day. For some, it's cuddly toys, others it's hearts and roses. Be open to all these ideas but not pressured by them. Use all the materials around you to authentically create and manifest love in the world. Choose to do this every day not just on 14th February. It may not be about expressing love for a partner, but for love for yourself. There are many permutations, the important thing is that it's rooted in your heart and is an authentic expression of what love and being loving means to you.

Raw Cacao is one of the main ingredients in this recipe and helps maintain healthy heart energy. Cacao is full of flavanols and polyphenols which are powerful anti-inflammatories and antioxidants. They can prevent hardening of the arteries and thin blood, to help circulation, blood pressure and blood clots. Cacao also contains two powerful mood enhancers. Anandamide, sometimes known as the bliss molecule, creates a feeling of euphoria; and Phenethylamine which releases endorphins and pleasure neurochemicals often triggered when we make love. Capture the feeling of falling in love by making this chocolate mousse.

TART CRUST

100g organic walnuts
50g ground almonds
150 oatie/hob nob biscuits
2 tbsp. agave syrup
A pinch fine sea salt

CHOCOLATE AVOCADO MOUSSE

3 very ripe avocados
15 very soft dates soaked in apple juice
4 tbsp. raw agave syrup
2 tbsp. high-quality raw cacao powder

You can make individual mousse servings by using a muffin tin or you can use a traditional pie tin and slice it up into servings.

First place the tart crust ingredients into a blender and pulse until combined. I like it quite chunky but give it more time if you like it fine. Press this mixture firmly into the base of a greased pie tin and leave to chill in the refrigerator for an hour. (Using a pie tin with a removable base makes it easier to slide onto a serving plate when finished) Next, scoop out the flesh of the avocado and blend along with the rest of the mousse ingredients until it appears as a creamy chocolate mixture. Spoon onto the pie crust/s. Place the finished dish back in the fridge to chill. When ready to serve, garnish with fruits such as raspberries, strawberries and redcurrants.

LOVE AND CHICKPEAS

Shame is an emotion that can keep you trapped, denying you the chance to enjoy the warmth, pleasure and freedom your body can bring. Maybe you did something you wish you hadn't or said the wrong thing at the wrong time. Perhaps, like me, you have a whole list of things you'd rather forget, usually for me, undertaken when I was full of bravado and gin. Things I wish I hadn't said or done, things I took part in fuelled by the desperate need to be accepted, understood and loved... all make me wince to remember. Some of them I was too young to prevent and some, too misguided to avoid. But, when I recall the times I'd rather forget, I shut my eyes, grimace, shudder, cringe and recoil.

These are all emotions that the heart protector will shield the heart from. The pain of the shame stops the heart from connecting, from experiencing true love. I invite you to support the heart protector by changing your belief about your memories. We often defend our hearts like an overprotective parent to a child. I can't change the past but I can forgive myself and others for the shame I feel today. One thing I have found helpful for this is the `ho'oponopono practice of reconciliation and forgiveness, which is to say "I Love you, I'm Sorry, Please Forgive Me, Thank you." Sometimes I say it to myself, internally, to my internal little girl who wasn't protected. Or to my inner teenager who couldn't protect herself. Sometimes I say it to the people I know I have wronged or hurt. I send it out to them, over and over again, believing that this will change things for them. I know it changes things for me because I feel differently. In the midst of feeling sad and broken, when I say this prayer, I feel human, with all its imperfections and dysfunction. My walls of protection melt and I feel love and connection for all beings, including, and most importantly, myself. Chickpeas also help.

When I am feeling unloved and ashamed, the temptation is to reach for sweet stuff. It brings momentary satisfaction on a crappy day but in the long term, chocolate cannot love you and will probably leave you feeling worse. So try a chickpea. Traditionally these pulses remove dampness and help stop sweet cravings. They are a perfect snack when you are down in the dumps and need to eat mindlessly. These chickpeas are coated in paprika, rosemary and thyme, all of which help with circulation and the heart. The little spicy kick will nudge you to loosen up the muscle around your heart, little by little, feeling loved, feeling forgiven, feeling safe, you can learn to love, without shame, without fear.

ROASTED CHICKPEAS

Serves 4

2 tins of chickpeas or 500g of cooked chickpeas
2 tbsp. olive oil
1 ½ tsp. sweet paprika
1 ½ tsp. smoked paprika
1 ½ hot paprika
½ tsp. fine sea salt
Grated zest of 1 lemon
1 tsp. chopped fresh rosemary
1 tsp. chopped fresh thyme

Prepare the marinade by mixing the paprikas, salt, lemon, rosemary and thyme into the olive oil. Spread the rinsed and drained chickpeas on a baking tray and pop them into a pre-heated oven at 180°C. After 10 minutes take them out of the oven, toss in the prepared oil, place back on the tray and bake for a further 20 minutes. Pull them out, and stir around before you pop them back in for a final 15-20 minutes. They should be crisp and dry, ready to munch. After they have cooled place in a container for storage and easy snacking.

ASIAN STYLE COLESLAW

Peyronie's Disease is caused when the penis or occasionally the prostrate has suffered physical trauma and scar tissue has formed. This doesn't have to mean a single dramatic incident, sometimes it's caused by minor repetitive injuries over time.

The body reacts to trauma and injury with inflammation and the depositing of plaque which forms scar tissue. This can happen anywhere in the body where there is trauma. Sometimes, following surgery, internal scars cause adhesions between the normal slippery organs and fascia causing constriction and restrictive movement. Pelvic inflammatory disease where the area becomes inflamed resulting from infection, affects the uterus, ovaries, bladder and the fallopian tubes which can lead to infertility and possible ectopic pregnancy. In the case of blood vessels, this inflammation from injury and stress can be deadly as plaque causes the blood vessels to narrow and harden, raising blood pressure and increasing risk of coronary heart disease. But for the penis, scar tissue and plaque can lead to pain during erection. The penis can become bent, shortened or in severe cases unable to become erect.

In Chinese Medicine, all these lumps and bumps impede blood flow and Chi, so how to dissolve them? Working on the fascia and connective tissue in the body by eating triple heater bitter, red foods will ensure good blood flow and oxygenated, hydrated fascia. Making sure you have plenty of collagen in the diet to aid elasticity and repair. by eating homemade bonebroth, the recipe for which is in "Jing" in the kidney/bladder chapter.

Avoid foods that cause inflammation in the body, the biggest culprit is sugar. Sugar causes inflammation and degrades collagen. Alcohol, also full of sugar, impedes the absorption of vitamins and minerals, weakens the liver, which is in charge of flexibility, tendons and ligaments and smooth flow of all energy and fluids in the body.

What strengthens flow around the body is food rich deep green in colour or vibrant yellow. Spinach, kale, watercress, chard and broccoli with a tart lemony dressing or homemade pickles are great examples. A sprinkle of seeds or nuts on the top adds to the oils and minerals such as zinc and vitamin E which protect and aid the production of collagen. The following recipe contains sprouted seeds which are a wonderful superfood. These are the embodiment of rising sap and vibrant energy surging upwards, perfect for a fully functioning penis.

ASIAN SLAW

Serves 6

50g toasted sesame seeds (black and white mix)
100g baby spinach
¼ head of red cabbage
1 pack bean sprouts
2 carrots
1 yellow pepper
150g sugar snap peas
100/150g fresh sprouted alfalfa or other seeds
25g pumpkin seeds
25g sunflower seed

Dressing

3 garlic cloves
1 fresh red chilli
2 cm ginger
1 lemon
100 ml organic sunflower oil
5 tbsp. tamari
2 tbsp. maple syrup
1 tbsp. tahini

Begin by assembling the dressing so that the strong flavours have time to meld, sweeten and soften together. Mince the garlic cloves, finely dice the ginger and red chilli and add to the sunflower oil, lemon, tamari and maple syrup. Using a fork blend the tahini into the mixture so that the dressing flows freely without lumps of tahini stuck to the ginger or chilli.

For the slaw salad, shred the red cabbage very finely and wash with the spinach and bean sprouts. Use a spinner to ensure that they are dried thoroughly. Finely slice the carrots, peppers and sugar snap peas, tossing them through the other colourful ingredients. Next using a frying pan with no oil, dry fry the sesame seeds for thirty seconds to a minute, shaking the pan continuously so the seeds don't burn but the aroma and oils are released. Sprinkle these over the prepared ingredients, pour over the dressing and toss again until all the seeds are distributed. To finish with a flourish, sprinkle the pumpkin seeds, sunflower seeds and alfalfa sprouts over the top and serve.

SACRED HOT CHOCOLATE

"When people participate in Ceremony, they enter a sacred space. Everything outside of that space fades in importance. Time takes on a different dimension, Emotions flow more freely, and the bodies of participants become filled with the energy of life and this energy reaches out and blesses the creation around them. All is made new, everything becomes sacred."

Sun bear, Native American medicine teacher

Sacred ceremonies using raw cacao chocolate have been performed in Central and South America for 1000's of years. Cacao was an intrinsic part of ancient Mayan and Aztec life. It was used in their economy and as part of religious ceremonies including death rites and sacrifices. It does not provide psychedelic effects but it does facilitate the opening of the heart area. The bitter flavour in Chinese Medicine points us towards the heart and because Cacao is predominantly used in group ceremonies I feel it can really help the heart protector in its job of keeping out harm and allowing in fun and joy. If the heart protector is not in balance we may feel easily hurt, isolated and even heartbroken. Only when the heart feels well protected is it able to experience connection and bliss.

On a physical level, raw cacao can have many health benefits such as thinning blood and slowing down platelet clumping that can block blood vessels causing heart attack and stroke.[19] Studies have also shown that cacao improves cognitive function and moods by increasing serotonin and blood flow to the brain.[20] All helping with heart function and boosting feelings of well being.

I have attended sacred cacao dance events where we all drank the following cacao drink as a ceremony before beginning to dance. Through this experience I found a deepening of my relationship with my partner and all those in the room. Perhaps it was the vulnerability as I danced with him outside of my comfort zone or perhaps it was the cacao, but I felt my heart soften and gratitude deepen for all human souls. Some tribes and groups use cacao to create an opportunity for lucid dreaming. You might like to use the recipe for a night of sacred love either with yourself or others. Perhaps you would like to discover what lies in your heart or help identify which areas cause you emotional disconnection and pain. Set the intention, use circulation of sexual energy on page 44 to stimulate the sexual energy, empty the mind and fill the heart. Drink this hot, chocolate drink in silence and without the intellect guiding, see what thoughts arise, what images appear and how you feel. Keep a journal handy so you can take notes of any dreams or sensory perceptions you may experience.

19 Researchers from Johns Hopkins University
20 https://www.ncbi.nlm.nih.gov/pmc/articles/PMC3575938/

SACRED HOT CHOCOLATE

Serves 2

450ml water
50g raw cacao
Pinch of sea salt
Pinch of cayenne
1 tsp. vanilla
2 tbsp. coconut sugar or maple syrup
½ tbsp. rose petals *(optional)*

Heat the water in a saucepan adding the raw cacao, salt, cayenne, vanilla, coconut sugar and rose petals. Don't let the water boil, keep it at a low to medium heat for about 10 minutes allowing the sugar to melt and the flavours to diffuse. I suggest serving in two large mugs, and drinking it with your partner in silence, facing each other, connecting heart to heart. You can place one hand on his or her chest whilst the other holds and drinks the silky, smooth, bitter chocolate. This might be outside your comfort zone for you and your partner but I guarantee from experience it will deepen your trust and acceptance for each other, opening your heart to feel the warm love vibration, emanating through your body.

I'm grateful to Paula Alup of Heart Ceremony Cacao, Dublin for her delicious, warm open heart space and fantastic Sacred Cacao.

ACUPRESSURE POINTS

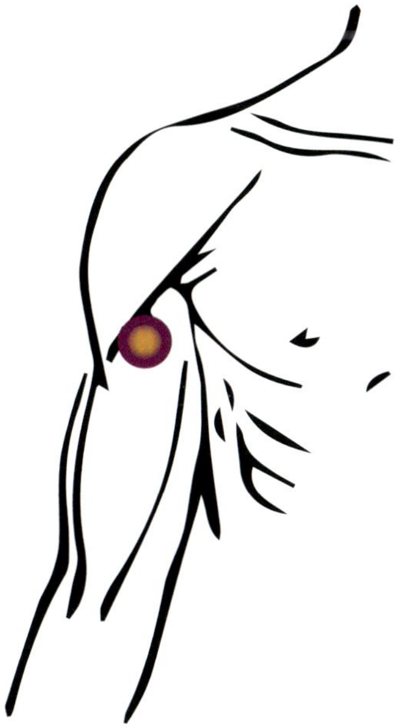

HEART PROTECTOR 2 – HEAVENLY SPRING

Encourages trust and reduces fear of intimacy

Find by using the middle line on the inner arm and measure two thumbs down from the deltoid shoulder muscle.

HEART PROTECTOR 3 – MARSH ON BEND

Removes heat from blood alleviating heavy menstrual bleeding and uterine fibriods.

Find by bending the elbow slightly, which will elevate the biceps brachii muscle.

The point is on the inner side of this muscle (closest to the body) at the crease of the elbow.

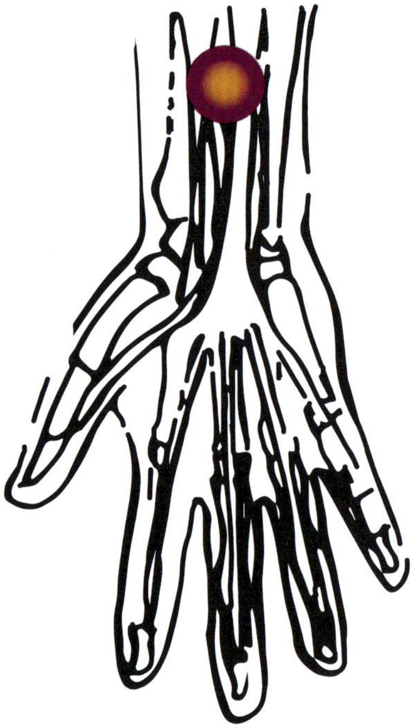

HEART PROTECTOR 6 – INNER GATE

Powerful calming point for the heart and mind reducing anxiety, palpitations, mood swings, depression and irritability.

Balances the inner ear preventing morning and travel sickness.

Used with kidney 6, this point opens the chest, promoting breathing, relaxation and heart connection.

Find the inner crease of the wrist and measure 3 fingers up the midline between the tendons of the inner arm.

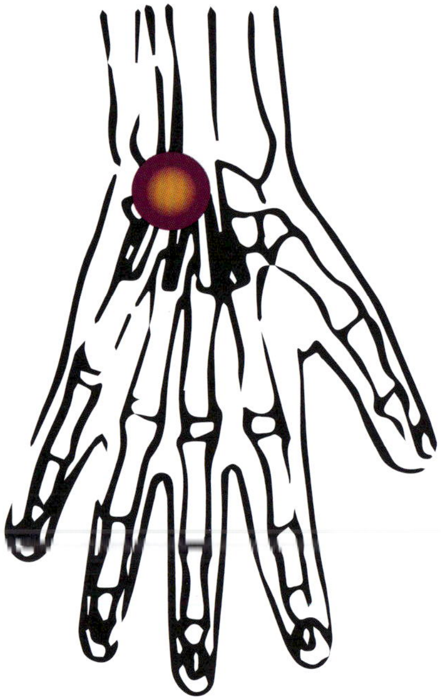

TRIPLE HEATER 4 – YANG POND

Helps excess fluids transform or leave the lower burner preventing dampness, stagnation, pain and fibroids. Helps the kidneys distribute Jing throughout the body assisting fertility, libido and all reproductive organs. Combined with Stomach 42 harmonizes the stomach and gives energy when exhausted.

Find by drawing a line on the top of the hand between the fourth and fifth fingers until you reach a depression on the bend of the wrist. This depression may become more obvious as you flex the wrist.

TRIPLE HEATER 9 – FOUR RIVERS

Helps clear the triple heater channel of phlegm and dampness especially in the neck and throat. Works well with CV6 to restore equilibrium and energy to the body.

Find by measuring one hand width from the elbow on the outer arm and locate the depression between the radius and ulna bone.

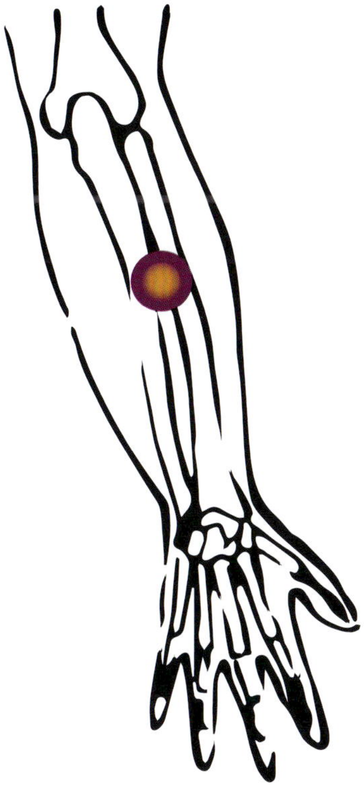

TRIPLE HEATER 10 – HEAVENLY WELL

Calms and cleats heat, transforms phlegm and sedates the whole triple heater meridian. When used together with Stomach 36, it strengthens the spleen meridian assisting change of habitual patterns and letting go of addictions.

Find by flexing the elbow to 90° and locating the depression just behind the elbow bone.

Summer

Huge giants silently lie
Basking surfaces burn
and the senses tingle

Awaken them to watch
them roar and stumble
Violent in their scorching
wrath
Arid tongue – eyes rolled
back
spitting sand to white

But when they settle soft
to sleep
Their thoughts fall as silk
Shyly stroking
Silently tumbling

Chapter 5

HEART / SMALL INTESTINE

My body is a pleasure
house
To lick from arch to armpit
And around to elbow as my
Senses stand erect on end
Yearning to softly receive
you
Like a sweet round cake
Half my body is yours the
other for me to enjoy
with its warmth, wetness
and silken exuberance
come to me
as the flavours mingle and
tingle on our tongues

OVERVIEW
HEART OF TRUE BEING

In Christian and Hebrew cultures, the flame is a symbol for the Divine and Holy Spirit. In other cultures, it represents wisdom, sacred purification and transformation. Within Chinese Medicine, ***the flame expresses our eternal light that never goes out. It is our spirit, our consciousness, it is called the "Shen." In the Tao and Chinese Medicine, we are born with this light of life and even upon death, this spirit cannot be extinguished.*** It is energy which merely transforms into another state. How that transformation is made manifest after death depends on your personal beliefs.

The Shen is a "unique treasure ... present in us all".[21] It is housed in the blood and specifically the heart and must be protected like a flame. The Shen cannot be fanned to an inferno by emotions or allowed to dwindle due to poor care and attention. Just like a fire, we must add fuel. The emotion that fuels the Shen, stored in the heart, is love. True blissful, expansive, tongue tasting, cheekbone grinning, joyful, bursting love. Hopefully, we have all felt it, the emotion that fills our heart as we radiate pure joy. Safe in the knowledge that all is well no matter the external circumstance.

In the west, the heart and the emotion of love are symbolized by Red Valentines or by cupid's piercing arrows. However, this type of love is usually for someone else, another person, a partner, a wife, a child, a dog or a family member. We rarely say that we are in love with ourselves. A healthy heart in Chinese Medicine is more about connection to your own spirit and the Divine, wherever that might be for you. Perhaps it's walking in nature, perhaps it's listening to your baby breathe, sitting in a comfy chair, baking a cake, perhaps it's on the dance floor. It is wherever you find unconditional acceptance with yourself. You don't have to be thinner, taller, richer or prettier. You simply feel good, which means the Shen is stable in the heart.

Spend as much time as possible connected to what makes you feel good. This practice generates love to illuminate our life. Our own connection to joy means less expectation of external relationships lighting the way for us.

There's nothing like the thrill of a chance meeting, a heart-stopping first kiss, the sensual brush of a lovers fingertips, the outburst of ecstatic joy as a baby arrives into the world, the contentment of holding hands or the heart tearing grief and devastation when a loved one leaves the world. ***We live our lives in relationship to others and cannot deny feelings they create in us but it is important not to let them overtake us.***

21 Shiatsu Theory and Practice: Carolla Beresford Cooke

We need distance from emotions so as not to overwhelm the Shen. If we make external factors the cause of our happiness and attach to outcomes, then the changing stories have power to swing us from ecstatic highs to suicidal lows. This damages the heart emotionally and physically. Chest pain, anxiety, palpitations, angina, high blood pressure, insomnia and dizzy spells may result. However, if we have perspective and don't take things literally to heart, then every person, place or thing can hold within it the possibility for our heart to expand with curiosity, love and compassion.

"In your heart there is love, don't love too deeply. In your heart there is hate, don't hate too deeply, because too much of any of these will attack the Shen"

Sun Simiao, "One Thousand Ducat Prescription Book"

Sometimes we are in the thick of emotions, trying to manipulate the story of our life, to get people to behave the way we want and control the outcome. This is conditional love with a healthy dose of limitation. We want to manage situations so that we can love safely and not get hurt. There is no avoiding suffering but if we are our own central light of love, it is much easier to ride the storm of heartbreak.

In Chinese Medicine the heart is the Emperor of the body. ***All the other organs are in service to the heart, physically and emotionally.*** It provides a home for our spirit and the light of our being. The heart's function in Chinese Medicine is to give vibrancy and life to blood. Because it is at the very core of our being it is essential to make sure the blood is healthy, that it is full of nutrients and that it flows evenly throughout the body.

Yin Organs	Yang Organs
The spleen makes the blood for the heart	The stomach transforms food into Chi used to make blood by the spleen for the heart
The liver cleans and stores the blood for the heart	The gallbladder stores bile - a pure substance which helps digestion and breaking down fats for good circulation of blood
The lungs transform breath into Chi for the heart which is then transported around the body	The large intestine removes waste for healthy circulation
The heart protector defends the heart	The triple heater is the communicator for the heart
The kidneys provide water to balance the heart fire	The bladder removes waste for healthy circulation

When we are not at ease with ourselves, housed in our heart, tension and stress occur. Resulting inflammation, speeding up physical degeneration, and allowing viruses to enter the body. It is within heart energy, free from attachment and external influence that we drop the armour of protection and become at peace and in love with ourselves. This emotional aspect is just as important as eating lettuce for a healthy physical body. A healthy heart creates a healthy body and mind. Being in the light of our being, connected to our Shen, free from external distractions is where our true love, intelligence, health and longevity lies.

The sage regards his/her body like a country: the heart is the ruler, and the jing and the qi are the citizens. If the heart does not abuse its superior position, if it remains centered and focused on the essential matters, the jing will flourish and the qi will be steady, noxious intruders will always be fought off, the dantian will be full with treasures, and every part of the body landscape will be light and at peace.

Unfolding the Mat with Enlightening Words
(*Tuipeng Wuyu*) , Ming dynasty, 1570:

My tongue longs for yours
It's muscle, thick and
flexible to touch crevices
creases of salty skin
Soft lips frame the flowing
movement as it snakes
around my body
stopping to flick and tease
until it returns
mouth to mouth
communicating, muscle
to silky muscle and a
thousand soft sensors
with a song at its tip to make
my heart soften and sing

HEART TANTRA
BLINDFOLD TASTING WITH THE TONGUE

Food is a main route to delight and enjoyment. The part of our brain that registers taste and sensations is the orbitofrontal cortex which is often referred to as the pleasure centre. A recent study on the science of pleasure[22] showed that food represents reward, identity and joy not just stopping hunger. By feeding yourself or your partner, you have delicious control over the novel flavours and textures of food. You can use anticipation, sound and touch sensation to heighten the experience of eating.

Because this exercise is done blindfolded, our other senses are heightened, so instead of our eyes being the sensory organ at play, the tongue takes its place. The ***Neijing*** states:

"The heart qi communicates with the tongue. If the heart is in a state of harmony, the tongue can distinguish the five essential flavours."

The five element chart at the beginning of the book sets out the five flavours and the colours to match. The heart in Chinese Medicine opens out into the tongue it can reflect quite physically the condition of the blood in the body. If it is a very deep red colour it can indicate heat and toxicity in the blood whereas a pale tongue signifies blood deficiency. A balanced condition would be light pink or red with a whitish coating.

The red colour of the strawberries make them food for the heart, igniting and exciting blood flow, stimulating all parts of the body, ready for play.

400g strawberries
3 tbsp. coconut oil
100g raw cacao powder
2 tbsp. agave syrup
½ tsp. vanilla
Pinch of sea salt

Melt the coconut oil in a bowl over a saucepan of boiling water. Then take off the heat and whisk in the cacao, agave, vanilla and salt. Take the washed and dried strawberries and dip them in the melted cacao mix. If the mix is not very runny use a teaspoon to paint onto the strawberry. Place them on a tray lined with baking parchment and pop them in the fridge.

As the cacao is cooling on the strawberries prepare the room for your Tantra experience. Remember as you or your partner will be blindfold the other senses will be heightened. Make sure that there are plenty of cushions with soft covers. Warm the room so that you don't shiver, apart from with anticipation. Set some music or sounds in the background. Perhaps download natural noises of a flowing river, a forest at dusk or rainfall in summer. Whatever sounds makes the body feel safe and secure. Then invite your partner to set some ground rules.

22 The pleasure of food: underlying brain mechanisms of eating and other pleasures. Morten L Kringelbach. Morten.Kringelbach@psych.ox.ac.uk. Flavour20154:20. DOI: 10.1186/s13411-014-0029-2. © Kringelbach; licensee BioMed Central. 2015; Received: 19 December 2014. Accepted: 30 December 2014

Where would they like the food to travel around their body?

Are there any out of bounds areas?

Is there anything they don't like the touch of?

How will you finish the experience?

Obviously, you can do this exercise by yourself. Enjoy the sensuality and the surprise of the touch of strawberries on the body and the lips whilst wearing the blindfold. If with a partner or in a group, mix up the experience by using different textures and foods. Try grapes or melon, brush their arms with a soft blanket or feather. Use the tips of your fingertips to touch their wrists and their lips. When you come to the end of the exercise remember that the person receiving may need to come back into the world of the visual senses slowly. Be gentle with the light and don't throw the curtains wide no matter how joyful and expansive you feel.

Heart / Small Intestine
RECIPES

BEETROOT, PEAR AND FETA SALAD

This salad says summer, the time of the heart. It is light, fresh and expands our energy as we eat it. Beetroot contains high levels of nitrate which our body transforms into Nitrous Oxide. The main purpose of nitrous oxide is to open the blood vessels and increase blood flow. This happens all over the body but especially in the tiny capillaries in the genitals. The release of nitric oxide relaxes narrowed blood vessels, increasing oxygen and blood flow. Viagra and other impotence medications also increase blood flow to the penis by influencing enzymes which enhance nitrous oxide.

You would have to eat a lot of beetroot to get the same instant hit that viagra gives but this book is about loving the body rather than popping a pill for a quick fix. Nitrous Oxide will expand the blood vessels which will help anybody who has high blood pressure, as it means the blood isn't forced through tiny spaces. However, if you already have high blood pressure it is advisable not to take viagra as the intensity of the drug forcing the blood into the capillaries can have common side effects such as a bloody nose, diarrhoea, difficulty breathing, headaches and pain around the eyes to rare occurrences such as hearing loss and blurred vision. Viagra is a drug and has to be processed by the liver and kidneys so it is preferable to take a natural food, which boosts the blood and aids circulation in a sustainable way. It seems shortsighted to take a pill to fix one problem that may cause another.

In Chinese Medicine, beetroot builds blood which helps the spirit settle. It aids circulation not only because of its high nitrate content but also by its high iron content which regenerates and reactivates red blood cells. The high copper levels make iron more available to the body, which means a greater supply of fresh oxygen to the whole body.

Raw beetroot and especially beetroot juice is a powerful solvent for inorganic calcium deposits that build up causing arteries to harden, reduce blood flow and increase blood pressure. Beetroot keeps the arteries flexible and open.

Mint aids expansion and uplift of energy, especially in the chest and stomach, aiding breathing and digestion. Openness, flexibility, expansion and healthy blood flow all sound like a very good place for a healthy sexual encounter.

4 good-sized beetroots
(Different colours;lif possible, scrubbed, peeled and cut into fine matchsticks)
3 ripe pears , peeled, cored and cut into matchsticks
(can substitute with apple)
200g feta cheese
1 large handful sunflower seeds

Dressing

1/2 lemon
5 tbsp. olive oil
Sea salt
Freshly ground black pepper
1 handful fresh mint leaves

Clean, peel and chop the beetroot into small matchstick shapes. Core, wash and prepare the pears, chopping them in the same way. You can substitute the pears with apples, which will only slightly change the energetic qualities of the salad but will markedly change the flavour. Crumble over the feta cheese and sprinkle on the sunflower seeds.

With the dressing, blend all the ingredients with a fork. Careful not to beat too forcefully or the oil will taste very bitter. Drizzle over the dressing and toss the salad, gently but thoroughly. As the beetroot is raw this salad keeps very well in a container. However, I doubt you will have any left over.

LIQUID VIAGRA

Just like beetroot, watermelon is sexually potent. Both the rind and flesh of this glorious fruit are packed with amino acids and citrulline, which relaxes the blood vessels and increases blood flow all over the body including to the genitals. I often recommend this food for people suffering from gout or other discomforts due to the build of deposits around joints as it reduces uric acid within the body. It also helps dissolve and pass kidney stones.

If you want to treat a certain condition attempt to view food as a medicine that you need to take every day to have an effect. A 250ml glass of this juice taken every day will increase citrulline and arginine needed for the bodies Nitrous Oxide levels. Enhancing nitric oxide is the function of many of the ingredients within Viagra. It increases blood flow to the penis, increasing sexual arousal, sensitivity and erectile function. However, just like any medication, there can be side effects. So if your kidneys are weak and you suffer from excessive or uncontrollable urination, this juice is not the place to start, try barley water in the kidney/bladder chapter and come back to this later.

Half a medium watermelon
2 peeled raw beetroot
Lemon or lime to taste

Use a juicer for the watermelon and beetroot. It is possible to use the skin of the watermelon as there are high concentrations of citrulline stored there but has a bitter flavour compared to the sweet flesh. Both these ingredients are very fibrous and I find using a blender for this recipe doesn't really work. The lemon or lime should be peeled before juicing. I often use a hand squeezer so I can regulate the taste. This juice will keep in the fridge for 2-3 days and whilst the enzymes will die fairly quickly after juicing, the minerals and vitamins will remain.

WATERMELON AND FETA SALAD

Serves 6

As in the previous recipe for Liquid Viagra, we covered how good watermelon is for increasing blood circulation but here I want to share its properties for reducing heat and inflammation in the body. Traditionally, in Chinese Medicine, watermelon removes summer heat problems; when joints become stiff hot, red and swollen due to lack of movement and blood stagnation. Too many fizzy drinks, alcohol and saturated fats can cause this condition and it is not sexy. Swap out the sugar and try a juicy sweet salad. It is an easy addition to barbecues but also goes well with Thai curries and Indian dahl's as the fruity, salty flavour combines with spices.

1 medium watermelon
100g feta cheese
1-2 red onions
Handful of fresh basil leaves
2 tbs. extra virgin olive oil

Chop into bite size pieces, triangle shapes work well. Slice the red onions into paper thin, half moons and sprinkle them along with the crumbled feta onto the watermelon. Scatter the basil leaves and drizzle olive oil over the top to finish.

Tip: Choose a watermelon that has wide spaces between the dark green lines – they're sweeter that way.

SEXING THE CHERRY

Cherries are such a sexy fruit. Roll them around your mouth use your tongue to push them around then bite into the deep blood red flesh. Practice consciously eating them and sharing them with a partner, mouth to mouth. They speak of sexual innocence and juiciness. Plus they are also very good for your heart.

The principal sugar in cherries, as in most berries and plums is xylose, which releases comparatively slowly into the bloodstream. They contain large amounts of antioxidants and anti-inflammatory chemicals, which help protect against heart disease and painful conditions such as gout.

As talked about at the beginning of the chapter, the heart in the upper part of the body represents fire, whereas the kidneys in the lower part of the body represent water. These two elements should be in balance. Water cools and Fire warms. When kidney Yin declines as we age, the heart fire can overpower us and we suffer from hot flushes, palpitations, insomnia and restlessness. Building up kidney Yin and Jing is vital. In fact, taking care of kidney Yin and Jing throughout our life is paramount. As classic Chinese Medicine texts say "it is too late to try to dig a well when one is already thirsty."

Luckily help is at hand with a cherry and a Goji berry. You will find these little berries pop up in all sorts of recipes throughout this book as their potent Yin tonic properties can support a range of organs.

CHERRY, MINT AND GOJI BERRY TEA

Serves 4

2 litres water
10-12 cherries
Couple of large sprigs of fresh mint
1 tbs. dried goji berries

Bring the water to the boil in a saucepan and add the cherries and Goji berries. Put the lid on and simmer gently for 20 minutes. The cherries should be soft enough to squish with a fork. Transfer the tea to a large jug and add the chopped mint. Drink hot or cold depending on your own body temperature. You don't need to strain it as you can eat the berries and cherries whilst drinking the tea.

HERB TART

Serves 4

This is another recipe that fortifies both kidney Yin and calms the firey heart. It builds both blood and healthy sexual energy.

Eggs in Chinese Medicine nourish the Yin of the body, which means they lubricate and moisturise. If you think about eggs they have everything they need within them to create new life so they are extremely potent to nourish Yin and tone the blood. They are even recommended for pregnant mothers to calm a hyperactive fetus.

In this recipe I have combined the heavy downward energy of eggs with the uplifting energy of herbs. Herbs tend to be green in colour, full of chlorophyll to stimulate the liver, detoxifying the blood. They are bitter in taste entering the heart and calming the mind. I have also added seaweed because it is fantastic for boosting the kidney energy and Jing which is responsible for brain development and function, including hearing, bone formation, the function of bone marrow, sexual activity, and capacity to conceive.

This recipes makes such a wonderful smell in the kitchen when all the herbs are out on the table. It feels like summer, full of light and freshness. It is however, not so quick to make so I usually make 2 or 3 at a time. Make one for your lovely self, one for the fridge and snacks tomorrow; and one for a neighbour or someone who you thinks needs a little cheering up. Be in love with yourself and with those around you.

Pastry Crust

350 plain/all purpose flour
175 butter at room temperature
Pinch of salt

Filling

3 large handful of flat leaf parsley, coriander, basil and chives.
Tarragon is another herb, very strong in flavour that works well here.
1 tbs. dried and chopped wakame
125ml double or single cream
125ml milk
4 eggs
Salt, pepper and grated nutmeg

Rub the salt, flour and butter together to make a bread crumb mix, making sure the butter is rubbed into the flour completely. Use 3 tablespoons of cold water to bring the dry mix together. If you need to add more water do so sparingly until the wet sandy mixture forms into a dough. With a rolling pin, roll out the dough onto a floured surface until it is approximately ½ cm thick and wide enough to fill your 30cm quiche tin. At this point let your pastry rest for half an hour as will tend not to shrink in from the sides when cooked if you include this step. After letting it rest, roll the pastry onto the rolling pin so you can manoeuvre it more easily onto the quiche dish. Gently press into place and trim the edges. Use any leftovers to plug gaps in the pastry.

Now to blind bake by placing a circle of baking parchment larger than the quiche on top of the pastry and fill it with dried beans. This will prevent the pastry from rising. Any pulse will do. Bake in the oven for 20 mins at 180°C, then take out of the oven and remove baking paper and beans. You can save the dried beans and use them for your next quiche and the one after that. Brush the crust with a beaten egg and pop back in the oven for another 10 minutes. This assures a crunchy thin crust to the quiche.

For the filling, beat the eggs, cream, milk and seaweed and leave to one side whilst you ¾ fill the pastry case with the chosen herbs you have chopped. Grate the nutmeg and sprinkle the salt and pepper over top. Pour the batter mix carefully over the herbs and place in the oven at 180°C to bake for 30 minutes until it is set.

This quiche accompanied by a large green salad with a tangy vinaigrette with further support the heart and balance out the dairy in the dish.

BE STILL MY BEATING HEART

In our busy lives, there is always more to do. Something new to learn, bills to pay, goals to reach... it is great to be aware and have a vision for a healthier and improved life but it can also become a source of stress. It can become about performance and pleasing other people. In Chinese Medicine, this is not good for the heart. Physically, it causes all sorts of problems such as insomnia, heart palpitations and premature ejaculation as we put ourselves under pressure to get it right, accomplish goals and be the best. Rather, please yourself first. From the freedom found there, your love will shine and you will please others effortlessly. Take it easy, less stress more joy, self-confidence and self-love.

Lettuce has an intensely bitter flavour which makes it perfect food for the heart, bringing the mind and body home to settle, calm and serene. It is full of iron which builds strong blood, full of vitality and vibrancy. In Chinese Medicine, healthy blood is essential to build a home for the energetic heart to settle. Anemia and weak blood lead to agitation, anxiousness, insecurity and insomnia. Sexually this means sperm count is low and if we are not settled in the mind and body it can lead to premature ejaculation and erectile dysfunction. Use this tea on a daily basis to heart centred, rested and relaxed.

LETTUCE TONIC

Serves 4

5-6 leaves of romaine or butterhead lettuce
1 litre water

Pour a litre of boiling water over the outer leaves of a head of, simmer for five minutes, leave to cool, strain and drink. It's a very refreshing tea.

LETTUCE JUICE

Serves 2

The juice of the lettuce contains Lactucarium which is a natural sedative so if you have periods of insomnia where your mind just cannot turn off, try juicing lettuce to reduce agitation and excitement of the mind. Lettuce is an excellent sexual tonic calming the nerves, reducing over-excitement which can lead to premature ejaculation.

1 head of chicory or romaine lettuce

Pass the lettuce through a juicer. Take a shot, approx 75ml, of this every night and every morning.

BITTER HEART OF AN ENDIVE

"Did I send flowers, that was nice of me"
"Nice to know you have feelings for me"
"I have feelings Richard, I just never have time"
– This book will save your life – a.m. homes

Just like many other people my days can be hectic, running here, shopping there, cooking everywhere. So when it comes time for bed it can be hard to be in the loving mood. Bedtime is often the only quiet space where my head has time to unpack the events of the day and ponder the plan for tomorrow. So the will, the desire and the impetus to focus and stir libido can be distracted by a wandering mind or an exhausted body.

In my Shiatsu clinic, both male and female clients, often request a cure for lost libido. They are looking for a magic tonic, food, or drink that will boost their desire and return them to the passion they once felt. There are foods and supplements that can help and support a boost of sexual energy such as ashwagandha, ginseng, maca and tribulus. Some of these are listed in this book within recipes but everyone is different so there is no single solution.

If you want to experience a rise in sexual energy, make time for yourself a priority. Understand your moods and sensibilities before making love. Being intimate isn't just about having sex. It's about being honest and being open and that begins with yourself. Being authentic is paramount to a healthy sexual libido. How do you feel? If you are sexual solo, how do you feel about your body, your soul, how are your energy levels? And if you are with a partner – how do you feel with them, are you honest with each other? Do you speak from your heart's desires? Are you accepting and understanding of each other's energy levels?

I know I often struggle with keeping my focus. In the day to day living, sometimes my mind slips to Saturday when it's only a Wednesday and I can be thinking about my kids and their problems when I'm kissing the man I adore and want to make love with.

A quick tip for me to get back into my heart and the present moment is to close my eyes and then open them and name the first five things I see, without judgment. Wall, Curtain, Hair, Window, Eyes. Not window that needs cleaning or cobweb that needs dusting, simply see five things and name the five things. Do this to become completely present where you are, be in your heart and know how you feel. Maybe you actually aren't in the mood for sex. Never be obliged or pressured to do things you don't want to do because you are afraid of the consequences. This is about being in the now without fear of the future. Maybe it's a cuddle you crave, a backrub you want to give, or a conversation you need. Completely accepting yourself is the best way to have a healthy libido and a circulating sex drive.

The Five Things technique mentioned previously, is a quick way to be in the heart and to be present, to be here and now – free to receive, give and make love. Being present, honest, and authentic helps with all areas of controlling sexual energy including premature ejaculation and erectile dysfunction.

The foods to support this authentic bravery in the body would be bitter foods and red foods. All foods that support the heart will calm the Shen, which in Chinese Medicine is our spirit, our consciousness. This becomes agitated and stimulates the monkey mind into thinking, thinking, thinking which is an avoidance technique from being in the heart and accepting how we feel, right here, right now. Sometimes feelings are uncomfortable and we resist them by filling our life with tasks and our mind with thoughts. Practicing non-identification with the feelings and not overthinking things, is helped by having a healthy heart, supported by the food we eat, and how we train the mind.

Here, I have chosen the bitterest leaf I know, endive. There are two types, white and red, both work in this recipe. Bitter flavours in food feed the heart. They calm body and mind, making sure the blood circulates serenely and freely whilst allowing the consciousness to settle and be present. The red of the pomegranate is fantastic for the heart. It is full of vitamin C and antioxidants. There is a slight bitterness to its juicy red sweetness which perfectly complements the mineral packed walnuts to relax and feed the nervous system. The antioxidants in this salad will help reduce cholesterol and cortisol in the bloodstream which can increase the production of testosterone and oestrogen which in turn will help physical sexual health and libido on a long term basis.

ENDIVE SALAD WITH POMEGRANATE DRESSING

Serves 4

- 1 red endive or radicchio
- 1 white endive or chicory
- 50g chopped walnuts
- 1 green apple
- ½ seeded pomegranate
- 50g blue cheese *(optional)*

Dressing

- 1 clove garlic, finely minced
- 1/2 tsp. Dijon mustard
- 1 tsp. honey
- 50ml pomegranate juice
- 50ml balsamic vinegar
- 100ml extra-virgin olive oil
- Salt and pepper to taste

Chop the stem from the endive and wash the leaves. Spin them dry and roughly shred by hand. Peel, core and chop the apple together with the walnuts. To seed the pomegranate, score around the top to make a little hat then score down the sides where they are slightly raised. When you remove the hat the segments of the fruit will open so you can take out the juicy seeds leaving the very bitter white pith. Dress the salad leaves by adding the dressing slowly and tossing then crumble the cheese over the top with the pomegranate seeds, walnuts and apple.

BLACK FUNGUS SOUP

Serves 2

Sometimes it's easier to be in a heart space, to feel joy and expansion when we are alone. Walking in nature, at the top of a mountain or drinking tea in the sunshine. There's no one to knock us off our cloud, to trigger feelings of inadequacy, anger, or shame. But to be alive means we have to interact with others and sometimes we are buffeted by their actions. The challenge is to keep a distance between ourselves and the emotions others evoke in us. Not taking other peoples actions personally helps, but sometimes its difficult and we feel shock and pain from how cruel and insensitive others can be with our delicate hearts, so if you feel hurt and you need to mend a tender heart this soup is perfect.

Black wood ear fungus has the ability to thin the blood by dissolving platelets. This helps to lower blood pressure thereby helping the heart to circulate blood. It is used for its texture rather than flavour and I recommend the shredded variety as the uncut variety can grow to frighteningly inedible sizes when rehydrated. Chinese red dates and Goji berries are packed full of vitamin C, which as we know is great for the immune system but often overlooked for its ability to repair the body. Delicate blood vessels can become damaged as plaque build-ups tear away from the artery walls, becoming dislodged by flowing blood. The vitamin C makes sure these are repaired quickly so the blood can nourish the organs and muscles in the body. To find vitamin C via food rather than chemical supplements is simple really, just visit the greengrocers instead of the chemist.

2 tbsp. dried wood ear fungus
4 Chinese red dates or 1 tbsp. of Goji berries
½ inch of ginger
2 carrots thinly sliced
1 litre water
3 scallions
1 red pepper
1 small chilli
Small bunch of coriander
2 tsp. light soy sauce
2 tsp. sesame oil
3 tsp. rice vinegar
2 large tsp. miso
Juice of 1 lime

Drop the fungus, red dates, goji berries and ginger into a large pot with the water, bring to the boil, then simmer with a tight-fitting lid for 15 minutes. Remove the fungus and chop finely (or buy pre-chopped). Add back to the water with the carrots, red pepper, scallions and let them soften for five minutes. Take a cup of liquid from the pot and dissolve the miso into it. Add the dissolved miso back into the pot with the soy sauce, sesame oil, rice vinegar, chopped coriander and lime. Take care not to cook the miso as this will kill the delicate good bacteria , just allow it to dissolve and warm into the body of the soup. The sour flavour from the lime will help liver function and assist the heart further by detoxing and cleaning the blood. All round, a great soup for a broken heart.

CARAMEL DATE ORBS

Serves 6

Sometimes when the heart is not calm and serene, it can be because the kidney energy, which is water, is not strong enough to balance the fire of the heart. This can lead to night sweats, anxiety and premature ejaculation. All the energy is rising and scattered instead of being grounded at the base of the body in the kidney governed, sexual organs. For women, this can mean loss of libido and vaginal lubrication. Ashwagandha, whilst originating in the Indian Ayurvedic herbal tradition can help strengthen kidney Yin and improve hormonal function, male semen and female fertility.

A test carried out in 2015 showed that out of 50 women tested, the 25 who were given the ashwagandha instead of the placebo showed signs of improved libido, lubrication and ability to orgasm.[23]

By boosting the kidney Yin using Ashwagandha we can reign in the excessive fire energy of the heart so that you can sleep better, calm anxiety, soothe the nervous system and prevent bodily damage from chronic stress. All this plus better sex and chocolate – what is not to love about trying this?

See Warm Cashew Milk in kidney chapter for more information on Ashwagandha.

190g walnuts
70g dates
85g raw cocoa powder
85g ashwagandha powder
100g shredded coconut

Soak the dates overnight so that they are thoroughly soft, drain them and keep the water. Blitz the walnuts in a blender until they are crumbed then add the dates so they combine. As the mix comes together add the raw cocoa and ashwagandha. When smooth take a teaspoon of the mixture and roll it in your palms to form a ball. Spread out the coconut on to a flat then roll the balls into the shredded coconut. Place in the fridge to set, resist them if you can for a couple of hours.

---

23 Dongre, Swati, Deepak Langade, and Souvik Bhattacharyya. "Efficacy and Safety of Ashwagandha (Withania Somnifera) Root Extract in Improving Sexual Function in Women: A Pilot Study". BioMed Research International 2015 (2015). Doi:10.1155/2015/284154

RED RICE AND MINTED PEA SALAD

Estrogen is on the increase and so are breast sizes. In 2016 the word moobs (man boobs) was added to the Oxford dictionary showing that this is true for men too. There are many types of estrogen in the male and female body but their job as a whole is to tell cells to grow and multiply. At major points of our life such as puberty and pregnancy, this hormone floods the body to assist with growth and changes. It maintains the sexual organs, stimulates fertility, breast growth and the menstrual cycle. However, if their balance is disrupted cells can multiply and lead to chronic inflammation and even cancer.

There is another type of estrogen that is not made by the body but absorbed by the body, through the skin, from petroleum-based products such as detergents, cosmetics, shampoo, furniture, carpeting and even from pesticides, herbicides and fungicides that are sprayed on our food. These synthetic estrogens can be stored in fat cells and accumulate over time, disrupting the normal hormonal flow by activating receptors to stimulate unnecessary hormones or block natural hormones from doing their job. At any time where weight, mood or temperature fluctuates in the body it is an important health indicator to notice. Take a good look at your diet and lifestyle and see where you could make changes. The first stage would be to do a liver cleanse so the cells detoxify and the liver can metabolise waste products and hormones. See Chrysanthemum tea in the liver chapter for more information.

In this recipe I have chosen red rice to help cleanse. The red colour comes from a potent antioxidant called anthocyanins which are found in deep red and purple fruits and vegetables. The red bran outer layer contains 95% of the minerals and dietary fiber. The white inner rice is mainly made of carbohydrates and protein. This red colour is perfect for the heart. It assists in pumping the blood properly, reducing temperature flashes and making sure organs, tissues and muscles are oxygenated reducing inflammation and heat. The minerals of magnesium, calcium and selenium help brain and nerve function. They make sure the blood vessel remains flexible and lower blood pressure.

This recipe also contains Mint and Peas. Mint is a summer herb, perfect for the heart. Its delicate fresh odour fills and expands the body. It makes any dish light and fresh. Together with the peas, which are rich in vitamin C essential for arterial health, they bring a lightness to the rice which can be heavy and hot, especially in the summer.

RED RICE AND MINTED PEA SALAD

Serves 1

50g red rice per person
50g brown rice per person
50g frozen peas per person
300ml stock
1 tblsp. fresh chopped mint
Juice of half a lemon
50ml olive oil
Sea salt and pepper

Ideally you should soak the rice for 8 hours before cooking. If you are short on time just rinse the rice. Put the rice and stock in a heavy based saucepan, with a tightly fitting lid, bring to the boil then turn down to the lowest simmer you can for approximately 40 minutes. At forty minutes, test if it is cooked. It should be chewy but not hard. Sprinkle the frozen peas on top of the rice, put the lid back on and allow to cook and allow to cook for a further 5 minutes. When the peas are cooked let the rice stand for two minutes which will allow it to fluff up naturally. Tip the contents into a bowl and lightly stir in the mint, lemon, olive oil and seasoning.

PUY LENTILS SERVED WITH BEETROOT AND GOAT CHEESE

Even though this recipe is in the index for erectile dysfunction it really is a great all rounder – it helps the blood circulate throughout the body, not just the penis. If you have cold fingers, pale toes, if you have headaches or you have a bruise that won't go away this will help shift and move blood to all the extremities, reducing pain by bringing nourishing life-giving blood. A woman's genitalia does not have to rise to the occasion but it still has to fill with blood and produce lubricating fluid for intercourse to be pleasurable. Where energy flows, blood goes – it is essential that blood travels to every part of the body to bring nourishing oxygen, energy and moisture.

Stagnation brings disease and death
Movement brings health and life
- Chinese proverb

As I mentioned in an earlier beetroot recipe, this fantastic little vegetable is great at getting the body to produce Nitrous Oxide, which helps expand the blood vessels helping flow. The lentils produce slow release energy, which will help to balance blood sugars and stop the onset of Diabetes, which can be a killer for erections. The fresh herbs, lemons and oils stimulate liver function, which further aids the flow of blood and Chi. Flat leaf parsley is an excellent source of vitamin c and calcium which is needed for the nerves to respond in both male and female genitalia to engorge with blood and fluid.

2 onions
2 carrots
2 sticks celery
2 cloves garlic
500g puy lentils
3 bay leaves
Large sprig of thyme
1 tsp. ground black pepper
1 litre vegetable stock

Dressing

3 tbsp. olive oil
1 tbsp. balsamic vinegar
Juice of lemon
100g flat leaf parsley, roughly chopped
4 cooked beetroots, chopped into bite size pieces
200g goat cheese roll sliced into disks
Handful chopped walnuts

Finely chop the onion, celery and carrot. Add the oil to a heavy-based saucepan and gently fry the vegetables for a couple of minutes so that they begin to soften. Tip in the puy lentils with the bay leaves, thyme, ground black pepper and vegetable stock. Bring to the boil then simmer for about 35 minutes until the lentils are tender and the stock has evaporated. Toss the lentils in the vinaigrette and pour out onto a large serving platter adding salt and pepper to taste. Scatter the goat cheese disks, flat leaf parsley, chopped walnuts and the bite-sized beetroot over the warm lentils. Salivate as aromas fill the air. Happy Munching!

LOVING THE TOMATO

I like to think of love as an energy which has to be generated internally. Like a dynamo light on a bicycle that only lights as you cycle. The harder you pedal the brighter the light becomes. This light is love and we have to generate that energy ourselves. If we use external situations, people, places and stories then the foundation of love is built on sand and can slip away as situations change, people and places move in and out of our lives. Instead of waiting for your divorce to finalize, your wedding day or the birth of your child to find love – be in love with your day, love who you are – take time to ask yourself, what would you like to do today, what would you like to eat today. The nitty gritty elements of life get in the way sometimes and we say to ourselves I'll take a walk on the beach when I've cleaned the house or I'll get some lunch when I've finished this project. In my life, there are things I don't want to do and I think this may be the case for others. But if I constantly put those things before the things I like to do I am sending signals to the body that I don't love it, that love can wait, that life is hard, a struggle, full of hard work. But life is a succulent, juicy cherry. Create the space to make love in your life, that is what a happy well-loved life is all about.

I like to sit outside and read a book, I don't like housework. I used to believe that I HAD to hoover before I could enjoy reading a book but from experience I now know that if I give time to read the book, hoovering isn't half bad. Or I hoover because I love to have a clean house in which to read a book. If I focus on the result, getting there becomes part of the love. My mistake previously was that I never got to the reading the book, there was always the bath to clean or the washing to fold. Some other drudgery that had to be done before I earnt the good times. But no more! Now I put my own love first, top of the list, as priority. It takes trust to believe that putting yourself first builds a happy life.

Falling in love takes courage especially when you fall in love with yourself. Treating yourself as a lover by paying attention to yourself, giving yourself compliments, respecting yourself by listening to your needs and doing things that make you feel special, takes bravery.

People who are in love with life seek out what brings them pleasure and attract their desires like a magnet. When you are in the moment and asking yourself what you want, life stops being a struggle. If you don't trust this is true just make a start, baby steps -make space twice a day, once in the morning, once in the evening to ask yourself what would you like to do right now? - go for a run, feel the air in your lungs and see the grand sky above you or time off from a run and an extra half hour in bed. What would you like to eat? - something delicious, nutritious and healthy or a Jaffa cake. Let life be fun, let it be joyous, let yourself be free to choose love at least twice a day and once you see that everything doesn't fall apart when you do what you want, you can build on that until your life becomes full of love and that light generated from using the internal love muscle.

How can I encapsulate all that self-love in a recipe? Rome for me is a city of love. Many great memories of adventures on Vespas through narrow streets, making hair wraps on the Spanish Steps, exploring the Vatican with an older man who would become my lover and traveling alone, church to church in quiet seclusion with a sketchbook and pencil, being brought to tears by the beauty of the sculptures. The following recipe is quintessentially Italian and reminds me of that city. It is a simple and fresh dish which if made with care for the ingredients, makes something elevated and graceful.

INSALATA CAPRESE

Serves 2

250g tomatoes
3 fresh mozzarella balls
15-20 basil leaves

Slice the tomatoes into disks, sprinkle them with the best quality sea salt. Leave them sit on a plater while you slice up the mozzarella cheese and tear up the fresh basil leaves. Depending on how much time I have will depend on how I arrange them on the plate. Even scattered quickly creates a tasteful look. Place the tomatoes on the mozzarella, sprinkle over the basil leaves and drizzle extra virgin olive oil over the ingredients to serve.

BAKED TOMATOES

Serves 4

This recipe is perfect to have in the summer months when tomatoes are at their peak and it is, of course, the time of the heart in Chinese Medicine. A tomato even looks like a heart with its blood-red outside and cavities inside. Tomatoes are a fruit but wisdom tells us not to put it in a fruit salad as it has a slightly bitter flavour and does not play well with grapes and pineapple. It is this bitter flavour that serves the heart in Chinese Medicine. In western medicine it is their high lycopene and potassium content that dilate and protect the blood vessels, meaning lower blood pressure and reduced risk of heart disease.

Studies[24] have also found that Lycopene causes significant membrane damage to Candida Albicans growth more commonly known as thrush. In this way, tomatoes have considerable anti fungal properties. Unlike other vegetables that lose their minerals when cooked, lycopene is more easily absorbed by the body when cooked so this recipe is fantastic for using up the delicious red fruit during an abundant summer and storing them for later use as the weather grows colder. I like to use cherry tomatoes for this recipe just because they are easier to cut but if you want to use larger tomatoes just cut them in quarters.

---

24 Journal of Microbiology and Biotechnology. [01 Nov 2007, 17(11):1797-1804].Type: Research Support, Non-U.S. Gov't, Journal Article

500g cherry tomatoes
Sea salt
50ml olive oil (optional)

Cut the tomatoes in half and place them on a baking tray, sprinkled with quality sea salt.

Pop them in a preheated hot oven at 200°C , then turn off the oven, shut the door and let them semi oven dry overnight. In the morning when the tray has cooled, scrape them with a spatula into a glass jar. If you want you can drizzle the olive oil at this point and they will keep for longer. If you want to keep the taste of summer over the winter you can cover them completely in oil, preventing the air from rotting these sweet, chewy tomatoes.

Before buying tomatoes, smell them, if they don't smell like tomatoes don't buy them. Leave them at home on a plate to ripen in the sunshine, this will make them all the sweeter. Never put tomatoes in the fridge.

PEA AND ROAST GARLIC SOUP

Serves 4

The physical heart can influence emotions and vice versa. If we are overweight, full of toxins or unfit, the heart has to work hard to circulate blood. This leads to shortness of breath, palpitations, dizziness which in turn creates emotions such as anxiety, fear, frustration and fuzzy thinking to name a few. It is important and easy to keep the heart healthy by eating plenty of fruit and vegetables, especially those that are grown in the summer. Pea's are perfect, I love the little sweet green balls bursting with vitamin C and sunshine. They remind me of happiness and summer days.

I recommend this next recipe to calm and open the heart. If you get over excited and climax too early you need to fortify the kidneys as well as pacify the heart. The warmth of the soup together with the fortifying garlic will help to tone your energy and stop you from climaxing quickly - the energy is a slow and steady release. If you want to make this in the summer you can use fresh peas adding mint to lift the soup and the parmesan in the winter for extra comfort. Joy is the antidote to the emotion of bitterness that damages the heart - so love your peas and all that is.

250g Marrowfat peas
1 tbsp. sunflower oil
25g butter
1 or 2 onions
1 stick of celery
2 inches Kombu seaweed
2 litres stock
1 Roasted Garlic bulb
Handful of chopped, fresh mint or 75g grated parmesan Cheese

Roast the garlic beforehand by cutting around the top of the bulb but not all the way through. You still want to be able to hold the garlic together using the central stalk. When you can see inside the tops of all the cloves, place on a baking tray and drizzle over the olive oil. Place in a hot oven 170/180°C for 20-30 minutes. When the garlic is roasted it will look a toffee colour and can even start to pop out of the papery casing of the bulb.

Soak the peas overnight in plenty of cold water. When you are ready to make the soup begin by chopping the onions and frying them gently in the oil and butter. After a few minutes add the celery and let them fry, stirring occasionally on a medium heat for about 10 minutes until they are golden and translucent. Next add the strained rehydrated peas, stirring them in with the onions, celery and the stock. At this point, you can add an inch or two of kombu seaweed to increase the mineral content of the dish and help the peas to cook. Bring the soup to a boil then reduce to a low simmer for at least an hour. Test to see if the peas are tender, if they are, squeeze out all the roasted garlic clove paste from inside the bulb into the pot, and liquidize the contents together, I find easiest with a hand blender. Now your soup is finished. You can add the mint or cheese or eat as is.

EXOTIC STRAWBERRIES

Vitamin C is essential for the production of collagen. This improves elasticity in cells throughout the body, including the arteries, which can harden and cause problems such as high blood pressure and heart disease. Collagen is probably most famous for keeping skin cells plump and resilient. Most fruits are high in vitamin C but this recipe is all about the sexy little strawberry. This special fruit also contains ellagic acid, which prevents collagen damage from overexposure to sun damaging UV-B rays and plenty of antioxidants to scavenge up those free radicals that circulate through our bloodstream. A study conducted by the Harvard School of Public Health[25] shows these antioxidants also reduce inflammation in the body.

In Chinese Medicine, strawberries are named as the queen of fruits. They are red in colour which benefit the heart and they nourish the kidneys and the Chi by cooling and bringing moisture to the body. Use strawberries as an aphrodisiac to get the juices flowing. Perfect for those intimate whisperings as they moisten all mucous membranes especially preventing dry mouth and throat. Strawberries are high in the B-vitamin, Folate and folic acid, which is recommended for women about to conceive or in the early stages of pregnancy as it helps with the development of the baby's brain, skull and spinal cord.

Strawberries shouldn't be refrigerated or washed until you are about to eat them. They will keep on a plate lined with a paper towel for a day or so before they start to go mushy.

400g thick natural greek yogurt
400g strawberries
2 tbsp. of agave syrup
2 tsp. rosewater (optional)
75g chopped pistachio

Hull and quarter the strawberries leaving them to marinade in the agave and rosewater for 4 hours. Take ½ of the soaked strawberries and mash with a fork. Gently fold the mushed strawberries into the yogurt so that the pink ripples beautifully through the white. Scatter the remaining strawberries and pistachios over the furrowed yogurt and spoon lovingly into the mouth.

Take care where you source your strawberries, those that are not ripened on the plant can cause an hay fever style allergic reaction with runny eyes, inflamed hot mucus membranes and a lot of sneezing. I know, I've been there. Sometimes they are pumped full of sugar to make them taste sweeter, which is debilitating for the stomach and spleen, creating heat and inflammation. Organic and/or homegrown are best.

25 https://www.health.harvard.edu/heart-health/eat-blueberries-and-strawberries-three-times-per-week

CHOCOLATE CHERRIES

The heart's emotion in Chinese Medicine is joy and expansion. So fall in love every day - find something that holds your attention and makes your soul sing, something that makes you feel good to be alive. Be grateful for the small things, the sunshine, the rain, your breath, your health, your mind. Don't wish them to be different. See them as they are and love them for the qualities that they have.

Food is a pathway to love. Ask yourself what you would like to eat and search it out. Use your wisdom and your heart to fill your life full of love. At this moment of typing, I am drinking coffee and eating Jaffa cakes because that is what I really wanted on my first day of holidays; no kids, no clients, no responsibilities - delicious - of course if I wanted that every day or if I felt I had to have coffee and Jaffa cakes to be happy then things would be off balance but I love my food, all my food, there is no good or bad food, just food that doesn't suit me at this time. Follow your heart, which is truly intelligent. Self-care and self-love is not all about candles, chocolates, holidays and massage. It is being really connected and truthful to the light of your being. That innate intelligence knows when to say yes or no, honouring and loving the decisions you make.

My favourite most orgasmic recipe at the moment is chocolate covered cherries. They are so simple yet so special. Cherries contain many antioxidants and the chemical melatonin which has a calming effect on brain neurons regulating regular sleep patterns and quieting the nervous system. They are red in colour and bittersweet in flavour, perfect for the heart in Chinese Medicine. They are full of antioxidants which helps the blood flow easier reducing gout and other conditions of heat and stiffness in the body. They also contain high levels of potassium which help reduce blood pressure and aid circulation.

CHOCOLATE COVERED CHERRIES

Serves 2

12-15 sweet cherries
50g fairtrade dark chocolate (75% cocoa)

Melt the chocolate in a basin which rests over a saucepan of boiling water. Holding the stalks of the cherries dunk and cover the fruit in the chocolate. Place them on a clean plate in the fridge to cool and harden.

There is no better lover
than a cool breeze on a hot
day
As it strokes my calves
And flutters against my
thighs
Cool along my lips
As I lie here naked
knees apart
sun heating me
where normally remains
dark and hidden

it is seen and beats with
blood and warmth
relaxing and opening
to allow the sun to be
swallowed
to enter

ACUPRESSURE POINTS

HEART 6 – YIN ACCUMULATION

As a major gathering point for Yin, it can moisten and reduce dryness in the body. It brings calming restfulness, reducing anxiety and night-sweats.

HEART 7 – MIND DOOR

Nourishes blood and brings the heart home for deep rest. Brilliant for insomnia, palpitations and anxiety. It aids a calm clear mind aiding the recovery of memories. It restores peace and love when the heart broken.

Find both points by drawing a line from the inner tip of the little finger across the palm to the inside crease of the wrist. Heart 7 is on the crease and measure one thumb width below for Heart 6.

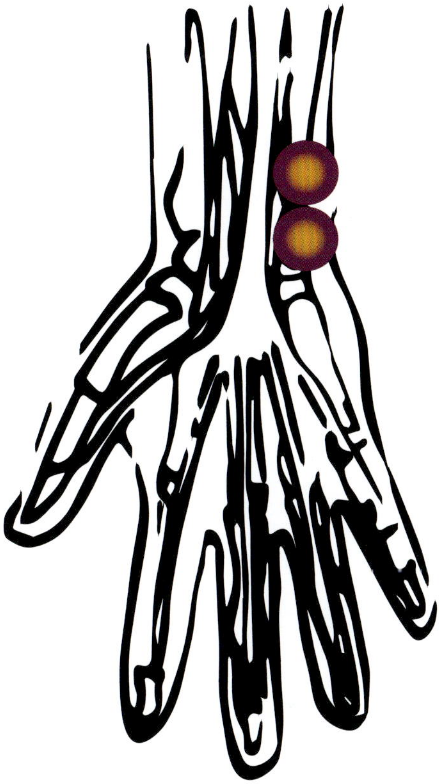

SMALL INTESTINE 17 – HEAVENLY APPEARANCE

Reduces glandular swelling and aids heartfelt communication by increasing circulation to the brain and opening the throat.

Find by first turning the head to the side so the sternocleidomastoid muscle is prominent, then find the space between the corner of the jaw and the sternocleidomastoid muscle.

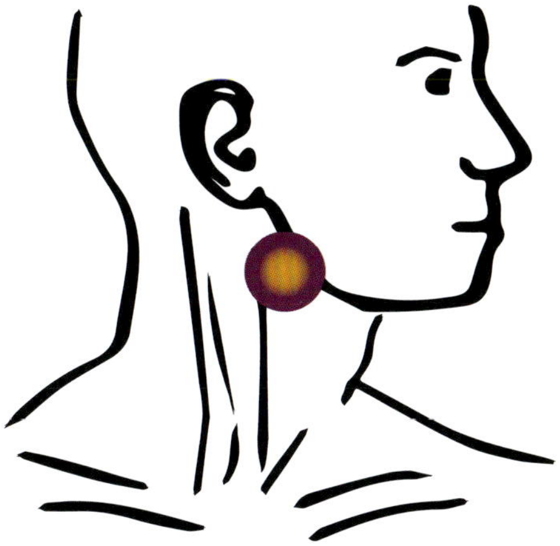

Late Summer Demons

Pack them up in boxes and
brackets
So there's no excuse for
Escape in the higgledy-
piggledy
Misjudgment of things
Neat and tidy
Order of the mind

But then what space
What openings for the deep
orange-brown
Sweet and warm orange
earth
To mix and mingle, shimmy
and pirouette
Wriggle and roar with
laughter
In the warm juicy wetness.

Chapter 6
SPLEEN / STOMACH

I haven't seen such
attractive hands for a long
time
I know those hands from
long ago
Unbelievably so
Strong, wide like paddles
That could carry an egg
softly across a dessert
Gentle fingers moving
independently
The pads touching
themselves
Softly brushing, gently
tapping
Down the hills of my ribs

OVERVIEW
THE ART OF ASKING AND RECEIVING

The stomach and spleen in Chinese Medicine represent the time of transformation when summer is turning to autumn. The berries are ripe and the earth is fruitful. In Christian and Pagan traditions this would be celebrated as harvest festival time when we give thanks to mother earth for the bounty she provides to us as her children. It is a similar energy in Chinese Medicine. The stomach and spleen are all about the bond between mother and child. It's how we cherish our bodies and nurture it as a mother would take care of a child, with deeply loving touch and embrace. Stomach and spleen are in charge of the flesh of the body, its tone and texture. The body loves to be touched, hugged, stroked, and held. In western medicine, the spleen and pancreas are responsible for the production of insulin and regulates blood sugar. It is no coincidence that the flavour for the spleen is sweet. However, rather than reaching straight for the chocolate bar, which may give momentary satisfaction, try wholesome sweet flavours within grains such as millet or rice. Mix them with starchy roasted root vegetables such as carrot, butternut squash or sweet potato.

From the Chinese perspective, there is nothing wrong with sweet food but if we overindulge, as with any area of life, it causes problems. My body is very wise and it speaks to me with its cravings. Just like a mother whose child is constantly asking for sweets, I know I cannot live on chocolate ice cream alone. I use cravings as a message from my body and apply Chinese Medicine to interpret and take responsibility for meeting my own needs in the most loving way possible. The free interactive tool found on www.joannefaulkner.ie can help you assess how you are feeling and what you need. ***The spleen with its sweet flavour, reigns over satisfaction but unless we are truly in touch with our desires and take action to fulfil them accordingly we can feel a constant craving like an addict with an emptiness that can never be filled with Oreos or orgasms.***

There are many ways in which to support the spleen but only when we learn to connect with the abundance of the earth and our own heart/body wisdom. But only when we learn to connect with the abundance of the earth and our own heart/body wisdom, can we discern what we need to feel truly satisfied and loved. Once you know what you need and ask for what you want, the challenge is in knowing how to receive. The stomach together with mouth, saliva and gastric juices transform food for the spleen to assimilate the nutrients. It's all about receiving. No matter how much healthy food we eat, unless we are open to receive, the spleen cannot collect, accept and metabolize the gifts of the Earth.

It can be difficult to ask for support in our lives and sometimes just as hard to receive it. Even if someone has cleaned the house for you, peeled the potatoes, mowed the lawn or made you a cup of tea, maybe it is not done quite the way you like it, it didn't come at the right time or in the right mug. Instead of feeling gratitude for the care of a thoughtful cuppa, we reject it and the person who made it. This is only a small example of how perhaps the world, with all its gifts and bounty, doesn't meet our needs in exactly the way we would like and we feel dissatisfied, unfulfilled and uncared for. These barriers to receiving create cravings and deep longings that are difficult to fill if care and love come with conditions.

By communicating our needs we are more likely to have them met, but to communicate means making ourselves open and vulnerable. We take a risk by really saying what we want because perhaps we will be judged and abandoned. Sometimes it is more comfortable to be a victim– unsupported, alone and misunderstood. The feeling of isolation may be preferable to possible rejection as it gives a mistaken sense of control. It is always more painful in the long term to deny who we are, what we feel and what we need, even if it satisfies someone else's need or placates our fears of rejection in the short term.

Managing and satisfying needs in life and relationships is not always easy. The bumps in the road are opportunities to explore and deepen the understanding of who you are and how you can love yourself more.

How can you improve and develop relationships with everything and everyone around you unless you relish the experience of what you don't want? That will bring true clarity of what you do want and propel you in that direction.

Ships operate on feedback loops. They constantly change direction to compensate for tides and currents. They have a fixed destination but to reach it they must constantly change the way they get there. Our journey throughout life is similar. We may have goals such as peace, happiness or long term love but how we get there will change due to external experiences and internal perceptions.

Enjoy the ride, keep talking, keep communicating, especially with yourself. Observe your process and ask for what you need, then have faith that you are completely loveable and fantastic, and deserve to receive it.

Sometimes low self-esteem makes it difficult to receive. We think we are not worthy, we don't deserve the gifts or compliments given to us. Perhaps the culturally-induced idea that nothing comes for free means that open-heartedly receiving can be difficult. The idea that giving and receiving is conditional upon effort or worthiness is often deeply, culturally ingrained. Practice seeing what's already there and being grateful. The more you acknowledge what you have the more you will receive. I often focus on the one little bit that's missing rather than seeing how fantastic the bigger picture is; the one recipe that didn't work out, the poor grammar in the sentence I wrote, my belly which is too wobbly, the kitchen table always needs clearing and the floor which is always grubby. I'm grateful to write this book, to remind myself that I am completely loveable, my house is secure and warm and that my body, even though it takes a pounding, still gets up in the morning and is beautiful. I love the power of words and that as humans we can communicate so well with them. I love that there are so many amazing stories to read, watch and write. I love that creating dishes and cooking comes easy to me; *gratitude is the key. We all have something to be grateful for, every day - water, sunshine, lungs, lips and toes.*

SPLEEN TANTRA
SACRED TOUCH, LIPS AND MOUTH

If spleen energy is out of balance the mind can become full of worry and anxiousness. It may be hard to settle as we constantly grasp for solutions. Incessant thoughts become distractions from the calm wherein true peace and satisfaction lie. As an antidote, we can use the breath as a tool to calm the mind. By placing our thoughts on the breath we allow them to disappear like clouds drifting across the sky. Clouds come and go, thoughts come and go, but during this exercise, we don't follow them.

The spleen meridian opens into mouth and lips, relating again to the mother and baby archetype where satisfaction is all about the mouth, from sucking the thumb in the womb to searching instantly for the mother's nipple. It is the sensory organ most used to self soothe, from eating and drinking to smoking and kissing. For the mother, when the nipples are stimulated by the child, the hormone oxytocin is released and the milk is let down. Oxytocin increases the bond between mother and baby and has become known as the love hormone or the cuddle chemical. However, this love hormone is not exclusive to new mothers and babies it can be produced by all of us using the spleen connected, sensory organs of the mouth, the lips and the flesh of the body. For all genders, sexual activity releases oxytocin even hugging and caressing will do the trick, increasing empathy and attachment. Research has shown that there are high levels of oxytocin in couples for the first six months of a relationship.[26] After which it was shown to decline. To maintain high levels of oxytocin try this exercise together with plenty of hugs to support your stomach and spleen. It encourages relaxation and trust, which enhances the body's ability to receive. It is the ability to accept the gifts given which will truly satisfy.

We must practice receiving touch every day. Too often we are in our head and forget how our body feels. Remember to feel the rim of the mug filled with hot tea against your lips, feel your thighs as you pull on your underwear, feel the earth or at least your shoes against the soles of your feet, massage your own shoulders and rub your own neck and chest remembering the feel of your own skin against skin. Understand that we are responsible for our touch and our own satisfaction. A good place to start is with stillness and silence. It is the Yin from which all Yang arises. Within the dark void of Yin, it is essential to use the breath.

26 https://www.ncbi.nlm.nih.gov/pmc/articles/PMC3936960/

To begin the exercise:

Sit or lie quietly and calmly breathe. If thoughts come let them dissolve with the breath. Then place your hands on your body; anywhere that is calling for touch and feels comfortable is a good place to begin. Apply enough pressure that you feel the body pushing back. Practice on yourself, stroke yourself so lightly it's annoyingly uncomfortable then push so hard the body tenses up and wants to shove you off. In the middle of those extremes is who you are and what you need. Use your hands to touch all of your body. Is it the same all over or are some areas more sensitive? Are there areas that want a vigorous rub? Or are some areas just calling to be held? *By listening to the body and what it needs, you will find surrender and receptivity.* Find the hollows of the body, such as backs of the knees, inner elbows, collar-bones, arches of feet, indents of ankles and hold them. Feel as they fill with energy, saying yes to loving touch.

There are many nerve endings in the vagina and on the penis which all feed pleasure chemicals to the brain. Through past physical or emotional trauma, the nerves can become damaged and different parts of the genitals inside and out can become desensitized or knotted and tense. Constantly asking and receiving gentle massages of the genital area without the aim of stimulation will allow the body and the nerves to heal and restore.

This practice is also very effective with a partner. This is not an exercise to attain orgasm, rather used to blend the Yin of the empty mind with the Yang of the body's energy. Both the giver and receiver can use the breath as a way to stay connected to the body in an open and spacious way. As your partner caresses and touches you, use the breath to stay conscious and connected to the body. Don't allow distractions by thoughts about your partner's expectations, reactions or feelings. Don't leave the body and start thinking about the plans for tomorrow. This is an opportunity to communicate and listen to your partner. By finding non-sexual ways of communicating with the body, you and your partner will better understand each other and become better able to explore and find new sources of connection and pleasure. It is important to remember that how you like to be touched is not necessarily how others wish to be touched. Together with essential feedback from the receiver, let your hands receptivity guide you and let the oxytocin flow. This practice can be done naked or clothed as you choose. It can be a five-minute quick back rub in the kitchen or a full day of silent exchange in the bedroom.

Then there is kissing. This satiates the spleen's sensory organ of the lips and connects the heart's sensory organ, the tongue. Kissing is a great way to relax and let go. Nerves, which stimulate the parasympathetic nervous system, are all over your mouth and lips. In this exercise, it's all about allowing your partner to explore your mouth and lips for a few minutes. Fully surrender to the experience of being kissed without having to give anything in return. Then switch, and immerse yourself completely in the act of kissing your partner.

Talk to them only with your tongue and lips; tell them who you are, how you feel and how you feel about them.

Spleen / Stomach
RECIPES

ROASTED PEACHES WITH DARK CHOCOLATE

Serves 2

Peaches are a wonderfully sexy food. They look like a super soft, fuzzy bum, so I am tempted to categorize peaches as an aphrodisiac for the index, especially as I prepared this special summer dessert with a lover in mind. But in Chinese Medicine, peaches are a potent fruit to clear stagnant blood and improve flow in the abdominal area. They are a warming, Yin fruit that brings moisture to the lower abdomen increasing bowel movements and preventing vaginal dryness.

For women, peaches can clear sluggishness of the menstrual cycle and improve the blood flow. This increased circulation means reducing period pain, hot flashes, uterine endometriosis and fibroids. For men they assist blood flow to the genitals, helping with erectile dysfunction, which is a common problem for those with diabetes and can reduce blood flow to the small capillaries in the penis. Peaches are a fruit packed with fiber slowing down the process of glucose absorption. Peaches are a sweet treat to strengthen the spleen without the blood sugar spikes.

In our modern supermarket shopping peaches can be a tricky fruit. We buy them rock hard and leave them sitting around for days, waiting for them to soften only to find as we looked away for a second, they have gone mouldy. This is a recipe to sweeten and soften those hard-to-ripen peaches. The recipe is much better with soft fruit but it will work with hardened flesh, it will just mean the stone is more difficult to remove. It is best not to keep fruit in the fridge, store it in a bowl on the countertop, in the sunshine. The stomach and spleen don't like cold food, they like warm, ripe, sweet stuff. I know that means that some food may ripen and rot but that is a good thing. Food is meant to do that. If it doesn't, it is not food, don't eat it.

5 peaches
50g fair trade dark chocolate
(at least 75% cacao)
150ml pressed apple juice
1 cinnamon stick
Tbsp. of maple syrup to drizzle

Cut the five peaches in half, removing the stones. Place them in a baking dish, flat side up so that they wobble. Pour the apple juice over top and drizzle the maple syrup to taste. Place a cinnamon stick into the juice on the bottom of the baking dish. Cover and seal with tin foil, sliding the dish into the oven for 20-30 minutes at 180°C: The harder the peaches, the longer the baking. When they are cooked, a sharp knife should pierce the flesh like butter. Using a large spoon, scoop out the peach halves intact and place them on a plate, use the lovely hollow in the center to place a small chunk of the dark chocolate and spoon over the cooking syrup from the bottom of the baking dish. These make a perfect romantic dessert as you can pick up the soft self-contained peach halves, feed them to each other and lick your sticky fingers afterward.

MANY WAYS TO EAT A GOJI

In the West, goji berries have become known as a super-food, full of antioxidants, helping to clean and nourish the blood, boost the immune system and stop macular degeneration of the eyes. In Chinese Medicine, they have always been a super-food tonifying and supporting many organs of the body. They are red so they nourish the heart, aiding transportation of the blood. They enter the body through liver channels opening out into the eyes, aiding vision and fat metabolism. Their sweet flavour nourishes the spleen, encouraging the building of blood and the balancing of blood sugars. Elevated blood sugar levels cause nerve and blood vessel damage, which impacts all areas of the body but especially the small blood vessels in the penis. This may lead to erectile dysfunction, as good blood flow is needed to enable and maintain an erection. The spleen also maintains the blood vessels, keeping them strong so the blood flows. Managing blood sugars is essential for all genital stimulation and lubrication.

Goji berries are mentioned for the first time in *Shen Nong's Herbal Classic* believed to have been written in approximately 2800 BC. A famous use is in the "Five Ancestors Teapills" which is a formula of 5 herbs created by Dr. Li ting in the Tang Dynasty (618 – 907 AD). The tea is still used for male impotence, premature ejaculation, infertility, premature greying and constant urination. All of the conditions listed for the tea relate to the kidney the organ, which is responsible for the production and management of semen. Traditional Chinese Medicine counts the production of semen in men and menstrual blood or pregnancy in women as some of the biggest strains on Jing. As discussed earlier in the Yin Yang chapter it is one of the three treasures. Jing must be nurtured. There are many recipes in which to use goji berries but you can munch them raw as well. They taste slightly sweet like raisins. In the following recipe, I use almond milk to further nurture kidney and lung energy and aid digestion.

As in all things beware of too much of a good thing. These little berries contain high levels of vitamin A which can interfere with other bodily functions if taken in massive quantities so I recommend 2-4 teaspoons per day is an average serving depending on your body size. They can thin the blood so take care if mixing with blood-thinning medication. As a member of the deadly nightshade family along with potatoes, aubergines, tomatoes and peppers, also check for allergies. Finally, if I haven't put you off these wonderful sweet gems beware of added colours. Some brands add extra red, which is not, in fact, extra healthy.

WARM GOJI SMOOTHIE

Serves 1

250ml almond milk or rice milk
2 tsp. goji berries
1 tsp. vanilla

Simmer all ingredients together for 5 minutes then blend until smooth.

SAVOURY CONGEE WITH GOJI BERRY

Serves 2

In western medicine, the spleen and pancreas are responsible for the production of insulin, which manages blood sugars. The spleen in Chinese Medicine is governed by the sweet flavour and the emotion is satisfaction. If the spleen isn't functioning properly it's easy to see how signals regarding sugars can become misinterpreted. We can get caught in the highs and lows of instant blood sugar hits such as chocolate, biscuits and cakes, looking for the spleen comfort and gratification that they bring. High blood sugars damage blood vessels and nerves but they also create a damp condition in Chinese Medicine, which can lead to an overgrowth of the Candida Albicans fungus causing Thrush. This common condition can occur in men as well as women and can make sex uncomfortable, even painful. To balance the blood sugars, whilst still giving the body a food hug, we can use starchy, whole-grains that release their sugars more slowly than simple processed white carbohydrates.

In Chinese Medicine traditional congee porridge is a very powerful food. The longer you cook it the more powerful it becomes. It is made from grains that are cooked to form a soupy porridge to which all sorts of therapeutic ingredients can be added.

Traditionally, congee is cooked for many hours and that's easy enough to do if you begin the night before in a slow cooker and let its magic work throughout the night. However, with the recipe below I use a quick(ish) version. Millet is much underused. It is a seed, very high in B vitamins. It's very soothing for the stomach and very easy to digest. I often use it in place of bread when making stuffing.

85g of Goji berries
25g red dates
1 inch of fresh ginger root
300g millet
1 litre water adding more later as the congee thickens
3 large handfuls of spinach
3 chopped scallions
1 tbsp. miso paste
Tamari to taste

Peel and chop the ginger, adding it with the goji berries, red dates and millet to the water in a medium sized pot. Bring the mixture to the boil and then let it simmer with a good fitting lid on, for at least 45 minutes, the longer the better. Stir every so often, making sure it's not drying out or sticking to the bottom of the pan. When you are ready to eat the congee dissolve the miso paste into some hot water from a recently boiled kettle. Add this to the mixture, stirring in the spinach, scallions and tamari. It's now ready to eat, so find a cosy soft spot and a big spoon.

SWEET CONGEE WITH GOJI BERRY

Serves 2 / 3

For this recipe, in addition to the goji berries, I have added Chinese red dates. They are not as sweet as palm dates but they are packed full of antioxidants and vitamin C. Traditionally they are given at Chinese New Year as a symbol of health and longevity. Red dates have long been used in Chinese Medicine for strengthening the spleen energy. Specifically, they help build blood and energy following chronic illness or childbirth. By building blood we can help to regulate menstruation and thereby increase the possibility of pregnancy. For men, they help with the production of healthy semen.

300g white rice, use short-grain white rice for slightly thicker starchier texture
1 litre plus more later as the congee thickens
50g goji berries
8 red dates
3 pears
50g palm dates

Begin by rinsing the rice several times until the water runs more or less clear. Add rice, water, goji berries and palm dates together in a heavy-based pot with a tight-fitting lid. Split open the red dates ensuring there are no stones left inside. Peel the pear, cutting away the flesh from the core and adding both ingredients to the pot. Bring to a boil and simmer on a low heat for at least an hour. Lift the lid occasionally to make sure it has plenty of water and that it's not sticking to the bottom of the pan.

For a new mum, this is a perfect dish. It's sweet and nourishing, easily digested and easily maintained. You can leave it in a slow cooker just heating away, taking a bowl when needed.

KISSABLE VANILLA DUSTING POWDER

Vanilla originates from Central America and was originally used by the Aztecs together with cocoa seeds to produce a much-loved drink made only for special occasions. Vanilla is used predominantly in baking and desserts. Its heady, sweet smell often reduces the need for extra sugar. The scent of vanilla is a powerful mood-enhancer. It induces feelings of pleasure and sweet satisfaction.

If you are buying vanilla make sure you get pure vanilla powder, pods, paste or liquid. Be careful as some are synthetic extracts.

- 50g of corn flour
- 25g of (powdered) icing sugar
- 25g of vanilla powder

Sieve all the above ingredients and store in an airtight container. A decorated glass jar looks pretty and can be kept in the bedroom rather than the kitchen. Although where you choose to play is entirely up to you.

This recipe doesn't keep forever so make sure you play with it regularly. Use a clean soft blusher or new paintbrush to dust all your favourite kissable spots on the body. It can get quite messy as the sugary dusting powder is light and airy so may fall onto the bed-sheets or the floor. I have found that first licking the spot on the body you wish to dust, helps the powder to stick to the body. Enjoy the romantic sensual play of dusting each other with an edible powder. See where the games take you but remember to set ground rules of where you wish to be dusted and where not. Is this powder for the kitchen or the bedroom, and do you really want to lie on your best, dry clean only blanket? Then enjoy the fun tickling and licking each other.

LICKABLE CHOCOLATE BODY PAINT

This is not necessarily the healthiest of recipes but it will address your spleen meridian and bring relaxing, pleasurable satisfaction whether giving or receiving.

6 tbsp. water
Pinch of sea salt
3 tbsp. date or agave syrup
6 tbsp. of coconut oil
4 tbsp. of high-quality cocoa powder
½ tsp. vanilla essence
200ml sterile jar

In a small sauce pan combine the date syrup, salt and water over a medium to high heat, without stirring, dissolve the syrup. Once the syrup has dissolved remove from the heat and add the coconut oil, whisking until combined. Then add the cocoa powder and vanilla, mixing until smooth and pour into the sterilized glass jar.

Test out the chocolate paint on your inner wrist using a pastry brush to make sure it is cool enough to paint it onto the body.

If there are leftovers you can store the jar in the fridge. When you want to use it again simply place the glass jar in a saucepan of water, heating it gently until the chocolate paint melts. I do not recommend a microwave for preparing any type of food, in any way, ever, but especially not for reheating this precious preparation. A microwave heats unevenly and you may end up with unexpected hot spots which can burn your bits.

BUTTERNUT SQUASH AND RED DATE SOUP

Serves 2

This recipe is especially good for anyone who has just given birth, has had recent surgery or just feels exhausted. It builds the blood and harmonizes the stomach. The root vegetables, with their slow-release sugars, give a sweet comforting flavour which nourishes the spleen but it's the Chinese red dates here that are special for building blood. Their red lantern-like appearance has long been used as a symbol of health and longevity. Maybe next time you are visiting a new mum and her baby you could bring Chinese red dates instead of chocolate. Or maybe as well as chocolate.

2 tbsp. of rapeseed or sunflower oil
1-2 onions
3 cloves garlic
1-2 inch fresh ginger root
2 tsp. ground cumin
½ tsp. ground turmeric
1 medium butternut squash
2 medium sweet potatoes
8 Chinese red dates
½ litre stock
1 tin coconut milk (400ml)
Salt and pepper to taste

Fry the chopped onions in the oil on medium heat until soft and translucent then add the garlic, ginger, cumin and turmeric until the spices release their aroma. Skin and de-seed the butternut squash, peel the sweet potato, chop both into bitesize chunks and stir all of these into the frying spices. Add the chopped red dates, cover with stock, pop the lid on, bring to a boil then simmer for 20-30 minutes until the veg is soft. Using a liquidizer or a hand blender, blitz until the soup is creamy. Pour back into the saucepan and add the coconut milk. Heat this through slowly adding salt and pepper to taste. On a very low heat let all the flavours mingle for 5-10 minutes. Take care not to boil the coconut milk otherwise, it will split. This is a great soup to soothe the stomach and large intestine. It is hearty without being heavy.

SWEET POTATO FALAFEL

Serves 10-12 falafel

This recipe was a revelation. It's so easy. I hate waste, which includes wasting space in the oven when I'm cooking. If I'm roasting a chicken you can be guaranteed, I'm also baking bread, making biscuits, probably roasting bulbs of garlic and as I turn off the oven, I'll pop a tray of halved cherry tomatoes for semi sun-drying overnight as the oven cools. Wrapping a couple of sweet potatoes in foil and popping them in empty spaces available in the oven makes me very happy. Scooping out the soft, sweet flesh when cooked, I pop into a squeeze lock bag in the fridge or freezer for whenever I'm ready to add it, to a Thai curry or to sweeten a tomato sauce. Here though, I use it for the perfect vegan snack food, falafel.

Sweet potato is packed full of complex carbohydrates and potassium. They can help with weight loss and balancing blood sugars. Because of their high potassium content, they help to keep your pH balanced. When the body is too acidic due to stress or consumption of acid-forming, refined foods the body looks for calcium, magnesium and potassium. It is far better your body finds it in the food you eat rather than your muscles, teeth and bones.

Too much refined sugar causes acid levels to rise, which encourages fermentation in the body. This decreases oxygen levels and metabolism at a cellular level of the body, meaning cells cannot function properly and we are left with acidosis where inflammation, energy loss, joint pain, yeast infections, liver congestion and arterial damage are common symptoms. The sweet potato, packed full of potassium, is one way to help the blood vessels carry blood properly around the body, reducing inflammation and improving erectile function. However sweet potatoes alone, I doubt, will cure erectile dysfunction. The amount of sugar, refined carbohydrates and other lifestyle choices will also need attention. Sweet Potato Falafel is a wonderfully comforting place to start.

2 medium sweet potatoes
1 tsp. ground cumin
2 garlic cloves
2 tsp. ground coriander
A handful of coriander leaves
½ lemon juice
100g gram (chickpea) flour
1 tbsp. olive oil

You can either leave the potato whole, pierce it with a sharp knife and place it on a baking tray or if they are rather large, you can slice them down the middle and pop them flesh side up to roast until they are softly mashable. After roasting simply scoop or peel them out of their skins and drop the flesh into a bowl. Mix all the other ingredients with the squidgy orange mash and roll them into balls with your hands. Use the oil to coat another baking tray and place the balls on the tray and pop in the oven at 180°C for 20 minutes, turning occasionally so they get brown and crispy all over. Eat hot or cold as they keep well in the fridge for a few days.

ADUKI BEAN AND KALE

Serves 4 as a side

Chi protects the body. When strong and active, it should stop viruses entering and work to expel them once they have entered the body. Protective Chi is warming and moving. However, if the body becomes damp it is difficult for protective Chi to flow. Too much sugar or the body's inability to process sugar creates this damp condition and so our immune system becomes impaired. We can feel heavy, bloated, confused, fatigued, foggy-headed, suffer poor memory recall and become sensitive or allergic to foods or substances in the environment. Also, when our immunity becomes impaired, invasive bacteria can take hold.

Our digestive system is full of bacteria, some of which assist our digestion and assimilation of nutrients like Lactobacillus, Acidophilus as well as others that are not so helpful such as Candida Albicans. It is normal to have some candida present but when it flourishes out of control in a damp intestinal system it prevents absorption of amino acid and stimulates the immune system to a point where it cannot cope. Autoimmune conditions such as arthritis, lupus, psoriasis, Crohn's disease and ulcerative colitis can occur as a result. Where immunity is impaired, this bacteria can travel around the body especially to the sexual organs creating common conditions such as thrush, vaginitis, prostatitis and anal itching, all of which can make sex uncomfortable. Promoting the health of the spleen and managing blood sugars is essential to prevent any fungal overgrowth and maintain the Yin Yang bacterial balance.

Aduki beans are great at removing dampness from the body. If you can't get them you can substitute kidney beans as both are high in fibre to cleanse the digestive tract, increase beneficial bacteria and remove excess cholesterol. In traditional Chinese Medicine however, the aduki bean is esteemed above all others. Recent research has made the connection between aduki beans and improved glycemic control in patients with type 2 diabetes.[27] So supporting the spleen.

2 tbsp. organic sunflower or rapeseed oil
1 onion
3 cloves of garlic
150g of dried aduki beans (450g cooked)
250g curly kale
3 tbsp. tamari
3 tbsp. water
Pinch of chopped wakame seaweed
1 tsp. black sesame seeds
1 or 2 tbsp. of sesame oil

It is possible to buy tinned aduki beans but it's always better to prepare them from scratch yourself. To do so, soak them overnight in plenty of water. Drain water and pop them in a pot with plenty of fresh water and a strip of Kombu seaweed. Bring to a boil and simmer for approximately 45 minutes until they are tender. They will approximately triple in weight when soaked and cooked so measure out approximately 150g of dried beans to make 450g. When they are cooked use in the recipe as follows:

Gently fry the chopped onion on medium heat until they are translucent. Add the garlic and fry for a further 2 minutes. Meanwhile, rinse the beans and add to the onions and garlic. Chop the kale into fine strips and pop into the pot. Mix in the other ingredients while cooking and add the water, the tamari and the seaweed. Place a good fitting lid over the pot and allow to gently simmer for 7-10 minutes depending on how crunchy you like your kale. When soft, remove the lid and let the remaining water evaporate. Toss out onto a large plate scattering over the sesame seeds and drizzle over the sesame oil.

This recipe serves 2 or 4 if you accompany it with rice to make a complete meal full of amino acids.

27 https://www.sciencedirect.com/science/article/pii/S0926669013005815
So, this study is from 2013, testing on rats. I did a quick search and found this from 2018 on humans: https://www.ncbi.nlm.nih.gov/pmc/articles/PMC5953312/

BIG BEAN SALAD

Serves 6 - 8

This salad is simple to put together. It works on multiple organs in the body. The soluble fibre within the beans is great for helping cholesterol and other waste products to bind and leave the body through the large intestine. Again, the fibre helps the large intestine to keep moving and expel those wastes from the body. However, it is here in the stomach/spleen chapter because of their balance of protein and carbohydrates. They are so good at providing a slow, steady source of energy preventing the peaks that can come after eating refined carbohydrates.

All dried beans work as a diuretic, removing excess fluid from the body but chickpeas specifically work on removing dampness from the spleen. Keeping candida at bay, which thrives in warm damp conditions and from excess refined sugars in the body.

Green beans are in this recipe to add colour and freshness to the dish. The silicon they contain is discussed further in the kidney/bladder chapter but here I've added them because they add a different soft texture to the dish. The warmth from the just-cooked green beans soothes the stomach and helps aid digestion. If beans are difficult for you to digest try adding a little seaweed to the dish as this will help to break down the beans during digestion.

250g french green beans
1 tin Borlotti beans (approx. 400g)
1 tin Pinto beans (approx. 400g)
1 tin chickpeas (approx. 400g)
2 large tbsp. of fresh/frozen thyme

Dressing

2 tbsp. honey
2 tbsp. balsamic vinegar
2 tbsp. rapeseed oil
8 finely shredded sundried tomatoes
Juice of 1 lemon
Gomasio (sesame salt) and pepper

Bring a pot of salted water to a boil and trim the stalks from the french green beans. An easy way to do this is to hold all the beans in your hands at once. Tap them on the chopping board so that all the stalks are even against the board then turn them onto their side and trim the top centimetre off, discarding the stalks. I like to leave the curly tips on at the other end. Who wants perfectly straight beans? Keeping the beans together, chop them into 2 centimetre pieces. Pop them into a steamer above boiling water and put the timer on for 5 minutes. Meanwhile, open and rinse all the tins of beans and chickpeas. Feel free to soak and cook your own, it's much better but if I did that I'd never get around to making this salad. Always look for tins of beans that have no added salt. Tip the rinsed beans into a large bowl, sprinkling the thyme leaves on top. In a small bowl mix the ingredients for the dressing, gently with a fork. By this time the green beans should be ready. Strain them, adding them immediately to the rinsed beans in the bowl. For the dressing, mix and leave the sundried tomatoes to infuse for at least 20 minutes. When everything is ready, pour over the beans, tossing frequently to ensure every bean is coated with this deep, rich, sweet sauce.

Tip: Keeping a bag of once fresh thyme in the freezer is a great way to always have thyme available as the little leaves take only minutes to defrost. It also means you don't have to fiddle around de-stalking as frozen leaves just fall off the stalk when you shake the bag straight from the freezer.

SPECIAL SPINACH WITH HORSERADISH

Serves 2

Erectile dysfunction is the failure of the penis to become and stay erect. It will affect a third of all men throughout their lifetime. There are many triggers for this condition including anxiety, depression, low testosterone production, nervous system disorders, as well as drug and alcohol misuse. However, it is usually a poor circulatory system that causes the greatest damage. For blood to flow smoothly it must be full of Chi and not too full of toxins or waste materials. High cholesterol manifests in Chinese Medicine, as dampness in the body and blood stagnation. This blood flow supplies oxygen and aids nerve impulses to muscles. As we age and stress our bodies, our veins and arteries can deteriorate. It is the spleen's job to make sure the vessels in which our blood travels are kept strong yet flexible. Like a hose, the vessels need to expand to handle the increased flow when we become aroused at the beginning of sexual intercourse. As mentioned in the heart chapter and the Beetroot Recipe, nitrous oxide plays a large part in the expansion of the smaller blood vessels in the body. It doesn't last in the body so the more antioxidants we can make, the more effective and stable nitrous oxide is. The recipes in this book are not a one-off fix. Dietary changes to fix long-standing problems must become a way of life for long term resolution.

This recipe is a perfect way to start. It works on many organs. The lightly wilted spinach builds and invigorates blood, clears heat, generates bodily fluids and drains dampness. The horseradish balances the stomach and increases circulation especially in the lungs which means higher levels of oxygen in the blood. Predominantly it balances the middle burner meaning that Chi energy flows smoothly. The stomach and spleen are at the horizontal midline of the body and their energy must always be in equilibrium. Stomach energy out of balance means energy rises instead of descending causing poor digestion, burping, vomiting and acid reflux. The spleen energy needs to keep everything up and in, poor function means easy bruising, hernia and prolapse. It is important to keep the Yin Yang of these organs in balance.

In this recipe, horseradish is a main ingredient. Often, horseradish is bought as a large stick like root. Once the horseradish is unwrapped from its packaging and peeled, contact with the air will kick start its pungency. The longer you leave it open to the air the more ferocious its flavour becomes. I grate the whole horseradish into a sterilized jar and pour over mixed oil, vinegar and soy sauce until it covers the horseradish. The ratio of the marinade remains the same 1:2:1 no matter how much is needed. Once the horseradish is covered with the liquid, the oxygen has no access and the horseradish remains pungent without being mind-blowingly hot. This dressing will keep well in the fridge for a couple of months and can be used in wraps and on all sorts of meats and vegetables. Try it with the Barley and Avocado Recipe in the kidney chapter as an alternative dressing. It hits the spot.

250g Spinach
150g Kale

Dressing

1 tsp. fresh, grated, horseradish
1 tbsp. soy sauce
2 tbsp. rice vinegar
1 tbsp. sesame oil
1 tbsp. sesame seeds

For this recipe simply bring a medium-sized pan of water to a boil. Place a steamer on top to steam the kale. Prep the kale first by stripping it from the stalk and tearing it into bite-size pieces. Let this steam for about 5-10 minutes before adding the spinach either directly on top of the kale of add another steamer on top. The spinach only needs to wilt for a couple of minutes. When all the ingredients have wilted but before they have lost their vibrant green, liver loving, chlorophyll, tip them into a large bowl and toss through the amount of dressing desired.

MACA SMOOTHIE

20 years ago, on the northwest coast of Mexico, and I had woken up on New Years Day feeling very queasy. I couldn't work out if the tilted feeling came from the ominous grey storm blowing through our 3 and a half walled hut or from the 3 different sets of fairy lights all playing jingle bells at slightly different speeds in the house next door. More than likely though, it came from the festivities the night before. I needed to hydrate and feel like I wasn't at sea. This led me to my first coconut. Green coconuts are plentiful in Mexico and it didn't take long to find a guy who would chop off the top with a massive machete and stick in a straw. After I finished the coconut water, he broke the coconut in half and I at the white squishy jelly that, if left to dry, becomes the hard white coconut we are familiar with in stores. Because the flesh of the coconut contains calcium magnesium, phosphorus, potassium and sodium it rehydrates the body rapidly. It has a structure very similar to human blood and has reportedly been used intravenously to save human lives[28]. My life didn't need saving but I certainly felt better.

In this recipe I have combined coconut with maca root to stimulate sexual desire and create a sweet and stomach-soothing, smoothie.

Maca originated in the high Andes of Peru and is a national heritage food of Peru. It is not a food traditionally used by Chinese herbalists and it is not native to China. Since 2003 it has been illegal to transport whole roots or seeds outside of Peru.[29] Sometimes you can find illegally cultivated Chinese Maca, so check your Maca before you buy.

Maca root contains a wide array of vitamins, essential minerals such as calcium, magnesium, manganese, zinc, selenium and 19 amino acids, which boost the kidney energy and the libido. For it to be effective, it is recommended to take two teaspoons every day for a month, take a break for a week, then begin again.

250ml coconut water
3 frozen bananas
Blueberries or raspberries or strawberries to taste
2 tsp. maca powder

Defrost the bananas to make sure your drink isn't too cold and that the mix doesn't break your blender. Pour all ingredients into a blender and whizz. Makes a yummy sweet satisfying drink.

I love freezing bananas. Sometimes the kids love bananas and can't get enough, other times they sit on the counter and grow black. At their blackest is the perfect time to freeze them. Peel, chop and store them in a zip lock bag with the air squeezed out.

---

28 https://www.abc.net.au/science/articles/2014/12/09/4143229.htm
29 https://www.theguardian.com/global-development/2015/feb/09/peru-maca-indigenous-root-china-biopiracy

SEA BUCKTHORN FIZZ

Serves 4

Vaginal atrophy sounds scary, like a frozen, deteriorating dead vagina. In western medicine it is seen as a natural consequence of menopause and aging. As estrogen levels drop, the reproductive system ceases to function in the same way so the body can become stiffer and less lubricated. But it doesn't have to be that way. There are ways to keep that juicy Jing flowing and pulsing. Practice *Circulation of Energy* from the Yin Yang chapter, create a routine of self-care exercise and stretching. Take time to do things for yourself that you love. Be open-minded, learn and taste something new. Smile at the sun or the rain.

These are all powerful tools to help the body feel balanced and loved. Add to that the breast and testicular massage from the heart protector chapter and the body will begin to respond. Self-massage is so important. As the vagina becomes dryer and the walls thinner, the breasts can become smaller and/or looser. Keep the Chi and blood flowing together with the whole glandular system by massaging the vagina, testes and the breasts. Remember, your vagina and your balls are not alone, they are part of the body and will respond as a system if you stay in connection to the whole body during the massage.

There are foods that will help the situation. Although it is important to remember the Japanese saying:

"There's no point in forging weapons when war has begun."

Avoid things that will stress and create an acidic environment in the body such as drugs, medication, additives, preservatives, sugar, coffee, overwork and take more alkalising minerals found in leafy greens, seaweed, seeds and nuts. It is more difficult to reverse this condition than prevent it. But you have to dig where you stand and if you have vaginal dryness then sea buckthorn oil or the Love Lube on page 105 will help moisten and lubricate the mucous membranes and vaginal epithelium.

Sea buckthorn is a plant that flourishes in coastal areas and produces a bright orange berry. It is difficult to gather as the berry skin is delicate and there are many protective thorns. In Chinese Medicine, the oil or dried berries are traditionally used to treat chronic pain, digestion issues and improve blood circulation by clearing the liver and strengthening the spleen. They are a warming fruit, moving blood and Chi around the body. Wherever the blood flows there is oxygen and life for the cells.

In recent times it has become a superfood as it is the only known plant containing all four essential fatty acids including omega-7 fatty acid which helps healthy skin, hair, nails and cardiovascular function. Its massive array of antioxidants helps remove cholesterol and promote blood flow. For men this means longer-lasting penile erections and the lycopene present in the berries means reduced prostate problems.

Bottle of Champagne or Sparkling Elderflower Presse
100g sea buckthorn juice (or to taste)
50ml maple syrup (optional)

Usually, I use food as a way to take in vital nourishment for the body but this beautiful little berry is hard to harvest and so I recommend buying from health shops or online, a high-grade quality oil, which has the omega 7 and the moisturising ability. I was inspired by Homebrew from the Hedgerow,[30] and went foraging to sample these berries in the flesh. Here I share my instructions from experience.

Arm yourself with thick gloves and secateurs to collect bags full of the bush. Don't bother trying to pick the berries they are too delicate and pop instantly. Rather cut the branch where they grow and place the berries, still on the branch, in the freezer. When frozen they fall off easily. Wash them to defrost. You can either simmer them with maple syrup to sweeten the very tart juice or as I like to do, simply push through a small sieve with the back of a spoon straight into cold champagne and drink immediately, giving thanks and celebrating all that is delicious in this life.

30 River Cottage foraging expert, John Wright,

HIGH ENERGY OAT BARS

Serves 12

Diabetes is a condition that often includes not being able to obtain or sustain an erection. Over time, high blood sugar levels damage nerves and blood vessels. This means the small blood vessels which take blood to the penis cannot dilate and the penis cannot fill with blood and become erect. Women with diabetes can also suffer from lack of vaginal lubrication, arousal and sensation for the same reason, lack of blood flow and nerve damage to the genital area. A sure way to exacerbate this condition is to smoke. Tobacco and nicotine narrow blood vessels and reduce levels of nitric oxide in the body that dilate blood vessels and allow blood flow. Alcohol with its high sugar levels is also best avoided if suffering from erectile dysfunction. Increasing physical activity helps to regulate blood sugar levels in the body. If you are physically fit and active daily, even after eating something sweet, the spleen-pancreas can stabilize quicker. Exercise also releases nitric oxide into the blood, which relaxes and widens the blood vessels.

Initial sexual desire releases hormones and stimulates the nervous system. The nerves within the penis cause the dilation of the deep arteries, which bring large amounts of blood and engorge the penis with blood, which in turn compresses the veins, stopping the blood from draining away and therefore maintaining an erection. If the nervous system is impaired, erection and blood flow in the genital and clitoral area become impaired. Deep breathing and deep relaxation practices can help with the nervous system as well as foods for the kidney/bladder.

In this recipe we use one ingredient that helps both the kidneys and the spleen—cinnamon. This warms and tonifies all the lower areas of the body including kidneys and Mingmen. It supports the spleen which helps calm the grasping energy of a body that is not satisfied and is looking for gratification in all the wrong places. Sugar, nicotine, drugs, alcohol, caffeine, all highly addictive and ultimately unsatisfying. They take vitality from the body rather than nourishing it. Supporting the spleen will help reduce cravings and dependence and help manage blood sugars to reduce the impact diabetes has on blood circulation. A strong spleen will keep the vessels in which the blood is carried robust and flexible. Studies have shown that cinnamon reduces glucose entering the bloodstream after a meal and that it can reduce insulin resistance[31] which is great for those with type 2 diabetes but don't think it is a miracle cure. Addressing the emotional as well as physical aspects of a weak spleen is essential.

31 https://www.ncbi.nlm.nih.gov/pmc/articles/PMC6425402/

Reducing refined sugars and refined carbohydrates is essential for spleen health. Even though coconut sugar is absorbed by the body slightly slower than cane sugar and it does retain minerals such as iron, zinc, calcium potassium, along with some antioxidants it is still sugar. Remember there are no good or bad foods, simply foods that do not serve us at this time. Sugar is not of itself bad, but our dependence on it can be unhealthy. Keep all areas of your life in balance and energy will flow. Where energy flows, blood goes. To reduce the sexual impact of diabetes bring your attention to all areas of support for the spleen. If all the tantric and dietary advice seems too overwhelming to take on, start with two teaspoons of cinnamon on your porridge every morning. Every journey begins with the first step.

I love this recipe. I make it if I am going camping – it makes a great snack that keeps me full for hours and if it falls apart in the container it becomes breakfast granola. It has plenty of ground cinnamon which mixed with the oats and the sweet dried fruit feed the spleen and stroke the nervous system into sleepiness.

100g dates
45g dried apricots
45g dried cranberries
200g oats
45g pumpkin seed
30g sesame seed
30g ground almonds
3-4 tsp. cinnamon
1 tsp. clove powder
100g olive oil
1 tbsp. barley malt
1 tbsp. syrup
100g coconut sugar

In a blender chop up the dates, apricots and cranberries. Rub them into the oats, seeds, ground almonds, cinnamon and clove. In the meantime put the oil, malt, syrup and sugar into a heavy-based saucepan and melt together over a medium heat. After ten minutes the mixture should bubble like lava, then it's ready to mix into the dry ingredients of oats, seeds and spices. Use a spatula as the mixture will be very hot and could burn the skin. When mixed thoroughly and slightly cooled, press into a tray 20x30cm which is lined with baking paper. Bake in a preheated oven at 170°C for 30 minutes. Allow to cool in the tray scoring into sections whilst the mix is still warm and soft. This will help with cutting through the mix when it is completely cool and you take it out of the tray.

LOADED SWEET POTATO

Serves 2

Sweet potato is the sweetest of sweet. It is delicious and nutritious, full of love. Even though food cannot love you, I think sweet potato comes close. When you've had a baby or you feel put upon, when everything and everybody is on the take, take, take; when the world and it's sister wants a piece of you; your stomach and spleen organs will become depleted. Where will you find comfort and love? Rather than reaching for chocolate, try sweet potato.

In my experience many young mothers find it difficult to put down the chocolate. After I had my twins I was 14 stone. I'd like to say it was baby weight but it was tubs of ice cream. Out on daily perambulatory walks, I'd have a magnum morning fix and chocolate at night to calm me down. They were treats for me. This was my time, my pleasure, my enjoyment. I had no energy for painting, reading, massages or sex. A cup of tea and a chocolate biscuit was as much as I could manage; a short, sweet pleasure fix. Though these quick energy surges were not providing me with any lasting enjoyment. I felt fat, stodgy, lethargic, pale, sore, full of candida and at my most unsexy ever. It's the catch 22 of sugar. We feel tired and lethargic, unsatisfied and unloved which means we can sometimes use food and especially sweet food to make us feel better; but the sugar just makes us feel more tired, more lethargic and unlovable, and so it goes on. This can go on for many years, this giving, giving, giving, and stomach and spleen will suffer, meaning a greater risk of diabetes, anemia, pelvic floor prolapse, hemorrhoids, weak bladder, sagging skin, arterial damage and bruising easily.

We don't have to have young children to get caught in this trap. Putting others first doesn't just happen when we have children. Caretaking of others can be an addictive pattern. It means we don't connect with how we feel and what we need. Sometimes it seems easier to ignore our own needs and focus on others but this never works out well. We mask our own needs with all sorts of avoidances in tobacco, food, drink and kissing. From an early age, we are taught that we can be soothed through the mouth. Even as babies when we cry we are often put to the breast, given a dummy or a piece of food to keep us quiet.

Constantly caring for others can be an escape from how we feel. So next time you reach for the sweet stuff, think about what you need, is this how you reward yourself, how you soothe yourself and how you love yourself? It is very easy after having a baby to put sex on the back shelf and I'm not suggesting sex is the answer but don't divert your needs for love and physical affection because you are putting the baby's needs before yours. Teaching children to love themselves is essential and this begins with us loving ourselves and making ourselves a priority. Take time for yourself and do things you love to do.

The sweet potato is full of potassium, it's a powerhouse of orange, spleen supporting energy which helps to reverse the acidosis of refined unbalanced blood sugar. The spinach in this recipe and the chickpeas help drain the body of excess fluid which reduces dampness and the climate for candida, eczema, water retention and abdomen distension.

2-3 medium or large sweet potatoes
2 tbsp. butter
1 medium onion or bunch of scallions
1 bag fresh baby spinach
60ml Greek yogurt
½ tin chickpeas
100g grand Padano cheese
Salt and pepper to taste

Cut the sweet potatoes, lengthways and roast at 180°C for approximately half an hour. They may need 5-10 minutes more depending on the size of the sweet potato. When they are ready the knife will pass through the flesh like butter and you can scoop the insides out into a bowl. Place the hollowed empty skins back onto the baking tray, drizzle with olive oil and bake for a further ten minutes. Meanwhile, gently fry the chopped onion for ten minutes, adding the spinach for the last minute and allowing to gently wilt. Tip them to the bowl with the butter, greek yogurt, chickpeas, salt and pepper. Coarsely mix and smash the ingredients together. You can leave the chickpeas fairly whole and crunchy. Scoop the mash back into the crispy sweet potato skins, sprinkle over the cheese, and place back in the oven for a further 20 minutes until the cheese is bubbly and ingredients are meltingly, comfortingly warm and gooey.

NO SHAME MILLET MUFFINS

Why wouldn't we put our enjoyment, our pleasure, our satisfaction first? Perhaps because from past experiences, there's hurt all wrapped up in how we feel and it is uncomfortable to feel it. Easier to mask the pain with food, drink, caring for others or various excessive behaviours. It is important also to consider that opening our intimate bodies to another human being or even touching, caressing and being intimate with ourselves is a very vulnerable act. We are sharing our sensitive precious souls and if we have been hurt or damaged in the past it can be easy to avoid this pain by shunning intimacy or putting the needs of others first.

However, connecting with how you feel is at the core of *Shiatsu and Conscious Cooking*. You are responsible for your feelings, emotions, reactions, satisfaction and happiness.

In the past, feelings of underlying shame have stopped me from taking responsibility for my own pleasure. I hoped my lover would do something or suggest something I would like. I have hoped that telepathically, I could communicate or he would guess how I would like him to move or what I would like him to do. I was embarrassed and afraid to move his hand, lick his thumb or suggest something new. It's scary to put yourself out there to explore what you like in the moment, to see how things feel and to move in honest flow with another human being. It requires honesty and connection to know how are you feeling. To communicate that to your partner takes bravery.

From an early age, I loved being touched. Don't we all as babies? We need to be held secure. The physical bonds of connection develop the emotional and neurological pathways in the body. I would go into a trance, and still do if somebody strokes my ears or plays with my hair. So, I didn't think anything of it, when I asked my mum to stroke me in the same way that my grandad did because I liked it. I was about three years old. Obviously, my mum was not as enthusiastic as I was about Grandad touching my vagina and a family meeting was called. My Grandad made a promise to my family that it wouldn't happen again, but it did, for years, until I was about 11. I don't know why I kept going back or why my family kept taking me. I think we were all in denial. My memories from when I was 7 onwards are quite clear, although feelings were confused. My Grandad would engineer a time when I was alone with him and I didn't resist him. Something in me liked it, I liked the physicality of it and I liked the attention. My parents found out again and again. They didn't understand either. My father said "I don't understand what it is you do," the blame was put at my feet. I was an intelligent girl, why did I allow it to happen? So, growing up my idea of physical pleasure was mixed up, I loved being touched in any way, but I was told it was bad. I was given the message that physical pleasure was wrong and it was my fault it was happening. I felt ashamed.

At age 11, I found a sexually explicit pornography magazine which I found hugely exciting. I was still searching to understand what I was feeling so I went looking in the dictionary, at school, for words such as sexual intercourse, orgasm and lesbian. My headmaster found me and instead of explaining what these words meant, he told me off, saying that I shouldn't be interested in this kind of thing. I was so embarrassed.

At 13 my school friends covered a Valentine's card, I was too chicken to send, with sexually explicit graffiti. I took it home and hid it. My dad found it and thought I'd written it. He furiously said he was bitterly disappointed and I was humiliated.

The area I grew up in had a drastically high teenage pregnancy rate, one in four girls would become pregnant before 16. This was not because everyone was having sex it was because no one used birth control. Being on the pill or carrying a condom meant admitting you were having and/or enjoying sex. This was a Catholic community and that was wrong. To have unprepared, unexpected sex without responsibility was acceptable, but a girl who was having conscious, protected, enjoyable, sex was a slag and an embarrassment.

There are many ways to get messed up and confused about sex and intimacy. I could share more and I did debate whether or not to include any of these in this book. Who wants to hear a strangers intimate mistakes and pain? I'm sure you have your own but I thought if I shared mine it may lessen the weight of yours. This is a book about healthy, physical and emotional sex. These experiences I've shared have been my foundation for learning. Over the years I have used them for my healing. I love the little girl who took off her clothes wherever possible. Who loved, and still loves, being naked with the sun on her bum, without shame or fear. I love the teenager who is scared of rejection but brave enough to stand and be seen. I love the young woman who chose men who were not able to care for her. I love the older woman who makes poor choices and has had hilarious tinder experiences, all in my search for acceptance and love.

With space and time I have come to love all my terrible choices, and accept the experiences that have made me. They match my flashes of deep, unconditional, unwavering love. There are so many different conflicting messages of what it is to be a loveable human being. Only we can find our path, only we know what it is to love and be loved. This changes day to day, just as tastes change as the palate ages. I have made some terrible decisions when it comes to relationships. Some I'm not proud of, some I didn't honour myself and some still owe me money. With some experiences, I really hurt myself, but I got up, I'm breathing, I am alive and I am constantly learning how to love myself more. I am not ashamed, just at times, cringingly honest and if I am honest I don't always eat the right things, sometimes I drink too much gin and eat too many biscuits. Here though, are lovely little shameless bites of sweetness which are perfect for supporting the spleen. When we need a little bit of comfort or feeling down in the dumps, instead of reaching for the large tub of ice cream try these perfect little mouthfuls without an ounce of guilt or regret.

MILLET MUFFINS

Serves 12

280 whole-wheat flour
60g raw millet
1 tsp. baking powder
1 tsp. bicarbonate of soda
½ tsp. sea salt
225 plain yogurt or buttermilk
2 large eggs
120 butter melted
1 tbsp. honey
Grated zest and juice of a lemon

These are so simple to make they have been firm favourites in all my cooking classes.

Begin by measuring the dry ingredients of flour, uncooked millet, baking powder, bicarbonate of soda and salt into a bowl. In another bowl pour the buttermilk or yogurt, the large free-range eggs, melted butter, honey, lemon zest and juice. Beat together the wet ingredients until mixed and pour onto the dry ingredients. Using a spatula, gently stir wet into dry and using a tablespoon measure into a buttered muffin tin and bake for 15-20 minutes at 200°C. I like to use the very small silicone muffin trays for these with 24 muffins per tray, so they are tiny bitesize muffins, just enough for something sweet without weakening or dampening the spleen Chi. Receive, receive, receive.

LIQUORICE STICK

The spleen and stomach govern the area of satisfaction and comfort. Their energy spreads from the flesh tone of the body to the succulent lips and mouth. It's earthy and lustful. Think of peaches, blackcurrants and plums with the sweet flesh dripping, how we have to suck and slurp, licking our fingers just to stop all the nectar from dripping down to our elbows. When in balance, it's juicy and flowing but out of balance its energy is deep insatiable hunger.

When uncomfortable feelings arise we want to be reassured even pacified, as a mother would her baby. Sometimes instead of allowing a feeling to pass or examining why we feel uncomfortable, we go looking for any nipple that can relieve our anxiety and comfort us, smoking, drinking, eating and kissing they all involve the sensory organ of the lips. Restless and dissatisfied we can begin craving and set up a vicious cycle that can lead to addiction, whether that be to sugar, sex, alcohol or tobacco.

Many of these addictions have an emotional core and whilst food is very helpful for giving us energy and life it cannot love us. Food and drink have the potential to support us but it cannot meet our emotional needs, only we have that responsibility. We can employ food to nourish or punish our bodies. It is our use of the substance, not the substance itself that affects us emotionally. While, in this book, I recommend foods to support our emotional well being, they are not the only solution. The spleen loves touch and I recommend anyone caught in an addictive cycle, to spend time giving and receiving loving touch. If you aren't in a relationship find a good

masseuse, attend a certified cuddle party or think about enrolling in a massage course. If you can't manage touch at the moment, try counselling or a group that hears how you are, without judgment or a set of weighing scales. We all need to be accepted, heard and loved and there are some things a chocolate bar or a glass of wine just can't do.

Liquorice sticks can be bought in most good health shops and have a very pleasing sweet taste when chewed. The root, not to be confused with the black liquorice/aniseed flavour confectionery, contains glycyrrhizin which is used frequently in Chinese Medicine to sweeten herbal preparations and increase uptake of the medicine, directing it to the meridians in the body. It is anti-inflammatory, reducing stomach acid, heartburn and relieving indigestion.

Liquorice can also help regulate cortisol, the "stress" hormone, lessening the emotional and physical impact of a craving. It contains phytoestrogens which can reduce symptoms of pre-menstruation and menopause such as irritability, mood swings and hot flashes.

I am not heralding the liquorice stick as the great answer to all our cravings but it is great for strengthening the spleen while at the same time keeping our mouth occupied. Some teachers say the human mind is always addicted to something, so why not make it a liquorice stick as we make our way along the path to enlightenment and complete self-love.

ACUPRESSURE POINTS

STOMACH 18 - BREAST ROOT

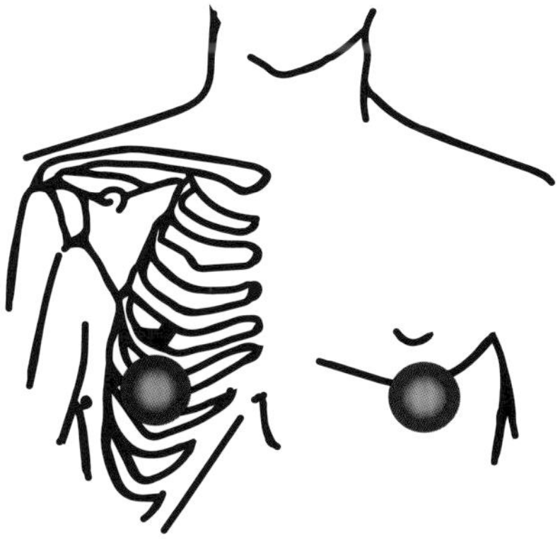

For use of pre-menstrual breast swelling and tenderness, reduces lumps and bumps, regulates lactation. It also loosens the chest muscles and aids breathing.

Find the point in the fifth intercostal space directly below the nipple.

STOMACH 28 – WATER PASSAGE

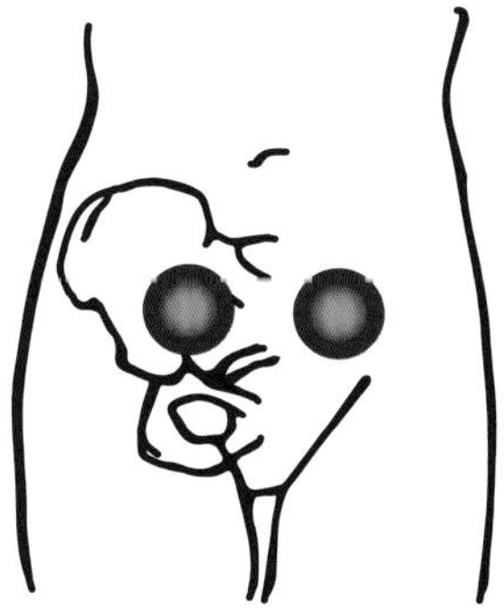

Stimulates movement of all fluids in lower burner. Great for water retention, swelling, difficult urination, and irregular, painful periods.

Find by measuring four fingers below the belly button and two thumb widths out from the midline.

STOMACH 36 – THREE MILE POINT

Raises Yang, invigorates the body and builds energy. Tonifies energy created by food and drink.

Strengthens immunity and defensive Chi, preventing excessive sweating. Together with CV6 tonifies prolapse in the body

Find by measuring four fingers from the base of the knee cap in between the depression of the tibia and fibia bones.

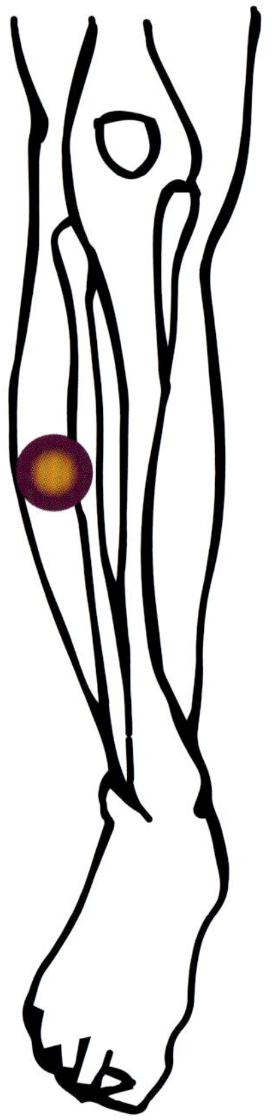

STOMACH 40 – ABUNDANT BRIDGE

Removes phlegm from all over the body, not only the chest but also intestines and uterus. Phlegm can also cause a mist in the mind causing brain fog and anxiety. Dispersement and movement is essential as left to accumulate phlegm can consolidate to form cysts, lumps and bumps around the body.

Find midway between the knee cap and ankle on the outside of the fibia.

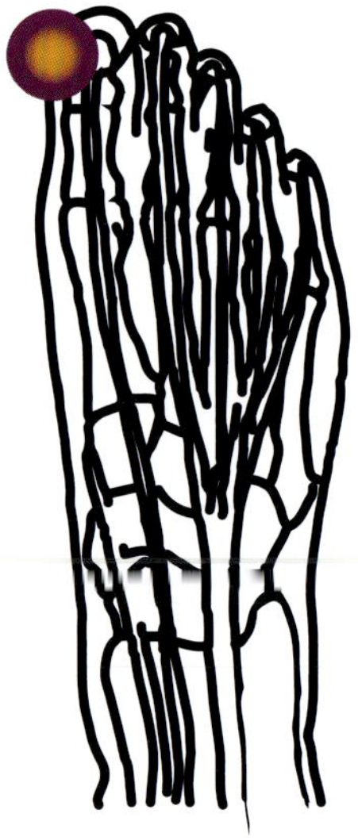

SPLEEN 1 – HIDDEN WHITE

Moves blood in the uterus regulating periods but has the ability to hold blood in the vessels to prevent blood loss from any part of the body, most importantly the uterus, intestines, nose or anus.

Find where the line of the base of the toenail mets the flesh of the outer toe.

SPLEEN 6 – THREE YIN MEETING/CROSSING

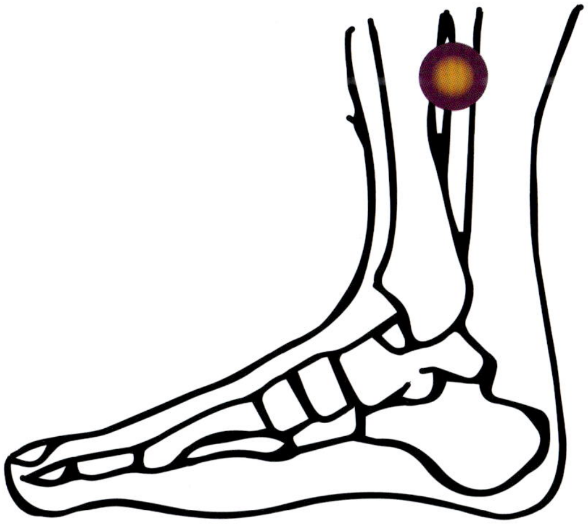

Nourishes, moves and regulates blood especially in the lower abdomen reducing pain and swelling. Relaxes the uterus and eases sexual intercourse.

Relieves damp cold and heat in the lower burner reducing candida, thrush, vaginal discharge, and itchy scrotum. Smooths the Chi for kidney, liver and spleen and builds kidney Yin essential for fertility and conception.

Reduces unwanted excessive sexual activity.

Use in conjunction with Stomach 36 to build energy for chronic tiredness and fatigue.

Find by measuring four fingers up from the ankle bone on the midline of the inner leg.

SPLEEN 12 – RUSHING DOOR AND SPLEEN 13 – MANSION COTTAGE

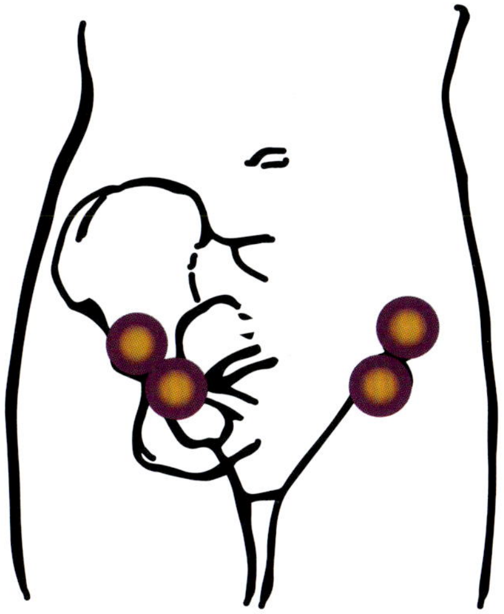

Both points good for impotency. Also use to clear and move energy relieving menstrual cramps, painful urination and abdominal discomfort

Find Spl 12 parallel to the pubic bone on the crease of the groin and Spl 13 one thumb width above and out from the Spl 13.

My heart fills with love for you
and my eyes fill with tears
As the mask goes on and I
see you drift away
So quickly into sleep
I've seen you rest and
kissed you in slumber a
million times
But this is different
You have drifted away
This is the sleep of the dead

Chapter 7

LUNG / LARGE INTESTINE

Autumn

Sleep running through
muddy mists
Leaden long skirts hold
heavy in the hands
Yet the swirling silk is held
aloft
By the time running down

And the minxes
They'll point and prod
Giggling unseen
At your bleary confusion

Light and giddy as a warm
feather
Cover their mouths and
squint their eyes
Yet caught alone they'll
melt with sobs
Grief of one hundred
fathers lost

OVERVIEW
BOUNDARIES AND CONSENT

Yin and Yang do not differentiate between good and bad, happy or sad, its all just energy swinging and dancing between the two poles. ***Our suffering is often caused because we are attached to emotions. We want to feel love, happiness and joy but recoil from anger, jealousy, sadness, and grief. It's good to remember that emotions are not fixed, they are Yang, constantly changing and active.*** Allow them to dance in your body, don't identify or become attached to them. Don't act them out unnecessarily or life can become full of drama, entertaining from the outside but exhausting to live from the inside. Constant emotional outbursts or agitated, passionate demonstrations of feelings are seen as one of the primary causes of internal disease in Chinese Medicine. The hot air of emotional Yang can manifest as ailments such as hormonal imbalance, loss of libido, high blood pressure, IBS, gall stones, inflammation of the liver and even heart disease. If we ceaselessly respond to our emotions they can become who we are.

Grief is a prime example of how emotion can completely consume us. Loss is a natural part of life. The leaves fall from the trees in autumn, preparing the soil for new growth in spring. It is the circle of life. This season governs the lung and large intestine in Chinese Medicine. Just like trees lose leaves, human life is about constantly letting things go. This might be the death of a loved one, a pet, a parent or relative. A relationship may end, we might lose a job, a house or a friendship. In the midst of grief, we feel isolated and alone in a world where we feel no one understands our loss, pain and tears. But grief is very powerful in the way it connects us to the things that matter.

Sometimes things happen to us we have no control over. They seem inexplicable and can cause great sadness. Natural disasters, for example like the 2005 tsunami in Thailand or man-made destruction such as the terrorist attack of the twin towers in New York on 9/11. These unexpected events with the loss of innocent lives caused great grief. Many people came together during these events to support each other and bear witness to each other's anguish. It felt like the whole world could feel the pain. ***The emotion of grief can bring us to a deeply human place where we recognise the ultimate truth, that everything changes, that life is fleeting and connections we have with others are fragile.*** Loss can focus the body and mind into living life and appreciating the things we have. It is important to let that emotion flow, feel the feeling but not to get lost in it - the danger is that grief can leave us disconnected, isolated and alone.

When we cry our breathing is shallow and short. Sometimes breathing deeply connects us to feelings we don't wish to contact but it is essential to experience Yang emotions before they become Yin ailments. There isn't one person who hasn't experienced bereavement, loss of a lover or a loved one. There is a natural order, a time to grieve and a time to live. The emotion of grief doesn't disappear, it often resurfaces, unexpectedly, with memories, smells or situations. By breathing deeply and connecting to how we feel, we don't eradicate uncomfortable feelings, rather allow the experience of them so they do not overwhelm or disconnect us from support and love.

This can be a vulnerable place but when the walls of protection come down it allows others to see us, support and love us.

"When correct breathing is practiced, the myriad ailments will not occur. When breathing is depressed or strained all sorts of diseases will arise. Those who wish to nurture their lives must first learn the correct methods of controlling breath and balancing energy. These breathing methods can cure all ailments great and small"

Sun Ssu-mo – Precious Recipes

The lung is our physical connection to the world around us. How we breathe says a lot about how we live. Is it rapid and shallow, on edge and afraid or is it deep, relaxed and expansive? The lungs have to be strong, not only to allow the exchange of oxygen and carbon dioxide but also to repel invading pathogens and viruses. The large intestine houses many receptor cells that detect invading pathogens. Resident tissue cells then release chemicals and enzymes which create an inflammatory response to kill invading viruses. ***In Chinese Medicine, these two organs are responsible for our boundaries, immunity and protection.*** Unexpected cold, dry nights plus damp soggy days of this autumnal season, can test the strength of our boundaries and immune system. In all areas of life, it is important to know your boundaries, how to say no and how to say yes.

It is what gives us a strong sense of self whilst at the same time gives us the strength to be vulnerable and open to connect with others.

Sexually it's important to be clear about boundaries, what you want and what you don't want, when you want it and when you don't. If you are clear with your NO then its easier to give an enthusiastic YES! There's a good analogy that explains sexual consent as though you were being asked if you want a cup of tea. Sometimes tea hits the spot but at other times it's not what you fancy. Sometimes you thought you wanted tea but by the time it arrives it is not what you fancy or you've fallen asleep. Sometimes you might want to try a different flavour of tea. Nothing wrong with the person making the tea but simply because they made you tea last week does not mean you want tea this week. The example of tea is saying to be in connection with your body and then be able to communicate how you feel and what you want.

If you are the tea maker there's nothing wrong with you if your tea is refused. It's just not that person's cup of tea at the moment. You can't force someone to drink tea. Get the idea? Its all about communication. Rejection can sometimes have consequences especially if we link our self-esteem and desirability to another's behaviour. Don't take their rejection personally, rather see it as an opportunity to open communication for other levels of intimacy - it can strengthen a relationship

Sometimes long term relationship sex can become habitual. We have tea at four o'clock simply because we've always had tea at four o'clock, but as energy and our bodies change, our needs change. I invite you to see what you want and to express it. Use the breath to quiet the mind and unwind the body. As we learned within the kidney Tantra exercise, it's easier to relax and be connected with how our body feels plus know what it needs, when we breathe. When we breathe properly we enter the parasympathetic nervous system, more parts of our brain are available for use, we can think laterally, having a greater perspective on situations and a clearer sense of self. Use this clarity to communicate with yourself in a journal, or your partner in a conversation. What does sexual intimacy look and feel like for you? Perhaps it's trying something new or perhaps it's reinforcing an existing routine.

Perhaps you need to say a definitive NO to something or gasp an orgasmic YES to something else.

Here is a technique that effortlessly fills the lungs with oxygen and allows the abdomen to relax, oxygenated and nourished.

CONSCIOUS BREATHING:

Take a regular breath in and as you exhale push out all the air from the lungs. With no more breath in your lungs, count slowly, silently, for four beats. When you release, the lungs will effortlessly take in air to fill your lungs deeply. Do this at least three times in succession so that the body is oxygenated and relaxed. Then simply sit with a straight back, breathing normally. Focus on the breath, when thoughts arise don't follow them, put them on the breath. Be aware of yourself breathing in and out. If done regularly this conscious breathing will build the kidney and the lung energy which benefit all areas of the mind and body. Deep breathing massages the internal organs especially the adrenals, which are often overused and abused. It allows greater oxygenation of the blood and enhances brain function. Instead of being stressed and narrow-minded in our thinking it allows us perspective and an open mind. This distance and perspective protects us. It strengthens healthy boundaries with the world and it's often overwhelming events and emotions.

Sea green eyes

It was far from a belly laugh
day
The water was churned
and although the surface
lays calm now
I know the sediment is held
suspended
Soft tissues still puffy
I will lead you to silent
shores
Only natural noises

I know you are numbed but
the sharp salty breeze shall
clean and cool you with it's
sting
It shall strip you of your
lead
Then I will give you time to
settle
and your eyes shall glisten
not from sobbing
but from knowing you are
home

LUNG TANTRA
MASSAGE

The lung and large intestine's sensory organ is the nose and sense of smell. For pleasure in this exercise, we use both the olfactory organ of the nose and the largest sensory organ of the body, the skin. The skin is seen as the third lung in Chinese Medicine. Quite often if I encounter a problem with either the lung or large intestine it will manifest externally through the skin as eczema, psoriasis, athletes foot and other fungal growths.

Smell is directly connected to the most ancient and primitive part of the brain, the limbic system, where deep-rooted emotional responses are stimulated, so don't underestimate the power of a fragrance. The skin is the physical boundary of our body. It keeps all our insides in and keeps germs and water out. Through the nervous system, our skin assesses our external environment and reacts accordingly. It keeps us cool when it's hot and warms us up when it's cold outside.

This exercise works with both sensory organs to give us a deep, connected sense of self. It's about taking control and responsibility for your sexual energy, with an understanding of who you are and what you need. This massage does not focus on or exclude specific body parts and its aim is not sexual arousal or orgasm, although both may happen. It's about experiencing your body, your energy and your boundaries so that they combine to live a full and juicy life.

First, choose a base oil which will carry the fragrance. I recommend sweet almond oil but you can also use grapeseed or coconut oil. Natural botanical oils work best on the skin so avoid mineral oils such as baby oil, as they are by-products of petroleum production. Next, select an essential oil. There are many to choose from; heart opening rose, stimulating cinnamon, classic aphrodisiac jasmine to cheap and cheerful lavender. Pour approximately 100ml of. the carrier oil into a bowl and add 10 drops of the essential oil. Use your fingers to blend the oil in the bowl.

Individual massage

This exercise can be done alone. First, get naked in a place that is warm and secure. Now ask yourself where the tension is in your body? Where would you most like to be touched and how? Perhaps the answer is your ankles and calves or perhaps it is your temples and scalp. Take some of the oil into the palms of your hands and rub, stroke or massage the place your body has called to you. Don't worry if the oil goes in your hair, it will wash out. The important thing is to really check in with yourself, see what you need and caress yourself accordingly.

Partner massage

Just as above, set up the room to be comfortably warm and relaxing then discuss who would like to receive and who would like to give. The receiver then checks-in to his or her body stating where to begin the massage and with what kind of touch. As the receiver, really check in with yourself; do you want to lie down, sit up or be held in the giver's arms? How is the quality of touch you want; light stroking, firm kneading or simply a hand on the shoulder? Don't forget to inform the giver of any areas that are out of bounds, where you don't want to be touched.

As the massage begins the receiver says yes and repeats yes as long as the physical sensation feels pleasurable. As the giver, you can begin to move slowly around the body, perhaps from the arm to the shoulder or from the belly to the breast. As long as the receiver is saying yes then continue. It is essential to hear a verbal "Yes" before continuing. If you hear nothing, take this as a no and massage another area or body part. As the receiver, be clear, if you are feeling yes, say YES and if you are feeling no, say NO. Also, you are encouraged to change your mind. As the receiver, you can also say "that is lovely but I've had enough on my feet could you rub my back" As the giver check in and ask if what you are doing is enjoyable. If you have been stroking their calves and want to work on their feet, you can always verbally check in with them again before you change. In this way, we are listening to our partner and they are being heard.

I would recommend that this is not a foreplay exercise, its goal is not a sexual climax. It is authentic connection with our partner in an atmosphere of unconditional giving and receiving. Set a clear time limit for the exercise. Perhaps an hour in the evening could be dedicated to one person receiving and the following evening the roles swap. Maybe it is twenty minutes each on a Saturday morning. Even clothed at the kitchen table for two minutes each can work. It is about creating space to express ourselves and have our needs met.

If you wish to learn more and experience unconditional touch with lots of people, fully clothed in a structured boundaried workshop environment check out where your local cuddle party is. Go, get cosy, comfy and cuddled.[32]

"Nurturing, welcoming consensual touch is good for you. Good for your body, heart and spirit. Good for your blood pressure, your nervous system, your emotional health, your ability to connect with and trust people, your ability to respect and care for yourself, your creativity, sense of safety and comfort and belonging. Infants who are deprived of touch fail to thrive; we never outgrow the need. We humans need touch that is not about sex."

Randy Ralston (Cuddle Party Ireland)

32 http://www.cuddleparty.com

Lung/Large Intestine
RECIPES

ANTI-INFLAMMATORY TEA

Serves 4

This tea has it all – take it for anything; Sore toes, ulcerative colitis, rheumatoid arthritis, a tickly cough... I recommend keeping all the ingredients in your store cupboard at all times. Taken regularly these ingredients keep you healthy, if you develop and illness or are attacked by a virus, this combination of ingredients is your army of defence.

In Chinese Medicine, turmeric stops blood stagnating and coagulating thereby reducing pain, swelling and stiffness all over the body. It helps the gallbladder produce bile, aiding the liver's detoxifying powers, invigorating blood and moving Chi in all areas of the body. In the abdomen, it reduces cramps and the pain of slow-moving menstruation blood.

Ginger has similar properties, warming and moving the Chi, especially in the digestive tract reducing wind/gas, irritable bowel, nausea, morning sickness and menstrual cramps.

The sour flavour of the lemon stimulates liver function whilst the vitamin C of the fruit helps fight infection by repairing damaged cells. Cinnamon helps balance blood sugars, and the maple syrup makes it taste good.

750ml water
½ a lemon, sliced or rough chopped rind included
(more or less to taste)
1-inch ginger root, roughly chopped
(more or less to taste)
1 tsp. fresh grated turmeric
1 stick cinnamon
1 tbsp. maple syrup
(more or less to taste)

Put all ingredients into a large saucepan, bring to the boil and simmer for 10-20 minutes. Strain and serve. Once strained I like to keep this in the fridge, filling half a mug and topping up with boiling water when I want a hot cup. It's a very pleasant drink to take warm in the winter or cool in the summer. Feel free to change quantities of ingredients depending on your taste or illness.

KIMCHI

As discussed in the last recipe, stagnation of blood and Chi can lead to swelling and pain. If there is internal dampness, the internal inflammation can become chronic. In Chinese Medicine, the use of antibiotics causes cold and damp stagnation. They kill both the invading virus bacteria and our own natural bacteria, disrupting the delicate balance within the large intestine. The animals we eat have often been fed antibiotics without even realizing it; we ingest small amounts of antibiotics. Antibiotics can lead to an increase of pro-inflammatory cytokines produced by the intestines mucosal membrane, leaving us susceptible to future invading viruses and a possibility that the body may start attacking itself with an autoimmune disease. An environment devoid of good bacteria can also lead to an overgrowth of Candida Albicans. This fungus aids nutrient absorption and digestion, it is supposed to be in the body. However, when the intestinal conditions are not kept in balance it can overgrow, break down the intestinal wall and migrate to different parts of the body such as the mouth, and vagina, causing thrush, vaginal discharge, incessant itching and even pain after intercourse. Eating a varied diet with plenty of fermented foods such as Kimchi, sauerkraut, yogurt, miso, pickles, kombucha, and kefir that contain natural probiotics, will maintain a balanced, internal climate.

1 medium head Chinese cabbage
100-200g sea salt
1 tbsp. grated garlic
1 tbsp. grated ginger
1 tsp. coconut sugar
2 to 3 tbsp. filtered water
1 to 5 tbsp. Korean red pepper flakes
1 tbsp. seaweed sprinkles or wakame
2 tbsp. tamari
10 radish or 3 inch of daikon, peeled and cut into matchsticks
4 scallions, trimmed and cut into 1-inch pieces
1 carrot
1 large glass jar with tight-fitting lid.

First finely shred the cabbage in a large basin or bucket and mix with good quality ground sea salt. Place a plate on top of the salty cabbage with something heavy on the plate. The cabbage will begin to pickle in the salt and release its water. Leave it under the plate for 4 hours then rinse and strain thoroughly 3 times. Wash and dry the bowl and put the rinsed cabbage back in. Meanwhile, in another bowl, not too far away, mix the garlic, ginger, sugar, water, seaweed and tamari into a paste using a spoon. Combine this paste with the cabbage, mixing thoroughly. I advise using gloves or a spoon as mixing the paste with the remaining veggies and cabbage can make your hands sting. Let the mixed ingredients sit in the bowl while you prepare the glass jar. To sterilize, wash and rinse out with boiling water, removing the rubber ring if it has one and place just the jar in a hot oven to 200°C for approximately 10 minutes. Allow it to cool, replace the rubber ring and empty the cabbage mixture from the bowl, including any spicy salty liquid, into the jar. Press the mixture down. The liquid should cover the cabbage, if it doesn't add a little more water. Close the lid and allow it to sit on the kitchen counter for anywhere between one day and a week, in which time you should see the fermentation begin to occur. Small bubbles will start to rise to the surface. Open the jar every couple of days to allow the gas to escape. After 3 to 5 days, depending on your room temperature, transfer to the fridge. You can eat it now or give it another 2 weeks to really come to its salty spicy, fermented prime.

Tip: This recipe seems a little involved but it keeps for ages in the fridge so you don't have to make it too often unless you love it and eat it all. Traditionally, in South Korea, where Kimchi is a national dish, families gather in autumn to make it together, strengthening bonds, connection and cooperation.

CHILLI SENSATIONS

These tiny red pods shout fire, sizzle, stimulated sensations and fun. They have long been associated with the pleasure/pain principle of sex, which with mutual consent, can bring an extra element of excitement and stimulation to your body. The physical sensation of eating spicy chilli stimulates the tongue's pain receptors from which mood-enhancing endorphins are released bringing a natural high, much the same as a consensual pinch, spank or tied down tickle.

Capsaicin, a chemical contained within small red and green chilli peppers, increases blood flow, heart rate and stimulates nerve endings. Capsaicin also helps with pain relief, as it is anti-inflammatory which blocks Substance P, a natural chemical involved in the transmission and perception of pain.

From a Chinese Medicine point of view, chillies disperse the stuck mucus laden energy of the lung and large intestine. Energetically, they help us let go of what is no longer needed, within past relationships or yesterday's dinner. When we let go of the old we can receive the new. Breathing it in with strong open lungs.

Almonds also appear in both these recipes and in Chinese Medicine are seen as fortifying energy, clearing and transforming mucous and stagnant energy in the lung and large intestine.

CHILLI PESTO

Serves 4

1-2 fresh chillis (*choose type depending on heat and required taste, small red chillis work well*)
2 cloves garlic
Large bunch fresh coriander
Large bunch fresh basil
50g ground almonds
50g whole almonds
250ml olive oil
Salt to taste

In a food processor blend all the ingredients, add a little more oil or water if it becomes too sticky. This is delicious tossed over some fresh spaghetti, stuffed into chicken breast or served with fresh grilled mackerel.

CHILLI RELISH

Serves 6

50g whole almonds
1 green or red bell pepper
2-6 red or green chillies
(*again depending on required heat and taste*)
1 red onion
1 tsp sea salt
100ml olive oil
Juice of half a lemon
1 tbsp. of maple syrup
Large handful of flat-leaf parsley

Begin by blending the almonds and pepper briefly in a food processor. Adding chillies, onion, salt, lemon, maple syrup and olive oil. I like to chop the flat-leaf parsley by hand to ensure the texture of this relish is left quite chunky. This relish goes fantastically with crackers and cheese, white fish, a large glass of crisp white wine and/or added to crunchy toasted quality bread.

GINGER BAKED POACHED PEARS

Serves 4-6

Sometimes known as "happy fruit," pears are popular throughout Asia and well known for their medicinal properties. They generate bodily fluids and moisten dryness, especially in the mucous membranes of the lung and large intestine. They also can transform and remove phlegm in these areas. The ginger and the cinnamon, in this recipe, warm the body from the inside out. If it's cold outside come on in, eat something wholesome, sweet and warm. There's no better way to feel loved.

300ml (½ pint) apple juice
2-3 cm fresh ginger root
1 tbsp. honey/maple syrup or apple juice concentrate
1 small cinnamon stick
4-6 medium pears

This is an easy dessert to make and it's a great way to use pears that are too stubborn to ripen. Simply cut the core at the base of the pear and place standing up in a Pyrex dish. It is great if they are standing snug but if they topple over it doesn't matter. Next, chop the ginger into thin matchstick strips. No need to peel it. Toss this and the broken up cinnamon stick around the pears. Pour the apple juice and drizzle the honey over the top of the pears. Cover, with the pears sitting in the juice, ginger and cinnamon with tin foil. Bake for between 30 and 45 minutes depending on the size and ripeness of your pears. When they are ready a knife should slide in and out like butter. It's that super, sexy simple.

WHEAT AND GLUTEN-FREE DROP SCONES

Serves 2

This is traditional style griddle bread – think blini rather than a risen fruit scone. They are simple enough to mix up in a minute. Perfect for Sunday morning breakfast if you want an alternative to gluten heavy bagels or croissants. There seems to be an increase in gluten sensitivity and sometimes I think it's not the gluten that our intestines have become sensitive to but rather the chemicals that have been used in the growing, refining and producing of wheat. If you are gluten intolerant, be sure to take care where you source your flour. Organic is always best not only for our sensitive bowels but for the planet, with all that slithers, crawls, flies and walks. Taking care of ourselves wholeheartedly means, in our actions, we take care of others.

Almonds are moistening and lubricating for the mucous membranes of the lung and large intestine. They can counteract dryness in the body which leads to constipation or coughing. In Chinese Medicine, they support the nervous and reproductive system as well as the Jing of the body promoting a strong, healthy, long life.

100g rice flour
25g buckwheat flour
20g ground almonds
½ tsp. baking powder
1 tsp. caster sugar
1 egg
150 ml goats milk or almond milk
1 tbsp. coconut oil for frying

In a large bowl, mix the flours, almonds, baking powder and sugar. In a jug, beat the egg with the milk then whisk the wet ingredients into the dry mixture until you have a thick batter consistency. Heat the oil to high on a flat pancake pan or large frying pan. Drop tablespoon size blobs of the mixture into the pan then turn down the heat to medium-low. After a minute or so the scones will have a few bubbles on the surface, flip them over so that they can cook on the other side for a couple of minutes. They should be golden crisp on the outside whilst warm, soft and doughy on the inside.

ONION PILAF

Serves 4

Chinese Medicine would say the pungent flavour strengthens the lung and large intestine. Physically and emotionally these are the organs concerned with our boundaries. In western medicine, most of the protective immune system can be found in the digestive system, specifically the intestines. Within this recipe, there are a plethora of pungent ingredients such as ginger, onions, garam masala usually containing cumin, coriander, fenugreek, cardamom, chillies and black pepper. All of which warm and disperse phlegm, which can build up in the lung and large intestine if we become cold and weak. All our connections with other humans can leave us open and vulnerable to infections and bugs. From door handles and toilets to smooches and sexual intercourse, we need to keep our physical boundaries strong when interacting with all the connections on offer.

50g butter
A splash of rapeseed oil
8 white onions
3 tsp. garam masala
1 small piece fresh ginger root,
250g basmati rice
1 bay leaf
The zest of one lemon
2 mild green chillies,
Salt and freshly ground black pepper to taste
375ml vegetable stock
1 tbsp. chopped fresh coriander
Lemon juice to serve

Heat the oven to 180°C. Melt the butter and oil in a heavy-based oven-safe, casserole dish over medium heat on the stovetop. When the oil and butter are hot, add the onions and fry on medium heat for 10 to 15 minutes until they are gorgeously yellow and beginning to caramelize. Add the garam masala and finely chopped ginger. As the spices become aromatic, slowly stir in the rice allowing the grains to soak up the spicy butter. Stir in the bay leaf, lemon zest, chilli, salt and pepper and pour over the stock. Give the pan a little shake to ensure the rice is settled and the stock covers evenly. Place the tight-fitting lid on top and pop it into the oven for 15 to 20 minutes. Do not stir the rice. To check if it is cooked, take a fork and lift the rice from the side of the pot to see if all the stock has been absorbed. If it looks too dry add more stock by pouring it in gently from the side of the pan. Again, resist the urge to stir. When the rice is cooked and the stock absorbed. Leave it to stand out of the oven with the lid on for 5 minutes so that the rice is fluffy and the grains are not stuck together. Finally, just before serving, sprinkle over the coriander plus lemon juice and fork through.

This recipe is one of my cooking class favourites. It's the one I'm told time and time again works for everyone in the family. It is adapted from a Simon Hopkinson recipe from the Good Cook Tv programme, where he lays smoked fish over the rice to steam as the dish cooks.

KASHMIRI CAULIFLOWER

Serves 4

One of the most influential men in my life, Eric Forsmark, bought me the World Food Café Cookbook. He was leaving a community development project we had created together in Dublin to live in Italy. I thought it was a strange gift at the time as I wasn't really cooking then, hadn't qualified as a shiatsu practitioner and didn't have any time for anything than the all-consuming development project. As it turns out, Eric's sensitive ability to see what was in my heart still fills me with admiration. It was a dark period in my life where I worked too hard. I ignored my own needs, my family and my health in the name of single-mindedness and a successful job well done. However, the heart's desire will not be suppressed. It was through the complete destruction of what I thought my life was, that made the journey of this book possible. My partner had an affair, I was forced to leave the community development project, I weighed fourteen stone instead of my healthy weight of nine; I had no sexual desire and gave no time to intimacy. My mind was completely consumed and I over-identified with the job. Eventually, I learned to let it all go and as I look back now, I can't believe I stayed as long as I did. I was clinging to a job and a partner, neither of which filled me with love. Today, in a work situations, I am much clearer about my limitations. Being a single mum with three teenage boys certainly tests my boundaries but I'm grateful to have the tools of food and Shiatsu for support.

Physically, the large intestine is all about letting go. In uncomfortable or stressful situations it's usually the organ that lets us know how we're feeling.

We can become constipated, experience severe pain, develop IBS, ulcerative colitis and even have diarrhoea due to emotional pressures. If we want to go with the heartfelt joyous flow of life we can't hold on to the past. Our large intestine must be functioning properly, letting go and moving on. The following recipe is from the World Food Café Cookbook and I'm very grateful for all the recipes, my friend Eric and how much this book means to me.

The first line of defence for the body is the skin and the mucous membranes. We are born with these defences, whereas bacteria and the digestive defence system have to grow and develop. The skin and membranes are waterproof and stop pathogens entering yet they can still excrete unwanted pathogens from your body through sweat and phlegm. This recipe can certainly make your skin sweat. It can be eaten with the Onion Pilaf on page 323, if you want an extra pungent boost and to create a little internal heat for the body. It is ideal if you are feeling cold, sluggish and unsexy. This recipe can spice things up and move things along.

1 white onion
4 cloves garlic
2 inches fresh ginger
6 medium tomatoes
6 tbsp. sunflower oil
1 large cauliflower
1 tsp. turmeric
1 tsp. cayenne pepper
1 tsp. ground cinnamon
½ tsp. ground cloves
1 tsp. ground cardamom
4 bay leaves
1 tsp. honey
1 tsp. salt
30g cashew
30g raisins

In a food processor, blend the onion, garlic, peeled ginger and tomatoes until they puree.

Place a heavy-based casserole dish on medium heat. Chop the cauliflower into florets and fry in the oil until they brown and begin to soften. Remove them from the heat and put aside in a bowl. Now place the already blended puree, turmeric and cayenne pepper in the pan. Fry on medium heat for about 3 minutes, adding the cinnamon, cloves, cardamom, bay leaves, honey and salt. Cook together for a further 5 minutes then add in the cauliflower, cashews and raisins. Heat the dish through until the cauliflower has the desired texture and serve. Simple and super tasty.

BLACK WOOD EAR NOODLE SOUP

Serves 2

Black Wood Ear Fungus - none of those words sound particularly appetizing, I even took the word fungus out of the title of the recipe just in case people passed it by due to its unpleasant sound. Who really would want to eat fungus? I urge you to give it a try. It is usually sold dried in Asian supermarkets and I would advise buying the precut type as the uncut can hydrate to frightening proportions. In Chinese Medicine, Black fungus supports the large intestine. They nourish Yin by bringing moisture to the lungs and large intestine. The black wood ear fungus can dissolve excess platelets in the blood ensuring a smooth, calm, healthy flow of blood. Blood is a Yin substance that nourishes and lubricates all areas of the body to which it flows.

There is a Japanese saying: "for every new food we try, we live another 7 days". Give it a go and think of the extra week you will gain! What will you do with that extra week of life? Include the other ingredients in this broth recipe and you might even get more than a week. Miso has an extremely salty taste and therefore is predominantly for strengthening the kidneys. It is a fermented product containing a plethora of healthy bacteria so it also supports the large intestine. Be careful not to boil the broth as this can kill the precious bacteria that strengthen the gut.

Buckwheat is not a wheat product or a grain as it sounds but rather the triangular seed of the Fagopyrum Esculentum (buckwheat) plant, related to rhubarb. It lowers blood sugars more slowly than rice or wheat products, which is beneficial for the inflammation of the blood vessels and it contains rutin, a mineral that can assist in lowering blood pressure. Seaweeds contain a wealth of minerals such as calcium, magnesium, iron, copper, selenium, and iodine to build blood. Seaweed is also an effective diuretic, reducing excess water from blood and lowering high blood pressure.

Increasing the transportation of nourishing blood around the body aids conditions such as Chilblains, Raynaud's Disease and erectile dysfunction. All of the ingredients in this recipe are Yin in quality. As discussed at the very beginning of the book, Yin foods are essential to hydrate, lubricate, open and relax the body. If you want to calm your sexual practice, balance your quick-fire, hot and heavy Yang with some smooth and cooling Yin nourished blood, try some Black Wood Ear Fungus.

2 handfuls of shredded and dried wood ear fungus
2 litres of water
2 handfuls of hydrated and chopped dulse (dillisk) seaweed
2 scallions
2 bundles of dry buckwheat noodles
2 tbsp. of dark miso paste
2 large handfuls of coriander
2 tsp. black and/or white sesame seeds

Bring the two litres of water to the boil and add the wood ear fungus. Simmer the water and fungus for about 10 minutes. After which, add the seaweed and the scallions to the wood ear fungus and water.

In a separate pan bring another 2 litres of water to the boil to cook the buckwheat noodles. The noodles only take a couple of minutes in which time you can take a mug full of the cooking water from the wood ear fungus and dissolve the miso paste into it. Add this back into the broth, turn off the heat and stir in well. Drain the cooked noodles, share into bowls and pour over the broth, finish off by sprinkling over fresh coriander and sesame seeds. Make sure you slurp and suck with your partner adding to the sensuality of the dish.

Here I have used dulse for its beautiful red/purple colour which blends well with the fungus. You can also add firm tofu, cut into small cubes when you add the seaweed as a nice optional extra. Seaweeds, black wood ear fungus and buckwheat noodles are a great source of easily absorbable protein. Even though meat products contain high levels of protein often they pass through the body without being digested and absorbed. Seaweeds and fungus are proving to be a healthier alternative protein food source.[33]

33 https://www.sciencedaily.com/releases/2012/10/121012074659.htm

GARLIC AND APPLE SLICES

"Let food be thy medicine, and medicine be thy food." It's a well-known saying attributed to Hippocrates, the father of western medicine. He understood the healing properties of garlic and prescribed it to treat a variety of medical conditions. It was given to ancient olympian athletes as a performance-enhancing drug. The Talmud, a collection of Jewish laws, ethics, and customs says that garlic should be eaten on Friday evening before the Sabbath because of its potency as an aphrodisiac. It also states that it satiates, warms the body, brightens a person's countenance, increases semen and kills parasites in the intestines. In Chinese Medicine, it is used extensively to treat diseases which occur mainly in the lung and large intestine such as the common cold, bacteria, candida, dysentery, abdominal obstructions, pneumonia, asthma, hay fever, dysentery and much more. It is truly a superfood. In recent tests, Garlic was shown to have an effect against the antibiotic-resistant MRSA[34] and in preliminary tests, it is being used against Herpes simplex type 1 and 2, Parainfluenza virus type 3, human Cytomegalovirus, Influenza B, Vaccinia virus, Vesicular stomatitis virus and human rhinovirus type 2.[35]

Allicin, an enzyme released when garlic is chopped or crushed, as found in the cited studies was found to have amazing antibacterial, anti-fungal, antiviral properties and it's the allicin that increases blood flow to the sexual organs.

Raw garlic is the best way to get the allicin as it's potency is greatly reduced after cooking. Unfortunately, the odour of raw garlic does not inspire romantic ardour so here are a few ways to eat raw garlic without too much odour.

The Spanish Way
Rub a peeled garlic clove and a couple of fresh halved tomatoes all over a couple of crisp toasted slices of bread.

Renata's Swiss Way
Slice an apple and a clove of garlic thinly, then make like a sandwich. Always with the garlic in the middle, this reduces the burning sensation in the esophagus and stomach.

The Sweet Way
Crush and chop raw garlic, take a dessert spoon and half fill with honey, mix in the chopped garlic and swallow on down

The Savoury way
Make the dressing recipe below: using a pestle and mortar, crush the chopped garlic with sea salt, pour over olive oil and use as a dip with delicious, rustic, crusty bread

Dressing
250ml olive oil
125ml apple cider vinegar
3 crushed and minced garlic cloves
1 tsp. Dijon mustard
Pinch of sea salt

If you are still worried about mouth odour after eating any of these recipes, try chewing fresh flat-leaf parsley afterwards. This works wonderfully for any bad breath and is packed full of vitamin C to boot.

34 https://www.ncbi.nlm.nih.gov/pmc/articles/PMC4458355/
35 https://www.ncbi.nlm.nih.gov/pubmed/1470664

LEMON CARRAGEEN POTS

Serves 6

In my first book ***Shiatsu & the Art of Conscious Cooking*** there is a recipe for Carrageen Moss which isn't very sexy. Instructions are to boil up the Seaweed into a gelatinous semi-transparent jelly which is eaten to clear phlegm from the chest, fight coughs colds and help relieve bronchitis. It's a traditional Irish cure to strengthen the immune system and has been used for hundreds of years. You can buy it, in dried form, in most supermarkets and health stores. Again just check the harvest location to ensure it comes from clean seas. Online is often a good place to buy Irish Seaweeds which as they are harvested off the Wild Atlantic west coast is a fantastic place to source them. For more information on seaweed look back to the Hummus and Seaweed recipe on page 90.

In this recipe, however, I am following the tradition from Jamaica and Trinidad where it is boiled with milk and served as an aphrodisiac. I have used goat's milk to lessen phlegm created in the lungs from cow's milk. Water can also be substituted. Carrageen Moss is a fantastic, cheap, healthy ingredient, that has a medicinal quality to disperse phlegm. Throw it into stews or brew into a tea to keep the lungs healthy in the damp beginnings of autumn.

This recipe is similar to an Italian Panacotta. It is delicate in flavour and light in texture. Perfect for a lover's meal where you want the sweet satisfaction of dessert but without the heavy sleepiness of a pudding.

1 Large handful of dry, clean carrageen moss *(approx. 20g)*
700ml goat's milk
Zest of 3 unwaxed lemons
1 tsp. vanilla extract
3 tbsp. castor sugar
2 eggs

Soak the carrageen in room temperature water for five minutes until it begins to swell. Strain the moss and check for any tiny shells or sand. Place the rinsed carrageen into a large pot with the goat's milk, vanilla extract and lemon zest. Bring these ingredients to the boil and then simmer very slowly for 20-30 minutes. Meanwhile, separate the eggs. Beat the sugar and yolks together in a separate bowl, whisk the egg whites until stiff.

Strain the milky moss mixture, making sure all the gelatine from the moss is pushed through the sieve. While the mixture is still warm, whisk in the sugary egg yolks. Allow to cool slightly then fold in the stiff egg whites. Pour gently into ramekins and allow to set in the fridge for at least 2 hours when it will be ready for you and your lover. Serve with the chocolate strawberries from the heart Tantra exercise on page 223.

See Hummus and Seaweed on page 90 for information on buying seaweed

GINGER COMPRESS

"Our body is made almost entirely of water, through which electrical discharges pass, communicating information. One such piece of information is called love, and it can interfere with the entire organism. Love is always changing."

Adultery - Paulo Coelho

All the tools of food and touch are a gateway to a deeper connection with yourself and how you feel. Using the recipes or exercises in this book can deepen trust and understanding of yourself and others. Allowing yourself to be vulnerable, to receive or to give unconditionally is the path to true love and great sex.

This recipe is not for eating. It is a treat for the body. It is usually given by one person to another however you can give and receive it for yourself. It is truly a remarkable therapeutic recipe. I suppose it is the Chinese Medicine equivalent of running a hot, scented bath with candles. The health benefits of this ginger bath, however, will penetrate deeper and last longer.

Ginger is a warming spice taken from the rhizome of the flowering plant. It can be eaten as a dry, ground spice or freshly cut from the tuber to speed up digestion and bring warmth and relaxation to the digestive system. It has fantastic antibacterial qualities and due to its pungent warming qualities is fantastic when you have a cold or flu. Use this recipe to strengthen the immune system, warm a cold body and clear mucus. It brings balance and reduces toxicity to the stomach, helping seasickness and nausea during pregnancy. Here the fresh raw ginger is employed to reduce inflammation, blood stagnation and muscle cramps. It penetrates deeply into the body, bringing warmth, movement, relief and ease to anything from period pains to injured knees, sore lower backs and cold, icy feet.

2 tbsp. fresh ginger root
2 litres water
Large saucepan
3 or 4 small towels

Grate the ginger and place in a muslin pouch, if you don't have one of these, a clean sock also works, held together at the top with an elastic band or string. Add the pouch filled with ginger to a pot of boiling water, instantly turning it down to a very low simmer. Leave it to infuse in the water for 15 minutes, remove from the heat and dip the small towels in the water. Wring them out and place directly on the body.

If using this recipe with a partner, use the guidance within the lung Tantra to set up the room so that it is warm and inviting. Ask if there is somewhere that is cold and calling out for touch and warm connection. If your lover is lying face down, lay the towels over the lower back and the soles of the feet. If they are on their back, lay the towels over the abdomen, the knees and wrap the feet. Once the towels are in place cover the receiver with a couple of blankets to keep the heat in. Leave for a few minutes until the small towels have begun to cool, remove, dunk again in the ginger water, wring out and repeat the process until you feel completely warm, comforted and loved.

When I die bury me deep down
under the earth
So that I am absorbed
like a heavy blanket falling on a
sleeper
Deep down into dark
unconsciousness
Thoughts slowing to stop as
silence kisses me

ACUPRESSURE POINTS

LARGE INTESTINE 11 – CROOKED POOL

Clears heat from all over the body especially in the urinary system. It clears stagnant menstrual blood and releases diseases and emotions that have been held deep in the body.

Find by flexing the elbow and on the outside crease of the arm you will find the point.

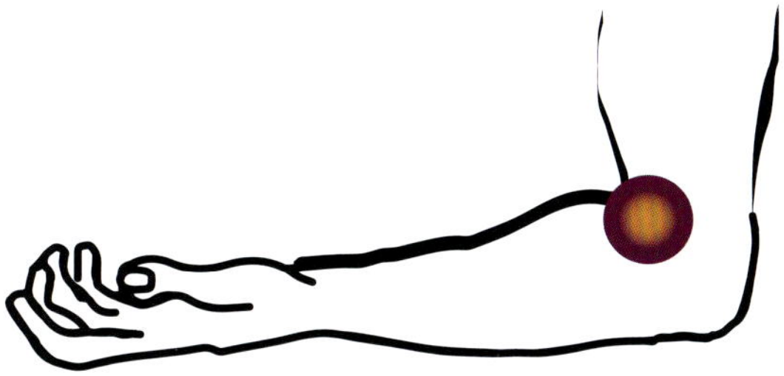

LARGE INTESTINE 4 – JOINING VALLEY

Removes physical internal obstructions in the colon and all along the meridian including neck and shoulder. Anti spasmodic effect for the intestines and uterus. Creates harmony in the body by helping to let go of the emotional past.

Combine with Liver 3 to reduce migraine and headache.

Promotes delivery during labour therefore contraindicated during pregnancy.

Find by pressing the thumb to the first finger to make a mountainous bulge, at the top of the mountain you will find L I4.

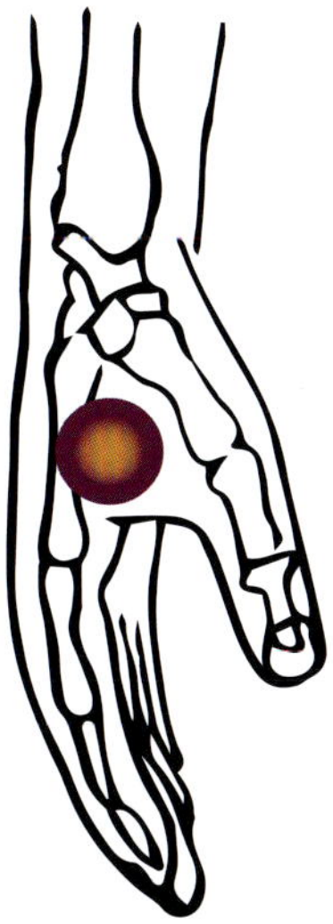

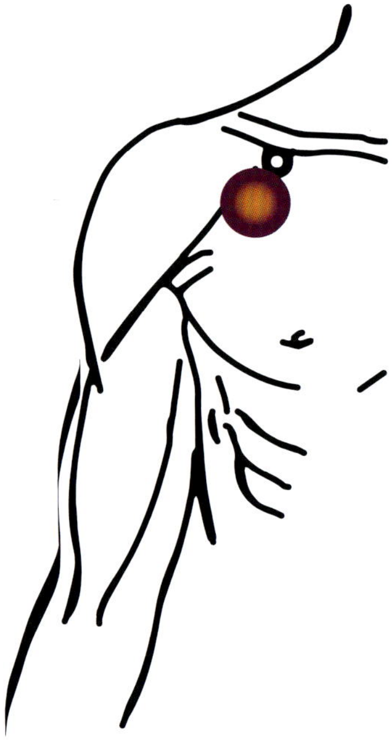

LUNG 1 – CENTRAL RESIDENCE

Connects and loosens the grip that grief, caused by isolation and loss, may have on us. Allows breath into the body for renewal and connection.

First find lung 2 in the depression where the clavicle meets the deltoid muscle. The depression is easier to find when the arm and shoulder is flexed forward. Lung 1 is a thumb width below and slightly lateral to lung 2 and can be quite painful when pressed.

LUNG 7 – BROKEN SEQUENCE

This point helps to open and relax the body so that the breath flows smoothly. Emotionally it helps release grief and other repressed sadness that may be held in the body. It strengthens boundaries so we are able to make healthy connections.

Used together with kidney 6 it descends energy, further nourishes Yin and supports all functions in the lower burner.

Measure 2 fingers up from the inner wrist and the thumb will fall into the point in-between the space of two tendons.

FULL CIRCLE

DEDICATION

An old boyfriend asked me to write some recipes for a sexual condition he wished to change. From that idea, this book began. Even though he has passed out of my life the gift he gave me carries on.

Intimate relationships are capable of stimulating great joy, connection, support and love but they can bring pain, heartache and frustration too. They come with feelings of vulnerability, inadequacy and sometimes, deep loss and sadness. It is all of these feelings I am grateful for, as I have found healing the wounds has brought me great love and learning.

I dedicate this book with gratitude to all the lovers that have come in and out of my life. With all the gifts they have given me, the greatest are my sons; Aaron, Zeph and Sam. They drive me crazy, they test my selflessness to the limit and I want to hug them all the time. They are my greatest lesson and they are my greatest love.

GRATITUDE

Faith Amon, effervescent, ceaseless friendship and amazing editing.

Davy Millard, teaching me sweet surrender.

Paul Congdon, Positive Life Magazine for my first opportunity to write professionally.

For my amazing circle of friends and their support in so many ways.

To my clients, without whom there would be no experience, no learning and no book.

My teachers of Anne Dreschler Hyland, Carmel Kelleher and Josephine Lynch who were exceptional and generous in the depth of their knowledge and their commitment to teaching. Anne was a leader in Macrobiotic Cooking and had set up one of the first Macrobiotic Café's in Ireland during the 1970s whilst Josephine was a skilled Chinese Medicine herbalist who taught, treated and supported me personally with food and Chinese herbs over many years.

RECOMMENDATIONS FOR FURTHER READING

At home in the Whole food kitchen
by Amy Chaplin

Ancient Kitchen, Modern Wisdom
by Yuan Wang, Warren Sheir and Mika Ono

Multi Orgasmic Man & Multi Orgasmic Woman & Healing Love through the Tao
by Mantak Chia

Great Sex Made Simple: Tantric Tips to Deepen Intimacy and Heighten Pleasure
by Mark Michaels and Patricia Johnson

Urban Tantra
by Barbara Carrellas

Change Your Thoughts, Change Your Life: Living The Wisdom Of The Tao
by Dr Wayne Dyer

Seaweeds,edible, available & sustainable
by Ole G. Mouritsen

Seaweed Kitchen
by Prainne Ratigan

Tao Te Ching
by Lao Tzu, translated by Stephen Mitchel

Sometimes it's not always easy to see situations clearly, especially if the emotion is strong. I have found The Work – Byron Katie to be very beneficial when I need help with perspective and alternative points of view. The website www.thework.com is full of free downloadable practical worksheets to help with transforming emotions.

AUTHOR'S BIO

Joanne Faulkner is a Shiatsu practitioner specializing in the energy of food in Traditional Chinese Medicine and runs a busy Shiatsu practice in Dublin, Ireland. Her Shiatsu & Conscious Cooking Demonstrations and Cookery Retreats regularly sell out. Currently she serves as Chairperson of the Shiatsu Society of Ireland, ensuring the standards of Shiatsu practice in Ireland. Blogging regularly on her food and health focused website www.joannefaulkner.ie, she is a published author of **"Shiatsu & the Art of Conscious Cooking"**: a modern cookbook full of recipes, ancient traditional medicine, acupressure points and meditations.

"Good Food, Better Sex" is the second book in the series of Conscious Cook Books. Both books give a unique understanding of how to use Food as Medicine. Joanne shares recipes that have health benefits, but more than that she illustrates how we can love and cherish ourselves with food.

Joanne, with her unique and extensive understanding of Chinese Medicine, explains this traditional approach to healing with food by using everyday ingredients in the modern kitchen. She makes the ancient system of Yin Yang with connected flavours, seasons, emotions and organs seem simple. Many systems borrow from this tradition, with Joanne you understand the foundation.

Contact her at www.joannefaulkner.ie

"In my life, perhaps like you, I have experienced heartbreak, panic attacks, sexual abuse, low libido, hormonal spins and hot flushes of peri-menopause but I am alive and very well without medication or trips to the doctor. Now in my 50s, I have yet to enter menopause and my sexual energy is better than ever. I put it down to using Food As Medicine and the Five Elements System of Traditional Chinese Medicine. It's simple and I share here how to use it everyday to stay healthy and in love."

Photograph: Patrick Bridgeman
@BestSelfPhotography